AA

THE AA GUIDE TO
Yorkshire

About the author

Andrew White is Yorkshire through and through. Sure he's travelled – working around the UK and Europe, including a spell in Rome – but Andrew's home and heart is in Yorkshire.

Born and bred in Doncaster, Andrew is a writer who is passionate about his home county, with countless articles and features about life, the landscape and the history of Yorkshire to his name. In his acclaimed radio podcast series *White around Yorkshire*, Andrew chats to people with stories all across the county, and through his award-winning film-making, Andrew has being putting Yorkshire in the frame for over 20 years.

After getting bitten by the bug at university, Andrew developed his passion for walking amongst the dales, moors and townscapes of Yorkshire – a passion which evolved into being the editor of the website *Walks Around Britain*. Now he has the luxury of devising routes and walking across the country as well as Yorkshire.

Published by AA Publishing (a trading name of AA Media Limited, whose registered office is Fanum House, Basing View, Basingstoke, Hampshire RG21 4EA; registered number 06112600)

© AA Media Limited 2016
First published 2014
Second edition 2016. Reprinted 2017
Third edition 2018

Maps contain data from openstreetmap.org
© OpenStreetMap contributors
Ordnance Survey data © Crown copyright and database right 2018

A CIP catalogue record for this book is available from the British Library.

ISBN: 978-0-7495-7947-0
ISBN (SS): 978-0-7495-7637-0

Cartography provided by the Mapping Services Department of AA Publishing.

Printed and bound in Italy by Printer Trento Srl.

Every effort has been made to trace the copyright holders, and we apologise in advance for any accidental errors. We would be happy to apply the corrections in the following edition of this publication.

The contents of this book are believed correct at the time of printing. Nevertheless, the publishers cannot be held responsible for any errors or omissions or for changes in the details given in this book or for the consequences of any reliance on the information it provides. This does not affect your statutory rights. We have tried to ensure accuracy in this book, but things do change and we would be grateful if readers would advise us of any inaccuracies they may encounter by emailing us at travelguides@theaa.com.

A05591

AA

THE AA GUIDE TO

Yorkshire

CONTENTS

USING THIS GUIDE

Introduction – has plenty of fascinating background reading, including articles on the landscape and local mythology.

Top attractions – pick out the very best places to visit in the area. You'll spot these later in the A–Z by the flashes of yellow.

Before you go – tells you the things to read, watch, know and pack to get the most from your trip.

Campsites – recommends a number of caravan sites and campsites, which carry the AA's Pennant rating, with the very best receiving the coveted gold Pennant award. Visit theAA.com/self-catering-and-campsites, theAA.com/hotels and theAA.com/bed-and-breakfasts for more places to stay.

A–Z of Yorkshire – lists all the best of the region, with recommended attractions, activities and places to eat or drink. Places Nearby lists more to see and do.

Eat and drink – contains restaurants that carry an AA Rosette rating, which acknowledges the very best in cooking. Pubs have been selected for their great atmosphere and good food. Visit theAA.com/restaurants and theAA.com/pubs for more food and drink suggestions.

Index – gives you the option to search by theme, grouping the same type of place together, or alphabetically.

Atlas – will help you find your way around, as every main location has a map reference, as will the town plans throughout the book.

INTRODUCTION

Yorkshire in the 21st century is a modern, thriving county, and the largest in the UK, covering over 2.9 million acres. It's also the proudest in the UK. Yorkshire Day, on 1 August, is celebrated across the county with civic ceremonies and special events. Yorkshire folk consider their home to be 'God's Own County', mainly because while around 80 per cent of the population live in towns and cities, there are miles of magnificent wide open spaces to enjoy.

Yorkshire has three National Parks – the Yorkshire Dales, the North York Moors and the Peak District – with some of the most remarkable landscapes and vistas in Europe. In 2017, the Yorkshire Dales National Park was extended by nearly a quarter – effectively linking it with its neighbour, the Lake District National Park. The new boundary includes parts of the Orton Fells, the northern Howgill Fells, Wild Boar Fell and Mallerstang to the north and, to the west, Barbon, Middleton, Casterton and Leck Fells. And for the first time, bits of Lancashire became part of the Yorkshire Dales National Park. So why do visitors come to Yorkshire? For a start, there's that

scenery. There's so much to explore, on foot, by bike, on horseback, or even by road – Yorkshire has some of the most scenic drives in the country over hill and dale, moorland and valley. And few modern railway journeys are as special as the trip from Settle to Carlisle, through breathtakingly stark and vivid landscapes ever seen from a railway carriage – and that's before you've even started on the scenic steam-hauled lines.

Then there's the villages, towns and cities. Yorkshire's list of places reads like a gazette of the most interesting, historic, busy, quaint and dynamic: Leeds, Sheffield, Huddersfield, Harrogate, Scarborough, Whitby, Hawes, Bedale, Coxwold, Goathland, Haworth, Settle, Grassington – all are diverse and famous for a variety of different reasons, with a history to match. Queen of them all is the fabulous medieval walled city after which the county is named – York itself.

Yorkshire's history is highly visible – you can see it in its proud castles and mansions, and explore its magnificent industrial locations and quiet, crumbling monastic sites. You'll find some incredibly well-preserved castles. Skipton, for example, on its 120-foot-high crag, has been the guardian of the gateway to the Yorkshire Dales for over 900 years and is one of the most complete and well-preserved medieval castles in England. The 90-foot-high great white circular keep at Conisbrough, with its six buttresses, is the oldest survivor of its type in England. Henry VIII tried to destroy Yorkshire's great religious buildings in the 16th century, but you can still piece them together at Fountains Abbey and Bolton Abbey, and at Roche, Whitby and Rievaulx, to name some of the best.

Yorkshire's many and varied museums outline different parts of the county's rich heritage, from Vikings at the Jorvik Centre in York to medicine at the Thackray Medical Museum in Leeds. You'll find five National Museums here – The National Railway Museum in York, The National Science and Media Museum in Bradford, The National Coal Mining Museum for England near Wakefield, Eureka! The National Children's Museum in Halifax, and The Royal Armouries in Leeds. Hull alone has eight free museums, and there's a whole host of municipal and borough museums that are well worth a visit, along with dozens of smaller, quirky museums too, covering anything from farming implements to quiltmaking.

People have visited Yorkshire to watch or take part in sporting events for many years. There's no better area in Britain for horseracing, with nine top-class courses holding over 170 meetings each year, all year round. The big course at York hosts the famous Ebor meeting, and Doncaster is the place to see the St Leger – the oldest of the 'classics'. Cricket is said to be part of the Yorkshire DNA, and the county is the birthplace of the modern game of football. Rugby League is Yorkshire born and bred since the classic Northern breakaway from the Rugby Football Union took place in Huddersfield in 1895.

Quality shopping is another major reason to visit Yorkshire; everything's here, from massive shopping centres such as the White Rose near Leeds and Meadowhall near Sheffield, to small boutique shops thriving in the heart of Yorkshire's towns. It's also worth coming for the local markets – with each place having their own dedicated market days, Yorkshire's markets are still very much at the heart of their communities. Doncaster's market won the Best Food Market 2015 at the BBC's Food and Farming Awards.

And you'll find some of the friendliest people in Yorkshire, all eager to show you their county. God's Own County.

TOP ATTRACTIONS

▲ York

Encircled within its medieval walls, York (see page 300) is an outstanding destination in itself, with museums from the funky (Jorvik) to the traditional (Castle Museum) to the bizarre (York Dungeon), and fabulous historic buildings from the magnificent Minster to the humble Shambles. Great places to eat out, too.

▼ Yorkshire Sculpture Park

A larger-than-life setting for larger-than-life modern art – it's no wonder that people come here in their droves to explore the sculptures placed against such a beautiful natural backdrop. It's about as far away from stuffy and dusty as you can get (see page 283).

◄ Yorkshire Wildlife Park

This wildlife park (see page 98) has visitors flocking to it from all over the UK. Amazing animals are spread over some 70 landscaped acres, including giraffes and smaller creatures you can walk among, such as lemurs and wallabies. The big cats – lions, tigers and leopards – are a huge draw, as are the park's four polar bears.

▸ Castle Howard

One of Yorkshire's favourite stately homes (see page 187), perhaps in part due to its exposure through TV and film versions of *Brideshead Revisited*, Castle Howard is undeniably grand in its own right and set in beautifully landscaped grounds.

◄ Royal Armouries

This is the Northern outpost of the national collection of arms, armour and artillery (see page 174), with displays over six galleries ranging from medieval tournament combat battleware to historic Oriental armour and weapons. Enactments take place outside, and there are lots of events throughout the year.

▲ Brontë Parsonage Museum

This modest shrine to three extraordinarily talented Victorian writer sisters is still one of Yorkshire's great attractions (see page 129), perhaps because of its touching authenticity – that really is the sofa where Emily died, the dress Charlotte wore, those are the spectacles that their father Patrick wore, their writing on those tiny little books, their etchings on the nursery walls. Their books are still familiar and widely known today, constantly filmed and reworked for the next generation.

▼ The Deep

The underwater tunnels of this amazing aquarium (see page 143) allow you to see around 1,000 different species of fish, themed into sections such as a tropical lagoon, Slime! and Endless Oceans. Walk through the Kingdom of the Ice, learn about the life cycle of the jellyfish, and watch sharks and rays all around you.

▲ North Yorkshire Moors Railway

Probably the finest heritage railway in the country, this is a ride back in time not to be missed (see page 206). Whether you're being hauled behind a powerful steam engine or a classic diesel locomotive, the NYMR travels through beautiful scenery, reflecting years of hard work by local enthusiasts. It even calls in at *Heartbeat* and Harry Potter destinations along the way.

▼ Yorkshire's ruined abbeys

Yorkshire is full of fascinating ruined abbeys. Fountains (see page 102) is surely the most beautiful; Bolton (see page 68) or Rievaulx (below, and page 231), the most complete; Whitby (see page 297), the most dramatic; Jervaulx (see page 155), the most tranquil; Roche (see page 246) the furthest south. Don't bother looking for one at Rosedale Abbey – there's nowt left.

◀ National Railway Museum, York

The world's largest railway museum (see page 309), packed with gleaming preserved locomotives, restored rolling stock, station signs, nameplates, signals and more. The museum hosts a range of special events throughout the year. Spotters will especially enjoy seeing *Mallard* and the Japanese Bullet Train.

▶ Flamingo Land Resort

Fancy corkscrewing horizontally through the air, like a caped superhero? If you do, you'll love the new Hero ride at Yorkshire's biggest theme park (see page 190). There are gentler rides and roller coasters that all the family can enjoy, plus a host of African animals and farmyard creatures.

◀ Eden Camp

This multi-award-winning museum (see page 188) is dedicated to understanding the hardships of day-to-day life during World War II. While social history is to the fore, there are lots of historic vehicles and even military aircraft on show. If you're lucky, you'll overhear veteran visitors reminiscing while you explore.

HISTORY OF YORKSHIRE

From the arrival of the first humans in roughly 7000 BC, Yorkshire has been a prized area of the British Isles – although back then it would have looked quite different. Most of the area was covered in thick forest, and these first Yorkshiremen hunted the plentiful wildlife that was around at the time, including boar and deer.

By 3000 BC the Stone Age people had arrived, and it was they who started to clear whole sections of land for farming. They were replaced by Bronze Age tool-and-weapon style farmers in around 1800 BC – and these folk stuck around for a while. The moors are still littered with the standing stones and rock art they left behind.

The next wave of people to come to Yorkshire were the Celts, in around 500 BC. With them they brought iron tools and weapons, and a more ordered and civilised society. Most of Yorkshire was occupied by a tribe called the Brigantes, who had their capital at Aldborough, near Boroughbridge. Eastern Yorkshire was occupied by a tribe called the Parisii, with a base at Brough.

Much of Yorkshire, as it is seen today, is down to the Romans, who conquered England in stages after landing in the south in

AD 43, although it took a while for them to get into Yorkshire. They first arrived in AD 55, building a wooden fort at Templeborough, near Rotherham, and remained there supporting the last ruler of the Brigantes, Queen Cartimandua, as she fought a battle against her estranged husband Venutius. As this family squabble got more heated, the Romans saw their chance and moved in to quell the ensuing civil war and take control.

By AD 71 a fort had been built at Danum (now Doncaster) and the Romans moved across the Humber from their base in Lindum Colonia (Lincoln) to Brough. Within the year a fort had been built at Eboracum (York). The Romans were big users of lead, and they quickly discovered large amounts in Nidderdale. As the Roman era marched on, Eboracum became increasingly important, growing to become the military capital of northern Britain. Constantine the Great was crowned Roman Emperor here in AD 306.

The Romans left Yorkshire in AD 402, and a quiet life was had by most – until the 8th century, at least. This is when the Vikings started their raids on England. By AD 866 they controlled the settlement of Eboracum (York), and with it the whole of the North. The Vikings created three 'ridings' (from the Norse *thriding*, or

◄ Cliffords Tower, York, at dusk (previous page)   ▼ Above Fryup Dale

third) which were administrative jurisdictions, and designed them to meet at York, which they renamed Jorvik. This Danish Kingdom of Yorkshire continued until AD 954, when Edred of England captured the area.

The Danes were not ones to give up lightly, and in 1066 an invasion force sailed up the Humber. They were ultimately defeated at the Battle of Stamford Bridge in September 1066 – the last time a Scandinavian army seriously threatened England. After his 1–0 win at Stamford Bridge, English King Harold raced back down to clash with the army of William, Duke of Normandy, who'd just landed on the south coast – and you'll know what happened at the Battle of Hastings, as he lost his shirt – and his life.

Yorkshire folk weren't much impressed with the new French King of England, and rose up in rebellion against him. William's answer was to march up the country and build a fort there to remind the people who was in charge. When he departed in 1069, the North rebelled again – and this time William's response was brutal and decisive: he burned all the stores of food and all the crops in the fields, and also killed domestic animals. It was a 'scorched earth' policy that knocked the region firmly back into its place.

▼ Civil War re-enactment, York Minster

▲ Scarborough Castle

Yet Yorkshire recovered, and in the 12th and 13th centuries many of the now familiar towns were founded – Barnsley, Doncaster, Hull, Leeds, Northallerton, Pontefract, Richmond, Scarborough and Sheffield. By the 1300s, many monasteries had been built, and Yorkshire was a fairly happening place, as they farmed sheep and built wealth.

The 14th century wasn't one to remember for Yorkshire. For a start, the area was involved in a long war with the Scots, with Robert the Bruce burning Northallerton in 1318. Then in 1349 around a third of the population were wiped out by the Black Death.

Fierce battles continued in the 15th century with the Wars of the Roses, which ultimately led to the defeat of the House of York in its quest for the English Crown. York and Lancaster have been – mostly friendly – rivals ever since.

Henry VIII's reign changed much of the landscape of Yorkshire as the monasteries were dissolved between 1536 and 1540. This is the period from which most of the ruins you can see dotted around Yorkshire come from – in all, some 120 religious places were closed across the region.

Yorkshire fared better under Elizabeth I, with a boom in population and major new industries springing up. By 1600 Sheffield had already developed into the major centre for cutlery production in England, and the farming communities started to set up small businesses in their dwellings – cottage industry was born.

The Gunpowder Plot of 1605 to blow up the King and Parliament has Yorkshire connections, with chief plotter, Guy Fawkes, being a York-born man, but in the Civil War of 1642, Yorkshire was divided between the two sides. The Royalists used York as their base, and the battles went both ways across the county until the Parliamentarians eventually won. Oliver Cromwell decided to dismantle many of the Yorkshire castles to ensure they couldn't be used again – which is why many are in ruins now.

The Industrial Revolution of the 18th century transformed Yorkshire, with the increasingly mechanised wool, mining, clothing and steel industries all playing a major part in the development of the county. Transport canals were dug, followed by the railways, and places like Doncaster and York became manufacturing centres of the new 'iron horses'. The leisure business started around the same time, with Harrogate flourishing as a spa town, and Scarborough becoming the first seaside resort in the county.

Yorkshire folk are known to speak their mind, and the region has always been at the forefront of the rights movements. William Wilberforce, MP for Hull, was central in the abolition of slavery in 1833, and the forerunner of the modern Trades Union Congress was started in 1866 in Sheffield.

World War II hit Yorkshire particularly hard. Sheffield was bombed heavily during the Blitz thanks to its importance in manufacturing, but it was Hull that became the most bombed city, with around 95 per cent of houses damaged or destroyed. The whole area was rebuilt after the War, and many towns and cities developed new suburbs thanks to the mass building programmes that followed in peacetime.

The most monumental change to Yorkshire came in 1974. Ever since the Vikings divided up the county into three, the West, East and North Ridings were a proud symbol of what it meant to be a part of Yorkshire. That changed in 1974, when county boundaries were reorganised across England. The ridings were split into North, South and West Yorkshire, while most of the East Riding was ripped from Yorkshire entirely to form the north part of Humberside. East Riding folk felt they were always part of Yorkshire and started an indignant campaign almost immediately to change back. In 1996 they were successful, and the East Riding of Yorkshire existed once more.

BACK TO NATURE

The natural geography of Yorkshire acts as the county's essential backdrop. The geology of the county is split into six major ages. The oldest rocks in Yorkshire date from the pre-Carboniferous period, a massive 370 million years ago. These can be found around Askrigg, Horton in Ribblesdale and Austwick in North Yorkshire.

These ancient rocks are surrounded by slightly younger rock from the Carboniferous era, which dominates most of the west of the county. This is the time, from 359 to 298 million years ago, when the millstone grit of the Yorkshire Pennines formed, and was covered with swamps and tropical rainforests. What would become the Yorkshire coalfields were created during this period, as well as the various limestone pavements, such as the one at Malham Cove.

Of course, Yorkshire wasn't in the place it is now, but some 30 degrees north of the equator – so the weather was quite different.

A narrow belt of magnesian limestone stretches down the east of the Pennines taking in places like Knaresborough, Wetherby and parts of Doncaster, while the Vale of York is made from layers of Triassic sandstone and mudstone, dating from around 250 to 200 million years ago.

◄ Idol Rock, Brimham Rocks
▲ Gannets, RSPB Bempton nature reserve

The North York Moors are dominated by rocks from the later Jurassic period, some 205 to 142 million years ago – mainly sandstone and limestone, which can be seen exposed on the coast around Filey and Staithes.

The Yorkshire Wolds consist mostly of Cretaceous chalk, giving a gentle rolling aspect to the landscape. The youngest part of Yorkshire – if that's really the word, as it was formed during the Ice Age, which ended around 10,000 years ago – is around the Humberhead Levels in South Yorkshire.

The native wildlife in Yorkshire is rich and diverse, and particularly prominent in the three National Parks, the National Nature Reserves, the many Areas of Outstanding Natural Beauty and Sites of Special Scientific Interest across the area. Some of these areas play host to the last stronghold of certain plant and animal species. Just in Yorkshire's Nature Triangle alone – an area between Selby, Spurn Head and Filey Brigg – you can see birds including guillemots, razorbills, puffins, ospreys, red kites, buzzards and barn owls. Rarer mammals like otters, water voles and roe deer are also to be found in Yorkshire, along with many species of frogs, newts and reptiles. Look hard enough in the right habitats and you might even find a grass snake – the North Cliffe Woods near Market Weighton are popular basking spots, if you're interested.

LORE OF THE LAND

As its place names bear witness, the Yorkshire landscape is redolent with devilish tales. There's the Devil's Punchbowl, a deep valley on the North York Moors, said to have been scooped out by the Devil, meaning to throw the earth at Scarborough. He also left his hoofmarks on the Cloven Stones – rocks at Baildon and Rivock Edge. He created Almscliffe Crag when he threw a stone at the giant Rombald during a fight on Ilkley Moor, and the cleft in the Great Rock above Hebden Bridge was created when the Devil, having wagered that he could straddle the Calder Valley, lost his footing.

Near the water, visitors need to take care, for the notorious Kelpie or water horse that inhabits the River Ure near Middleham, Wensleydale, has the reputation of taking the life of at least one human each year. Even more dangerous is the Bolton Strid, where the river shoots through a narrow gap in the rocks haunted by a Kelpie with evil intent. Only the foolish will attempt to jump it, whatever the water level. A fairy steed is alleged to ride through the Strid on May Day morning – a grim reminder that three sisters

◀ Rosedale Valley, from Blakey Ridge

– the heiresses of nearby Beamsley Hall – disappeared, never to be seen again, after keeping watch for it on that date.

Across Yorkshire, fairies lie in wait for the unwary, ever hostile to being discovered by humans. Among their most notorious haunts was Elbolton Hill, where anyone spotting them would immediately be turned blind, and Ilkley Moor where at White Wells one William Butterfield discovered in his bathhouse 'a lot of little creatures dressed in green from head to foot' who, when seen, went away 'helter-skelter, toppling and tumbling'.

Little helpers

Aside from the latest white goods and useful appliances, housework in Yorkshire is remarkably lightened by live-in Hobs – also known as Hobthrusts, Hobmen and even Hobbits – spirits who help with everyday chores. At Hart Hall in Glaisdale a Hob described as a 'little hairy man', wearing nothing but sacking, was seen threshing in a barn by some farm boys. Feeling sorry for his lack of clothing, they had a smock made for him, but after he had picked it up the Hob promptly disappeared forever. Why? Because he was offended by the idea of being clothed like a man.

Another Hob was equally offended on a farm at Upleatham, near Hob Hill, where a man's coat was accidentally left on a winnowing machine. But this was not the end of the story, for after the Hob deserted the farm the residents were tormented by a witch named Peggy Flaunders. Not only did she send a blazing pig to their doorstep, but smashed all the crockery and made their cattle fall ill and die. Only when the family took a black cockerel, pierced it with pins and roasted it alive in the pitch dark did Peggy's power over them cease.

Hobmen also live on the Yorkshire coast as at the aptly named Hob Hole at Runswick Bay, a natural cavern where children afflicted with whooping cough were regularly taken to be cured by the resident spirit, and at Markse-by-the-Sea. Here, an old church was due to be demolished, but every time the stones were removed Hobmen came by at night and replaced them.

Forces of evil

Belief in witches runs strong in this county, so much so that timber-framed houses were built with carved oak beams specifically designed as witch barriers, usually bearing the cross of St Andrew on top. Most famous of all Yorkshire's witches is Mother Shipton, born Ursula Southeil in a cave near Knaresborough, where her memorial remains. After Ursula's mother died in childbirth, the baby, who was afflicted by physical deformities, was brought up by a townswoman whose cottage became plagued by supernatural forces. Furniture moved, while food vanished from plates and visitors were forced to dance in circles and were even attacked by imps disguised as monkeys and armed with pins. Following her marriage to Toby Shipton in 1512 Ursula became famous as a fortune-teller, but as soon as people began prying into her affairs she took her revenge, sending goblins to pursue them or bringing on premature deaths.

Yorkshire witches took on other forms, like Nancy Newgill of Broughton who not only transformed herself into a hedgehog to suck milk from cows' udders overnight, but could empower other hedgehogs to do the same. Even more common were witches disguised as hares, like Au'd Molly of Guisborough, who used her powers to avert death by silver bullet – said to be the only ammunition that could kill a witch hare. Even more dramatic is the tale of Abigail Craister, a witch who lived in a cave on Black Hambleton and who, when pursued, jumped into Gormire Lake below Whitstone Cliff – only to emerge in a sinkhole nine miles distant. It's said that she still haunts the lake and can be seen riding over the district on her broomstick.

▼ Hole of Horcum, Levisham Moor near Pickering

Folk hero

Despite his Nottinghamshire associations, Yorkshire boasts many connections with the legendary hero, Robin Hood. Most notable of all is Barnsdale in the south of the county, renowned in the 14th century as a royal hunting forest and place of ambush, and used by Robin as a refuge from the jurisdiction of his arch enemy the Sheriff of Nottingham. In Yorkshire, too, he robbed the rich of their wealth, targeting corrupt clerics in particular. Later in life, Robin took refuge near Scarborough – not by forward planning but because a random arrow shot towards the coast determined his destination. Here a widow employed him as a fisherman, and though mocked at first by his shipmates for incompetence, he earned his place on board when he shot a Frenchman on an enemy ship. 'Twelve thousand pound of money bright' was the booty, with half given to his compatriots and the other half used to fund a refuge for the poor.

Eventually, even folk heroes' lives must end. Old and ill, Robin travelled to Kirklees Priory, near Huddersfield, to undergo bloodletting – a common cure in medieval times. But all did not go well. Robin was locked into his chamber, and although he

▶ Long Stoop on Pennine Way towards Stoodley Pike

managed to summon Little John with his horn, his end was near. Shooting an arrow through the window, he chose the site of his grave – where a stone still stands today.

Marking the year

Year in, year out, Yorkshire celebrations reflect its rich folklore, beginning on New Year's Day with first footing – bringing luck by being the first person to enter the house in the new year. For luck in East Yorkshire a first-footer needs to be dark haired, in North Yorks fair and in the West Riding a 'ginger nut'. In Driffield children are still thrown pennies to spend when they set out chanting:

> Here we are at our town's end
> A bottle of rum and a crown to spend
> Are we downhearted? No!
> Shall we win? Yes!

Plough Monday, the first Monday following Twelfth Night, is the prompt for farm labourers to seek donations. Adding a disreputable note in East Yorkshire were the dancer Besom Bet and her raggedy companion, Blether Dick. Armed with a bladder on a stick, Dick would beat the labourers, known as Plough Stotts, whilst performing a lewd dance.

On Good Friday, the people of Calderdale still dress in colourful costumes as characters including St George, The Slasher, Doctor, the Moroccan Prince and Toss Pot to perform the Pace Egg Play, vividly depicting the triumph of good over evil. On hearing the first cuckoo of spring (at least when cuckoos were commonplace, unlike today) any resident of South Yorkshire would promptly 'foot the cuckoo', gathering friends and barrels of beer to be consumed beneath the trees from where the bird was calling. Every three years, on May Day, Yorkshire's most famous maypole, at Barwick-in-Elmet near Leeds, is ritually re-assembled using ropes and ladders and topped with a weather vane in the shape of a fox.

Come summer, the residents of West Whitton in Wensleydale 'Burn the Bartle' on the Saturday following St Bartholomew's Day (24 August), parading a giant human effigy to the end of the village where it is ritually ignited. As winter approached, stray dogs were once driven out of town on 'Whip Dog Day', 18 October – St Luke's Day – while at Halloween girls in North Yorkshire would throw nuts into the fire hoping to see one that burnt fast – the sure prediction of a happy marriage. On Christmas Eve bell ringers in Dewsbury still toll the 'Devil's Knell', an arrangement designed to confer protection from evil and disasters of all kinds for the year ahead.

LONG-DISTANCE WALKING IN YORKSHIRE

With such a massive area to explore, it's little wonder the whole long-distance walking movement started here in Yorkshire. These are some of the best long-distance trails, which either start in or pass through Yorkshire.

Pennine Way National Trail

nationaltrail.co.uk/pennine-way

Let's start with the very first National Trail, the epic 268-mile hike which is the Pennine Way. The bright idea of a route from the Peak District to the Scottish border is credited to journalist and walker Tom Stephenson. He proposed the idea in an article in the *Daily Herald* newspaper in 1935, and began to lobby Parliament for the creation of an official trail. A year after he became the secretary of the Ramblers' Association, the Access to Countryside Act 1949 was passed which brought National Trails – or Long Distance Routes, as they were called then – into being. It was another 16 years before the Pennine Way was officially opened, with the final section of the path declared open in a ceremony held on Malham Moor on 24 April 1965.

The Pennine Way starts just outside Yorkshire in the Peak District at Edale, and heads northwards over the Kinder Plateau and into Yorkshire through Standedge and across the mighty M62 motorway. Once through Calderdale you're eventually into the Yorkshire Dales National Park, passing through Malham Tarn, Pen-y-Ghent and to the lonely Tan Hill Inn, and then across the North Pennines Area of Outstanding Natural Beauty out of Yorkshire. Continue on the trail, and you'll reach Kirk Yetholm in Scotland. The Way starts and ends at pubs – the Nag's Head Inn in England and the Border Hotel in Scotland.

Cleveland Way National Trail

nationaltrail.co.uk/cleveland-way

Britain's second National Trail is here in Yorkshire, too. The Cleveland Way, opened in 1969, stretches 110 miles from Helmsley in a horseshoe shape, skirting the North York Moors National Park and finishing at Filey Brigg. The trail's horseshoe line has led to several suggested routes to link the start and finish – making a circular trail.

Yorkshire Wolds Way National Trail

nationaltrail.co.uk/yorkshire-wolds-way

After the Cleveland Way the rest of the country wanted National Trails, and Yorkshire had to wait its turn until 1982 – but the prize was the Yorkshire Wolds Way. This is a journey from the Humber Estuary to the dramatic Cleveland coast through the gentle chalk hills of the Yorkshire Wolds. The 79-mile downland trail ends at

▼ Wolds Way sign, Thixendale

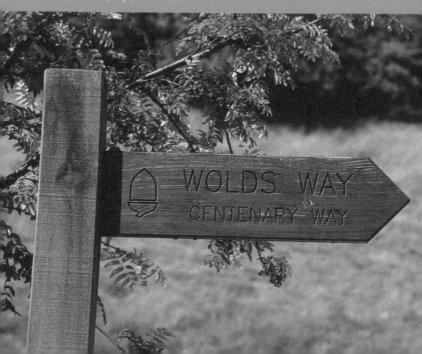

Filey Brigg – and by carrying on along the Cleveland Way you could enjoy a route from the Humber to Helmsley – a total of 185 miles of great walking.

Coast to Coast (C2C)

wainwright.org.uk

Alfred Wainwright's version of a Coast to Coast walk is the second-best known route in Britain, so for some it's a surprise to learn the C2C isn't a National Trail at all – but rather a Long Distance Trail. The difference? National Trails are the ones designated in England by the government-sponsored Natural England, and are cared for accordingly. Volunteers look after the other paths, which is where The Wainwright Society comes in. It has recently got most of this 183-mile trail waymarked with distinctive signs, making it much easier to navigate.

The path goes from St Bees on the Cumbrian coast to Robin Hood's Bay in North Yorkshire. In fact, roughly two-thirds of the route is through the Yorkshire National Parks – first across the Yorkshire Dales and then through the North York Moors.

You could attempt it in record time – which is a blistering 39 hours, 36 minutes and 52 seconds, achieved in 1991 by Mike Hartley – but most people take longer to soak up the atmosphere.

Dales Way

dalesway.org.uk

The Dales Way is another very well-known long-distance walk. Starting in Ilkley, West Yorkshire, the trail takes a fairly gentle route along Wharfedale, passing Bolton Abbey before crossing the Pennine Way to descend to Dentdale. After following the River Dee to Sedbergh, the Dales Way crosses farmland to reach Burneside and the River Kent, which is followed for several miles before the path branches off to the finish at Bowness, on the shore of Windermere in the Lake District.

At 78 miles, the Dales Way is a great trail to try for your first long-distance walk – with plenty of points along the route where you can stop off and stay, and a route profile that's not too demanding. Three Dales Way Link routes join the trail from Leeds, Bradford/Shipley and Harrogate.

Trans Pennine Trail

transpenninetrail.org.uk

Like Wainwright's classic C2C, this is a coast-to-coast journey – but it crosses the country slightly further south. It starts in Southport, then heads through Liverpool, Widnes, Warrington, Stockport and across the Peak District. Then it enters Yorkshire, passing through Penistone, Doncaster, Selby, Hessle, Hull and finally reaches Hornsea, after some some 207 miles.

There's also a north–south trail connecting the major centres of Leeds, Wakefield and Barnsley to the main trail at the Dearne Valley. This route then carries on southwards to Sheffield and Chesterfield.

The Trans Pennine Trail is mainly along disused railway lines, canal towpaths and well-maintained bridleways, making it easy to walk – and indeed cycle on, as this is a multi-user trail.

White Rose Way

whiteroseway.co.uk

Here's a 104-mile trail which goes through West, North and East Yorkshire, all the way from Leeds to Scarborough. Starting from the Black Prince statue in Leeds' City Square, the White Rose Way leads leisurely to Wetherby, then alongside the River Wharfe as it flows through Boston Spa and Tadcaster, before following an old Roman road into the suburbs of York.

The route continues out of York towards the Howardian Hills, an Area of Outstanding Natural Beauty, and into Malton and the chocolate-box village of Thornton-le-Dale. Once you're through the North York Moors National Park and the impossibly beautiful Dalby Forest, it's not too far to Scarborough's glorious South Bay.

South Yorkshire Way

southyorkshireway.co.uk

South Yorkshire isn't quite so well known for its walking, which is why this new trail made up of two interconnected routes was launched in 2014. The Boundary Route is 171 miles and starts in Bawtry, southeast of Doncaster – the traditional gateway to Yorkshire – and passes through the Humberhead Peatlands National Nature Reserve before heading west to Barnsley. Here the trail leads into the Peak District National Park to the highest point – High Stones (1,804 feet) – before skirting around Sheffield, passing Maltby and back to the start.

The 98-mile Central Route starts at Thorne North Railway Station and threads its way through Doncaster, Rotherham and Barnsley before joining the Trans Pennine Trail for a while and then through Sheffield until it joins the Boundary Route again at Totley Railway Station.

The trail has been designed so it can be walked in sections, with handy guides to the buses needed to get you to and back from each section.

▶ From the Pennine Way towards Stoodley Pike

YORKSHIRE DIALECT

On your travels around the county you may encounter some unfamiliar turns of phrase, so here's a brief guide to some popular Yorkshire-isms. Oh, and be prepared to be called 'loov', 'flower' and even 'petal' – they're all general terms of endearment.

'appen	*perhaps*, as in "'appen bus might turn up"
'eck	*heck* or *hell*, as in "by 'eck"
'ey up	could either mean *look out/be careful* or be the traditional Yorkshire greeting
'ow do	*how do you do?* Another traditional Yorkshire greeting
'utch up	*make more room* on a seat, for example
allus	*always*, as in "I allus goes there"
b'aht	*without*, as in "I'm b'aht car"
band	*rope* or *string*
beck	*stream* or *brook*, from the old Norse
belt	*to hit* or *thrash*, as in "I belted it"
butty	*sandwich*
callin'	*talking* or *gossiping*
causey	*pavement*, from the Yorkshire word for pavement, a causeway
champion	*excellent*, as in "I'm champion, I am"
chuffed	*very excited*, as in "I'm chuffed to bits"
courtin'	*going out with* in a romantic way
faffin'	*messing about*, as in "stop faffin'"
fettle	either *to make* or *to tidy*
flaggin'	*getting tired*, as in "I'm reet flaggin' now"
flayed	*afraid*
flit	*to move on somewhere else*, as in "they flitted around a bit"
flummox	*confuse* or *puzzle*, as in "I'm flummoxed as to where it is"
foss/force	*waterfall*

fratch	*quarrel*
gaffer	*boss*
gill	*stream*
ginnel	*narrow passageway*, from the old Norse
gip	*to retch* or *be sick*
kayli	*sherbert*
kaylied	*drunk*, as in "he's really kaylied"
loosin'	either *ending, finishing* or *clock or watch running late*, as in "loosin' time" – finishing time
lug	either *to pull* or *tug* or *a knot* or *tangle* in hair, from old Norse
lug 'ole	*ear hole*, as in "pin y' lug 'ole back"
mash	*to brew tea*, as in "are y' mashin' up?"
maungy	*spoilt* or *peevish*
midden	either an *outside toilet* or a *dungheap/rubbish tip*, from old Norse
middlin'	*moderate* or *average*, usually as a response to "how are you doing?" – "oh, fair to middlin'"
mind	*watch out for*
mither	*to fret*, as in "quit mitherin'"
nobbut	*only*
nowt	*nothing*, as in "nowt taken out"
owt	*anything*, as in "are y' doing owt?"
parky	*chilly, cold*
peff	*gentle cough*
pikelet	*crumpet*
playin' pop	*telling someone off*
pop	*fizzy soft drink*
reckon	*to think*, as in "what dus't a reckon?"
reight	*very*, as in "this is reight good"
shuft up	*to make more room*
silin'	*raining heavily*, from the old Norse, as in "it's silin' it down"
snicket	*narrow passageway*
spice	*sweets*
stalled	*out of patience* or *fed up*
sup up	*drink up*
ta	*thanks*
tea	*evening meal*, as in "what'll you have for your tea?"
think on	*remember*, as in "you must think on..."
thissen	*yourself*
Tyke	*Yorkshireman/woman/dog*, previously not always complimentary, but seen in a more positive way now
wang	*throw*

LOCAL SPECIALITIES

There's no better place to start than with the one dish everyone knows is from Yorkshire.

YORKSHIRE PUDDING
This savoury batter pudding is a mix of flour, eggs and milk, which originated in Yorkshire as a thrifty way of making a dinner go further. The tasty batter was served before the meat, so people filled up on this comfort food and, of course, the meat went further. Today it is a must-have with your traditional Sunday roast beef dinner. Lay sausages in it before you put it in the oven, and you've got toad-in-the-hole.

WENSLEYDALE CHEESE
Shot to fame by Wallace and Gromit, Wensleydale cheese has actually been around for several hundred years. It's a unique-tasting cheese, mild and fresh and crumbly, and it now comes blended with dried fruits such as apricots and cranberries for special occasions. Eat it with apple pie or fruit cake for something different. Look out for other Yorkshire cheeses – Shepherd's

Purse of Thirsk make Harrogate Blue and the creamy Mrs Bell's Blue; the Ribblesdale Cheese Company in Northallerton produces tasty goats' cheeses; and Swaledale cheese, made in Richmond, is flavoured with Theakston's Old Peculier ale.

YORKSHIRE CURD TART
This teatime treat is a kind of open pie, with the shortcrust base filled with a custard-like filling of milk-curds – something like cottage cheese – flavoured with currants, nutmeg and lemon. Bettys Tea Rooms in Harrogate and York serve up some of the best. Another teatime treat is the rather weighty, chewy ginger cake called parkin. It's made with oatmeal and dark treacle in the recipe, and is a traditional accompaniment to fireworks on Bonfire Night.

RHUBARB
They say that if you listen carefully enough, you can

◀ The Original Wensleydale Cheese & Wine Shop, Aysgarth
▲ Fish and chips and mushy peas

actually hear the rhubarb growing in Yorkshire – especially in the nine square miles of the Rhubarb Triangle, between Wakefield, Leeds and Morley. At one time around 90 per cent of the world's winter forced rhubarb was produced in the barns here. In 2010 Yorkshire Forced Rhubarb was awarded the status of 'Protected Designation of Origin' by the EU, placing it neatly alongside Champagne and Parma ham.

LIQUORICE

It seems strange that it was once used only for medicinal purposes, as the extract of the root of the liquorice plant is now completely linked with the popular multi-coloured sweet, Liquorice Allsorts, first manufactured by Bassetts of Sheffield. Possibly brought back by returning Crusaders, liquorice is actually known as a Pontefract speciality – or rather, making sweets from it is, thanks to the two large factories there. Pontefract or Pomfret cakes are sweet discs of liquorice, moulded and stamped like coins.

CHOCOLATE

Yorkshire is the unlikely birthplace of many chocolate brands that are now famous the world over. Rowntrees, for example, started in York in 1862 and developed Kit Kat, Smarties, Aero and Black Magic. Joseph Terry, also of York, brought the world All Gold, Neapolitans and – of course – Terry's Chocolate Orange. Luxury chocolate, toffee- and fudge-maker Thorntons started in Sheffield in 1911, and is now the largest confectionery-only group in the UK.

FISH AND CHIPS

Battered and deep-fried fish, served with fried potato chips, became a thrifty English staple at a time when Atlantic-trawled cod and haddock could be cheaply delivered around the country's rail network from the great white-fish ports of Hull and Grimsby. In Yorkshire, it's usually take-away fare, perhaps with a blob of mushy peas. But in 1931 Yorkshireman Harry Ramsden took this working-class basic to new heights in his Guiseley restaurant, styled on

London's Ritz Hotel and hung with chandeliers, where tea and bread and butter were the only menu extras on offer – but the fish and batter were superb. Alas, that glittering emporium is gone, but his name lives on in the multi-million pound fish-and-chip restaurant chain, which has now spread as far as Saudi Arabia.

YORK HAM

Salted and then dry-cured over a period of two months or more, York ham is known for its high quality and flavour. Some say it should be lightly smoked, and there are legends that link the original smoking to timbers left over from the building of York Minster. The truth is more prosaic – butcher Robert Burrow Atkinson laid claim to the process he had started in his Blossom Street shop in York in the 1860s, successfully upholding legal requirements that it should be cured within a couple of miles of the city boundary to qualify for the name. The style of curing is now recognised in European law, but the tradition has spread beyond the county boundary and it may be made anywhere.

YORKSHIRE TEA

It may not be grown here, but the county's name is proudly borne on the packaging of black tea blends produced by Taylors of Harrogate, founded in 1886 and one of the last remaining independent tea merchants in the UK. Sup it in any branch of Yorkshire's famous Bettys cafes, part of the same family concern.

▼ Yorkshire Tea produced by Taylors of Harrogate

BEFORE YOU GO

THINGS TO READ

Yorkshire is a magnet for writers and artists, and there's no shortage of books out there – both fiction and non-fiction – to show you its different sides.

Lee Hanson: *Edge of Heaven: The Yorkshire Coast* (2011)
A fascinating collection of writings about different aspects of the coastline, by a range of writers with something interesting and personal to say – from Margaret Drabble and Alan Plater to Blake Morrison. Illustrated with great photos, too.

Neil Hanson: *The Inn at the Top: Tales of Life at the Highest Pub in Britain* (2013)
Yorkshire is proud to be home of the highest pub in Britain, the Tan Hill Inn, and this book is the delightful story of a young couple who in the late 1970s, on impulse, became its new landlords without any experience of running a pub.

Mike Pannett: *Mike Pannett's Yorkshire* (2013)
Yorkshire-born ex-policeman Mike Pannett is the star of the BBC's *Country Cops* series. Here he combines stunning photos with warmhearted tales, on a personal tour of his home county, revisiting favourite places from his past which hold special memories. Mike's first popular autobiographical book, *Now Then Lad... Tales of a Country Bobby*, was published in 2008 and has been followed by several more.

James Herriot: *If Only They Could Talk*, etc (1970–77)
These memoirs of a country vet, written in the 1970s but based in the 30s and 40s, became so popular that they spawned a film and a long-running TV series, a museum in Thirsk and the term 'Herriot Country'. Today his observations of the Dales and the folk who lived there are just as sharp and entertaining.

▲ Holiday essentials

Emily Brontë: *Wuthering Heights* (1847)

Originally published under Emily's pseudonym of Ellis Bell, *Wuthering Heights* is an inspiring read, with its Yorkshire setting still recognisable in the moors above Haworth – Wuthering Heights is the name of the farmhouse where the story of Cathy and Heathcliffe unfolds. Although deemed a classic now, Emily's darkly romantic novel was overshadowed by her sister Charlotte's *Jane Eyre* – also to be recommended – and received mixed reviews at the time for its bleak themes, which focus on jealousy and vengefulness.

Peter Robinson: *Gallows View*, etc (1987–ongoing)

The first in a highly acclaimed series of crime thrillers set in Yorkshire, with Inspector Banks at their heart. The latest title, number 23, is *When the Music's Over* (2016). Several have been filmed for TV, starring Stephen Tompkinson. The author was born in Richmond.

Stuart Pawson: *Chill Factor* (2001), etc

Charlie Priest is a detective with a degree in art and a love of the Yorkshire moors. Pawson has set his highly successful detective stories around the fictional South Yorkshire wool town of Heckley, and with later titles including *Limestone Cowboy* and *Shooting Elvis*, you can expect some dry wit too.

Adrian Braddy: *How Yorkshire Are You? The Yorkshire Citizenship Test* (2017)

As the editor of Yorkshire's National Magazine *The Dalesman*, Adrian is just the person to test your knowledge of the county, and here you'll also be assessed on other Yorkshire traits such as frugality, tea-brewing and pudding-making.

Ian McMillan: *Neither Nowt Nor Summat* (2015)

Can a man from Barnsley often engaged as a 'Professional Yorkshireman' worry about his Yorkshire-ness? Having a dad from Scotland makes him only half-Yorkshire, but is that enough? So Ian sets out to discover the essence of the county – and whether the Yorkshire Pudding is worthy of becoming a UNESCO Intangible Heritage Site.

THINGS TO WATCH

Yorkshire has featured as the backdrop to several successful, long-running TV series, which can still be seen regularly in daytime repeats. *All Creatures Great and Small*, the veterinary tales of James Herriot in the 1950s, was based on Askrigg but shot all over the Dales. The comedy series *Open All Hours*, which starred Ronnie Barker and David Jason, used Balby, Doncaster as its backdrop – as does its modern version *Still Open All Hours*, while Roy Clarke's other great TV success, *Last of the Summer Wine*

– which holds the record for the longest-running sitcom in the world, at 37 years – is forever associated with Holmfirth.

Heartbeat, the rural detective drama set in the 1960s, was based at Goathland, and used locations across the North York Moors. Its sister hospital-based series, *The Royal*, was largely filmed in Scarborough. All shared a gently humorous view of doughty, warm-hearted Yorkshire folk.

The crime drama *DCI Banks* presents a more serious urban and up-to-date view of Yorkshire, using many locations including Leeds, Huby, Bradford and Huddersfield.

Yorkshire's most recent starring role has been in the BAFTA award-winning gritty police drama *Happy Valley*, which first aired in 2014. The series uses many West Yorkshire locations including Todmorden, Luddenden, Mytholmroyd, Bradford, Keighley, Sowerby Bridge and, of course, Hebden Bridge. It was written by Huddersfield-born scriptwriter Sally Wainwright, who also penned the sharp and witty *Last Tango in Halifax*. While this series used many locations around Greater Manchester, Halifax itself features more often in the second series.

Two notable movies about Yorkshire hit the big screen in the 1990s, both comic tales of post-industrial depression. *Brassed Off* (1996) depicted the fortunes of the Grimly colliery band after the pit closed – and any rumour of similarities with the real life story of the Grimethorpe Colliery Band are fed by the fact that the real band played on the wonderful

▼ Sid's Cafe from *Last of the Summer Wine*, Holmfirth

CAFE

THE WORLD FAMOUS SID'S CAFE
LAST OF THE SUMMER WINE
is **OPEN** for
TEAS AND COFFEES AND A WIDE SELECTION OF
SNACKS AND SANDWICHES,
GIFTS AND SOUVENIRS
TRY SID'S FAMOUS SCONES
TOPPED WITH REAL FRESH DAIRY CREAM
AND FRUIT, DELICIOUS !!

sound track, the real Grimethorpe Colliery entrance was seen on screen, and it was filmed all over Rotherham, Doncaster and Barnsley.

The hugely successful film *The Full Monty* (1997) dealt with unemployed steelworkers in Sheffield, and the city provided most of the filming locations for real.

Yorkshire's comedy gold streak continued with *Calendar Girls* (2003), based on the true story of a Yorkshire Women's Institute group's fund-raising efforts which became a worldwide sensation – Rylstone was the original setting, but nearby Kettlewell took most of the screen glory.

Films of the Brontë sisters' novels are a great way to access images of Yorkshire – but ignore the first, classic version of *Wuthering Heights* (1939), where Vivien Leigh and Laurence Olivier were firmly stuck on a Hollywood lot.

Emily's *Wuthering Heights* and Charlotte's *Jane Eyre* are the most frequently seen (both most recently in 2011), but there has been an adaptation too of Anne's *The Tenant of Wildfell Hall* (for TV, 1996).

The coal mines of Barnsley also played an essential part of the 1969 film *Kes*, written by South Yorkshire-born Barry Hines and directed by Ken Loach. The film, about 15-year-old Billy Casper and his love of a kestrel, is ranked seventh in the British Film Institute's Top Ten British Films.

It's worth mentioning two children's films with good Yorkshire backdrops. The real star of Edith Nesbit's *The Railway Children*, filmed so memorably in 1970, was of course the Keighley and Worth Valley Railway – the Brontë Parsonage got a look-in too. Allerton Castle, north of Harrogate, provided exterior shots for the 1993 version of Frances Hodgson Burnett's *The Secret Garden*, and Fountain's Hall is also in there somewhere.

Back on the small screen, and the documentary series *The Yorkshire Vet*, which follows the real-life vets at James Herriot's former practice, is currently a big hit on Channel 5, while the walking series *Walks Around Britain* regularly features Yorkshire locations.

For a slice of drama-filled rural Yorkshire soap life, you won't want to miss *Emmerdale*, aired five nights a week on ITV.

These days the exteriors are filmed on a cloned set, built on the Harewood Estate, and you can take a tour on weekends between April and October – for a price. Or if you prefer, you can visit Esholt – the real village where it was filmed, back in the days when it was called *Emmerdale Farm* and the plot lines centred on the fictional farming community of Beckindale.

THINGS TO KNOW

With a county so large, so beautiful and so historic, there are many fascinating facts to share:

▶ Tourism in Yorkshire & Humber is worth over £7 billion – which is more than the whole tourism expenditure in Ireland.

▶ With claims dating back to the early 17th century, Scarborough is said to be Britain's first seaside resort – welcoming holidaymakers for over 360 years.

▶ The highest point on the east coast of England is at Boulby, near Staithes in North Yorkshire, where the cliffs reach over 600 feet high.

▶ With the North York Moors, most of the Yorkshire Dales and part of the Peak District, Yorkshire contains nearly a third of the total area of all the National Parks in England.

▶ The Yorkshire Dales is home to England's largest single drop waterfall, Hardraw Force, with a drop of around 100 feet. It also has Britain's highest pub, the Tan Hill Inn, at 1,732 feet above sea level.

▶ The Humber Bridge is the longest single-span suspension bridge in the UK, second longest in Europe and fifth longest in the world. It was the longest in the world when completed in 1981.

▶ Yorkshire can claim to be the birthplace of both club football and rugby league.

▶ The West Yorkshire Playhouse in Leeds stages more productions each year than any other theatre outside London.

▶ Yorkshire has six Michelin Star restaurants – which is more than any other region outside London.

▶ York Minster is the largest Gothic cathedral in Northern Europe. It took 252 years to build and contains the biggest expanse of medieval stained glass in the world in its Great East Window.

▶ Standedge Tunnel in Huddersfield is the highest, longest and deepest canal tunnel in the country, at around 3.75 miles long.

▶ Leeds and Sheffield can claim to be two of the greenest cities in Europe.

▶ Doncaster's railway works, known as The Plant, constructed two of the world's most famous steam locomotives – *Mallard* and *Flying Scotsman*.

▶ Yorkshire has two UNESCO World Heritage sites: Fountains Abbey and Studley Royal in North Yorkshire, and Saltaire village in West Yorkshire.

▶ The Turkish Bath and Health Spa in Harrogate, now restored to glory, is one of only seven remaining 19th-century Turkish baths in the UK.

So there you have it, plenty of possible answers to pub quizzes in the future...

THINGS TO PACK

First you'll need suitable clothing. That doesn't necessarily mean thick duffle coats, but really layering – several thinner layers which you can remove when the heatwave comes – and waterproofs, of course, just in case. These are especially necessary if you're venturing for a walk, which you surely will.

Sensible footwear is a must, too – Wellingtons and walking boots allow you to take full advantage of the opportunities to explore the countryside. However, smart shoes could be required for that elegant evening meal...

You'll be needing a good camera of course, to take photographs of all the sights and to remind you of the great time you had in Yorkshire. It's worth bringing extra batteries and memory cards, although often you'll be able to pick up what you need locally.

Camping or beach or general outdoor gear is always useful – with 45 miles of coast, you'll need some beach stuff. Folding chairs, picnic baskets and cool boxes and – of course – buckets and spades, are in order. You'll often see those collapsible stripy windbreaks on the beaches of Yorkshire, and those wide open, windy beaches are great for flying kites. And although you might not think of it to start with, bring a wetsuit and a surfboard if you're into that scene. A number of Yorkshire's beaches have great surf, including Cayton Bay.

If cycling is your thing, then you can have great fun with your bikes in Yorkshire. There are hundreds of miles of cycling lanes, bridleways and trails to explore, both on the levels and in the high places. Of course, you could hire them locally as you travel around the region.

If you are a walker, then the correct AA Walker's or Ordnance Survey Explorer map is a smart idea, showing the footpath details you need. With Yorkshire's massive size, though, you'll probably need more than one if you are walking far or moving across the county. The AA produces several excellent books of circular walks around Yorkshire, including *50 Walks in North Yorkshire* and *50 Walks in the Yorkshire Dales*, which have maps already included for each route.

▼ Don't forget your walking boots

▲ Cleveland Way on Easby Moor

BASIC INFORMATION

The best time to visit Yorkshire really depends on what you want to do when you're here, and who you're coming with. From the weather point of view, Yorkshire's climate is a couple of degrees cooler generally than, say, Cornwall and suffers from the typical unpredictability of the English weather. The summer months between May and September are usually best to promise sunny days and the temperatures are quite mild. As for rain, the huge towers of the Pennines act like a bit of a rain shield, with less rain in the areas as you travel eastwards in Yorkshire – in fact, the east coast is one of the driest parts of the UK. Also, there are relatively low rain averages found in the Vale of York and around the Doncaster area.

It's highly unlikely therefore that it will rain solidly for two weeks, but if it does, there's a wealth of places indoors to keep the kids entertained. Most towns and cities have a good choice of cinemas as well as useful indoor play areas to visit, and a great number of the larger visitor attractions throughout the county are either located indoors or have a large indoor area.

If you're not too bothered about the weather – and don't have children – the best times to visit are in the school term times, as the family-friendly tourist attractions especially get very busy in school holidays. There are great offers at hotels and bed-and-breakfasts outside the major tourist times, and although several attractions might have reduced opening hours, they sometimes have a reduced entry fee to match.

The road network around Yorkshire is very good, with most of the big towns and cities connected by either motorways or primary roads. The A1 – the major route from both the north and the south to Yorkshire – has been upgraded to motorway status for most of its length throughout the county. The M1 is the alternative way from the south, and the west to east running trans-Pennine M62 is now fairly free-flowing at all times, thanks to the new managed motorway section. The M18 is less well known, but joins all three, with 26 miles of road around South Yorkshire.

Yorkshire's rail network matches the motorway in destinations – and travelling to, from and around Yorkshire is easy by train. From London, Scotland, and the southeast, the main operator is Virgin Trains East Coast, which operates plenty of services to Doncaster, York, Wakefield and Leeds – along the very line on which the historic *Mallard* and *Flying Scotsman* ran. From the southwest, the Midlands and Scotland, Cross Country pass through Sheffield, Doncaster, Wakefield, Leeds and York. TransPennine Express straddles the width of the

country, bringing visitors from Lancashire as well as Manchester, Liverpool and Cleethorpes. East Midlands Trains covers from Merseyside to the East Midlands and Lincolnshire – they also operate to Sheffield from the splendid St Pancras Station in London.

A little known fact is that between Yorkshire and London there are two smaller operators who run to some fantastic destinations previously unloved by the InterCity network: First Hull Trains and Grand Central. Check them out, as they have services which call at Doncaster and York, as well as Hull, Thirsk, Northallerton, Halifax and Bradford, and can be quite competitive on price.

The vast majority of train services between Yorkshire stations are run by Northern, and their Rail Rovers and Ranger multi-day tickets are a great value way to travel around the county.

The county has two airports; Leeds Bradford International and the newer Doncaster Sheffield Airport. Neither airport has a direct train connection, but there are good bus services which link up to the rail network at Leeds and Doncaster respectively for onward travel.

Coach travel to Yorkshire is easy too, with National Express operating regular direct services to York, Leeds, Sheffield, Doncaster and Hull.

FESTIVALS & EVENTS

There are so many Yorkshire festivals that it's impossible to list them all, but here's a small selection.

▶ FEBRUARY

Jorvik Viking Festival
jorvik-viking-festival.co.uk
The largest Viking Festival in Europe celebrates York's Norse heritage and sees over 40,000 visitors experiencing family-friendly events, lectures, guided walks and battle re-enactments.

▶ APRIL

Harrogate Spring Flower Show
flowershow.org.uk
The Spring Flower Show is one of the highlights of the gardening world. Famous for its daffodil show and early season tulips, it provides a showcase for garden designers, nurseries and growers from across the country. The Autumn Flower Show takes place in September.

▶ MAY

Malton Food Lovers Festival
visitmalton.com/food-lovers-festival

Known as Yorkshire's Foodie Glastonbury, the Malton Food Lovers Festival is a celebration of the county's finest produce and cooking, all set along the streets of Yorkshire's Food Capital – Malton. Expect delicious street food, talks, tastings, celebrity chefs, demos, cookery lessons and loads of music.

▶ JUNE

The Dales Festival of Food and Drink
dalesfestivaloffood.org
Come along and experience local food and drink at its best. The event is based in Leyburn, Wensleydale, and includes a food hall, real ale, farming displays, cookery demonstrations and guest speakers.

▶ JULY

Burton Agnes Jazz and Blues Festival
burtonagnes.com
Three days of the best jazz and blues around, in the Elizabethan Hall and its beautiful grounds.

Bradford Festival
bradfordfestival.org.uk
The lively annual Mela has been incorporated into a bigger, more inclusive event, with international acts taking to the stage in the town centre City Park.

Rotherham Real Ale and Music Festival
magnarealale.co.uk
How does three days to experience more than 250 real ales and 80 different types of cider, wine, perry and lager appeal? Sounds like a great challenge. Each year the festival raises over £100,000 for charity.

Tramlines
tramlines.org.uk
One of the largest music festivals in the UK, Tramlines is a major event on the Sheffield and South Yorkshire music scene. Gigs are held in many different venues across the city.

Go Racing in Yorkshire Summer Festival
goracing.co.uk
Go Racing brings together all nine Yorkshire racecourses for a week-long celebration of horseracing and open days.

The Great Yorkshire Show
greatyorkshireshow.co.uk
This is England's biggest traditional agricultural show, drawing visitors from near and far to the showground on the outskirts of Harrogate. Here you can admire livestock, browse the stands and enjoy the fun of the show ring.

▶ AUGUST

Whitby Regatta
whitbyregatta.co.uk
Four days of yacht racing, rowing races and free entertainment ending with a firework display from what may be the oldest regatta on the northeast coast.

Whitby Folk Week
whitbyfolk.co.uk
The North's premier folk festival, with some 600 lively events in 30 different venues, based around traditional song, music, dance and storytelling.

Leeds Festival
leedsfestival.com
Yorkshire's biggest music festival takes place in Bramham Park, near Wetherby, attracting the megastars of the pop/rock world and up to 90,000 fans.

▶ SEPTEMBER

Richmond Walking & Book Festival
booksandboots.org
More than a week's worth of walking, talks and book-related goodness. Join in with the walks and meet celebrated walking authors, based around this lovely town on the edge of the Yorkshire Dales National Park.

St Leger Festival Week
visitdoncaster.co.uk
Doncaster's annual 10-day festival is a celebration of racing, music, fine food, arts and culture. For the local children, the highlight is the St Leger Funfair.

York Food and Drink Festival
yorkfoodfestival.com
Around 10 days of celebration of delicious local produce and the joys of good things to eat and drink from Yorkshire and around the world. There are also lots of cooking demonstrations.

▶ OCTOBER

Harrogate Comedy Festival
harrogatetheatre.co.uk
Starting back in 2009, the popular Harrogate Comedy Festival has become a firm favourite in the funny calendar, mixing well-known established names, cult stand-ups and rising stars.

▶ DECEMBER

Grassington Dickensian Festival
grassington.uk.com
For three Saturdays before Christmas, Grassington is transported back to the age of Charles Dickens. The village square is transformed into a Victorian-style market, with shopkeepers, villagers and visitors in costume, and musicians, dancers, street entertainers and country crafts.

CAMPSITES

For more information on these and other campsites, visit theAA.com/self-catering-and-campsites

Skirlington Leisure Park
▶▶▶▶▶ HOLIDAY CENTRE
skirlington.com
Skipsea, YO25 8SY | 01262 468213
Open Mar–Oct
This large park is close to the beach in meadowland with young trees and shrubs. The site has a supermarket and an amusement arcade, plus occasional entertainment in the clubhouse. Amenities include an indoor heated swimming pool complex with sauna, steam room and gym, a 10-pin bowling alley and indoor soft play area.

Vale of Pickering Caravan Park
▶▶▶▶▶
valeofpickering.co.uk
Carr House Farm, Allerston, YO18 7PQ | 01723 859280
Open 5 Mar–3 Jan
Family park with facilities including a shop and woodland walks. Children will enjoy the play area and large ball sports area. The park is in countryside bounded by hedges, with manicured grassland and seasonal floral displays.

Flower of May Holiday Park
▶▶▶▶▶ HOLIDAY CENTRE
flowerofmay.com
Lebberston Cliff, Filey, YO11 3NU
01723 584311 | Open Easter–Oct
A high-quality family park with top-class facilities. Grass and hard pitches are available. There's a full range of recreational activities for everyone, including an indoor swimming pool, leisure complex, games room and adventure playgrounds. The best part, though, is the 'Scarborough Fair' museum, with a collection of restored fairground attractions.

Golden Square Caravan & Camping Park ▶▶▶▶▶
goldensquarecaravanpark.com
Oswaldkirk, Helmsley, YO62 5YQ
01439 788269 | Open Mar–Oct
A popular and spacious site with very good facilities in a quiet rural setting with lovely views over the North York Moors. Terraced on three levels and surrounded by trees, it's great for families, with excellent

play areas and plenty of space for ballgames. Country walks and bike trails start here, and you're also close to York.

Old Station Holiday Park ►►►►

oldstation-masham.co.uk
Old Station Yard, Low Burton, Masham, HG4 4DF | 01765 689569
Open Mar–Nov
An ex-railway station, with enthusiastic owners who have maintained the railway theme. The cafe, in a carefully restored wagon shed, provides a range of meals. A major attraction of this park is the fact that the town of Masham, home of the Theakston and Black Sheep breweries, is very close.

Grouse Hill Caravan Park ►►►►

grousehill.co.uk
Flask Bungalow Farm, Fylingdales, Robin Hood's Bay, YO22 4QH
01947 880543 | Open Mar–Oct
A spacious, terraced park on a south-facing slope overlooking the North Yorks National Park. The site has solar-heated toilet blocks and a woodland adventure play area, and is an ideal base for serious walking. No hardstandings for tourers, only grass pitches.

St Helens in the Park ►►►►►

sthelenscaravanpark.co.uk
Wykeham, YO13 9QD | 01723 862771 | Open 15 Feb–15 Jan
(Nov–Jan shop/laundry closed)
This delightful landscaped park has some stunning floral displays. If nights under canvas don't appeal, camping pods are available. A cycle route leads through the Wykeham Estate and the Downe Arms Country Inn is nearby.

Robin Hood Caravan & Camping Park ►►►►

robinhoodcaravanpark.co.uk
Green Dyke Lane, Slingsby, YO62 4AP
01653 628391 | Open Mar–Oct
This pleasant, well-maintained, grassy park is on the edge of Slingsby. There is electricity for every pitch, and a centrally heated toilet block. Treasure trail and play area for children.

Goosewood Holiday Park ►►►►►

flowerofmay.com
Sutton-on-the-Forest, YO61 1ET
01347 810829 | Open Mar–2 Jan
Set in woodland, six miles from York, Goosewood is a relaxing park with a lake and seasonal fishing. Patio pitches are ideal for those who like their privacy. The whole family can gather at the indoor swimming pool, club house and games room.

Ladycross Plantation Caravan Park ►►►►

ladycrossplantation.co.uk
Egton, Whitby, YO21 1UA
01947 895502 | Open Mar–Nov
Ladycross is set in 30 acres of peaceful woodland. The pitches are sited in small groups in clearings around two smart amenity blocks. The site is well placed for visiting Whitby and exploring the North York Moors.

A–Z of Yorkshire

▶ Addingham MAP REF 327 E4

Unless you're looking for a nice place to retire to, what'll make you want to stop here is the cosy, welcoming pub. Addingham is an amalgamation of three separate communities between Ilkley and Skipton that grew together as the textile trades expanded – Listers adapted their mills to weave parachute silk in World War II, but the mills are long gone, leaving an attractive backwater. The picturesque St Peter's Church stands at the eastern end, close to the River Wharfe. Rombald's Moor lies to the south.

EAT AND DRINK
The Fleece
fleeceinnaddingham.co.uk
154 Main Street, LS29 0LY
01943 830491

In a great location, where several well-tramped footpaths meet, The Fleece is a sturdy, stone-built 17th-century coaching inn. Sadly damaged by a major fire in 2015, the pub has been carefully restored and brought back to its former glory. Now run by the Seafood Pub Company, it offers great local produce including (naturally) the freshest fish, (which can be pre-ordered) as well as a wide choice of pub classics, from steaks and pies to slow roast pork belly. In addition to the traditional bar with its open fire and flagstone floors, there's a stylish, contemporary gin and champagne bar on the first floor.

▶ Askrigg MAP REF 335 D4

It might only be small, but the appealing stone village of Askrigg, nestled in lovely Wensleydale, certainly has a long history which goes back at least as far as the Domesday Book. No doubt it benefited from the misfortunes of its neighbour, Wensley (see page 285), which was almost wiped out by the plague in 1563. Askrigg quickly nabbed the weekly market concession, and local industries boomed, including clock-making, brewing, spinning and dyeing.

Prosperity was fleeting, for Wensleydale's railway station was built at Hawes (see page 125) – a mere three miles away, but just far enough to switch the main tourist focus to Hawes, where it remains to this day. However, Askrigg got the last laugh in 1977 when location scouts were scouring the area for an unspoiled Dales town to represent Darrowby in a TV version of James Herriot's veterinary tales. *All Creatures Great and Small* was a smash hit, running until 1990 and still sometimes seen today, putting the village firmly on the tourist map.

SADDLE UP

Wensleydale Equestrian Centre

wensleydaleequestrian.com
Bainbridge, near Askrigg, DL8 3DB
01969 650367
How about seeing the area from a different perspective? The Wensleydale Equestrian Centre at Bainbridge offers trekking and hacking out, from short-lead rein hacks to full day treks – and you don't have to be experienced to join in.

EAT AND DRINK

The King's Arms

kingsarmsaskrigg.co.uk
Main Street, DL8 3HQ
01969 650113
If you have long memories and remember *All Creatures Great and Small*, you could drink here and pretend you're at James Herriot's favourite watering hole – Drover's Arms – as The King's Arms doubled for it in the BBC series. There's a big inglenook fireplace in the oak-panelled bar, where photographs show cast members relaxing between takes. In reality it's an elegant 18th-century coaching inn, owned by hotelier Charles Cody. The menu is written up daily on an impressive mirror behind the bar, and is based on top-quality produce, such as game from the surrounding moors, and fish fresh from Hartlepool. Look also for loin of local lamb, pan-fried salmon, and wild mushroom risotto.

▼ Dry-stone wall, near Askrigg

▶ Aysgarth   MAP REF 335 E4

Aysgarth is a village of two halves. The larger part is set along the main A684, while the other half is set around St Andrew's Church. It's worth looking inside – it contains the spectacular choir screen brought here from Jervaulx Abbey, down the dale (see page 155), when it was closed by Henry VIII. Like the elaborate stall beside it, it was carved by the renowned Ripon workshops.

Aysgarth Falls are just outside the village on the road to Carperby. A must-see Wensleydale attraction, they are well signposted. There's a National Park Centre here, together with a good-sized car park and a busy cluster of shops and cafes.

There are three sets of falls at Aysgarth – Upper, Middle and Lower – each with different characters depending on the width of the River Ure. These aren't exactly Niagara – they are gentler, more understated – a tumble perhaps, rather than a fall – but still extraordinarily beautiful, and the Upper Falls are best of all. These featured in a key scene in the film *Robin Hood, Prince of Thieves* (1991), when Robin (Kevin Costner) and Little John (Nick Brimble) fought here with staves.

▼ Aysgarth Falls

As the waterfalls are on private land, there's a small admission charge by way of an honesty box for access to the best viewpoints. Don't bother trying to avoid the charge by walking round to view the falls from the nearby road – the view just isn't worth the saving.

Before heading off to look at the rest of the falls, pick up the useful walk leaflet from the National Park Centre, which provides lots of information about the woodlands you'll be walking through and the local wildlife. The name Aysgarth means an open place marked by oak trees, and as you walk through the woods to view the Middle and Lower Falls you're strolling through remnants of the ancient Forest of Wensleydale, which once covered most of the countryside in the area. Today the art of coppicing is being revived here.

GET OUTDOORS
Aysgarth Falls National Park Centre
yorkshiredales.org.uk
DL8 3TH | 01969 662910
This visitor centre is usefully stocked with maps, guides, walks and local information. Interactive displays explain the history and natural history of the area. It's perfectly situated close to the waterfalls on the River Ure. Various guided walks begin here throughout the year.

TAKE IN A GARDEN
Aysgarth Edwardian Rock Garden
aysgarthrockgarden.co.uk
Asygarth, DL8 3AH
Take time out to visit the Grade II listed Rock Garden, a walled site commissioned in the years before World War I by Frank Sayer-Graham - who owned the cottage opposite. Listed in 1988, the current owners are raising funds through donations to restore these fascinating gardens to their former glory.

EAT AND DRINK
The Coppice Coffee Shop
coppicecafe.com
Aysgarth Falls National Park Centre, DL8 3TH | 01969 663763
Known locally as Karen's, this cafe has long been a welcome sight to visitors to Aysgarth Falls. Right next to the National Park Centre and the car park and bus stop, it's an ideal place for a light lunch. Filled jacket potatoes are popular – and locally sourced ingredients are used whenever possible.

The George & Dragon Inn
georgeanddragonaysgarth.co.uk
DL8 3AD | 01969 663358
Inside this 17th-century listed building is a proud, centuries-long tradition of Yorkshire hospitality. Keep cosy in winter by the fireside, and in summer enjoy your drinks and meals out on the flower-filled patio. Well-kept real ales are served, and the inn has a great reputation for its traditional food, including steak pie and fish and chips.

▶ Barnsley MAP REF 323 F3

Barnsley is a medium-sized former mining and industrial town lying between Leeds and Sheffield. Enthusiastic remodelling in the 1960s left the town centre with few buildings of architectural note, but the imposing town hall is the exception – constructed in 1933 and built out of gleaming white Portland stone, it now houses a splendid new museum of local life, Experience Barnsley, which opened in 2013.

Barnsley owes its existence to monks from the monastery of St John in nearby Pontefract who relocated nearer to the River Dearne, at a hub of significant roads. Barnsley grew significantly in the 17th century, developing as an important stopping-off point between Leeds, Wakefield, Sheffield and all routes south. Barnsley's history as a centre for coal and glassmaking is still at the heart of the town today, but the last pit closed in 1994, and only one glassmaking company remains – business parks and call centres have replaced the old industrial base.

Barnsley is the home of the world-famous Grimethorpe Colliery brass band, who featured notably in the 1996 movie *Brassed Off* – not just playing the BAFTA-nominated soundtrack, but providing real brass-playing extras who helped bring the story to life on the big screen.

TAKE IN SOME HISTORY
Monk Bretton Priory
www.english-heritage.org.uk
17 Abbey Lane, S71 5QD
0370 333 1181 | Open daily
The priory was an important Cluniac house, founded in 1153. The considerable remains of the gatehouse, church and other buildings can be seen.

VISIT THE MUSEUM
Experience Barnsley
experience-barnsley.com
Town Hall, S70 2TA | 01226 772500
Open Mon–Fri 9–4, Sat 10–4,
Sun & BH 11–3
Discover the town's history, from the Roman invasion to the miners' strikes of the 1980s and beyond.

CATCH A PERFORMANCE
The Civic
barnsleycivic.co.uk
Hanson Street, S70 2HZ
01226 327000
Since reopening in 2009, this lively performance space has hosted a diverse range of entertainment, exhibitions and events. For an up-to-date list of what's on, check the website.

GET ACTIVE
Barnsley Metrodome
www.bpl.org.uk
Queens Road, S71 1AN
01226 730060
Barnsley's multi-activity leisure complex has fitness suites, dance studios, squash courts, a sports hall and a Ten Pin Bowling Alley. The main leisure

swimming area is called the Calypso Cove waterpark.

PLAY A ROUND
Barnsley Golf Club
barnsleygolfclub.co.uk
Wakefield Road, Staincross, S75 6JZ
01226 382856 | Open daily
Undulating municipal parkland course with easy walking apart from the last four holes. Testing eighth and 18th holes.

Sandhill Golf Club
sandhillgolfclub.co.uk
Middlecliffe Lane, Little Houghton,
S72 0HW | 01226 753444
Open daily
Attractive, easy walking parkland with views of the surrounding countryside. The course has strategically placed bunkers, the fourth hole having a deep bunker directly in front of the green.

▶ PLACES NEARBY
Just outside Barnsley you will find Cannon Hall, Elsecar Heritage Centre and Worsbrough Mill.

Cannon Hall Museum, Park and Gardens
cannon-hall.com
Bark House Lane, Cawthorne,
S75 4AT | 01226 790270 | Gardens and park open daily; check website for museum opening times
This old country house is set in some 70 acres of beautiful parkland, west of Barnsley. For nearly 300 years Cannon Hall was home to the Spencer and Spencer-Stanhope family before being turned into a

10 famous sports personalities from Yorkshire

▶ **Geoffrey Boycott**, Yorkshire CCC and England cricketer – Fitzwilliam, near Barnsley

▶ **Alistair Brownlee**, Olympic gold medallist 2012, world champion in triathlon 2011 – Dewsbury

▶ **Jonathan Brownlee**, Olympic bronze medallist and triathlon world champion, 2012 – Leeds

▶ **Ed Clancy**, Olympic gold cyclist, 2012 – Barnsley

▶ **Jessica Ennis-Hill**, Olympic gold medallist, 2012, and heptathlon world champion – Sheffield

▶ **Alan Hinkes**, mountaineer, first Briton to climb the world's highest 14 peaks – Northallerton

▶ **Kevin Keegan**, footballer and twice European Footballer of the Year – Doncaster

▶ **Anita Lonsbrough**, Olympic gold swimmer, 1960 – York

▶ **Ian McGeechan**, Scottish Rugby Union legend – Headingly

▶ **Mike Tindall**, England Rugby Union Captain and husband of Zara Phillips – Otley

museum in the 1950s. You can see local ceramics, glass, furniture and paintings here – and an original painting by Constable, a portrait of 'Mrs Tuder'. The park and gardens are excellent for a relaxed walk, family days out or a picnic.

Elsecar Heritage Centre

elsecar-heritage.com
Wath Road, Elsecar, S74 8HJ
01226 740203 | Open daily 10–5

Elsecar Heritage Centre has an interesting variety of antiques shops, craft workshops, artist studios and small traders. Take a ride on the Heritage Railway and check the website for information about special event weekends.

Worsbrough Mill

worsbrough-mill.com
Worsbrough Bridge, Barnsley,
S70 5LJ | 01226 774527

Open weekends 10–4; school holidays & BH daily 10–4. Tea Room Tue–Sun 10–4; Country Park open daily all year round

Set in 240 acres of quiet parkland, this 17th-century working water mill is a great place to learn about the milling process, and you can even buy their premium quality flours to bake with at home. The 60-acre reservoir is a haven for wildlife and regularly attracts birdwatchers and anglers – try to time your visit for a day when the Millers Tea Room is open.

▶ Bedale MAP REF 336 B5

Many people miss Bedale as they drive into Wensleydale – but visitors are in for a treat in this attractive old market town, full of characterful local shops, cafes and eateries.

With its 14th-century market cross, there's plenty of history to discover around this town. On the wide main street stands Bedale Hall, a Georgian mansion which today serves as rather grand council offices. Inside you'll find tourist information and a tiny local museum, whose chief exhibit is a fire engine dating from 1748. The 400-year-old bell in the church was rescued from Jervaulx Abbey (see page 155) after the Dissolution – to find out more, pick up a Heritage Trail leaflet.

Bedale is a station on one of Britain's newest railway lines, the Wensleydale Railway. It runs from Leeming Bar in the Vale of York to Leyburn and Redmire (for Bolton Castle) in Wensleydale. The original line, axed in the 1960s, was reopened in 2003 when campaigners leased some 22 miles of old track and began running trains again for themselves. Bedale Station is now served by diesel rail car units every couple of hours in summer, and at weekends in winter. There are ambitious plans for the railway to link up with the east coast mainline at Northallerton, and for restoring the Settle–Carlisle link – some journey that promises to be. See wensleydalerail.com to check their progress.

To the south of Bedale, off the B6268, is Thorp Perrow Arboretum, which has more than 2,000 species of plants and trees in its 85 acres of garden.

61

BEDALE

VISIT THE MUSEUM
Bedale Museum
bedalemuseum.org.uk
DL8 1AA | 01677 427516
Check website for opening times
Located in a building that dates back to the 17th century, this is a fascinating museum. The central attraction is the Bedale fire engine of 1742. Other artefacts include documents, toys, craft tools and household utensils, which all help to give an absorbing picture of the lifestyle of their times.

MEET THE ANIMALS
The Big Sheep and Little Cow Farm
bigsheeplittlecow.co.uk
Bedale, DL8 1AW | 01677 422125
Open daily 10–5.30; farm tours throughout the day
A great family-run farm visitor centre with a unique hands-on farm experience. The farm tours allow children – and adults – to hold and feed the animals. The whole family can come and play together – whether in Wooly Jumpers Play Barn or outside on the go-karts, or even in the large sandpit. Take home some ice cream or Dexter beef from the farm shop.

GET OUTDOORS
Thorp Perrow Arboretum
thorpperrow.com
DL8 2PS | 01677 425323
Open mid-Feb to mid-Nov daily 11–5, mid-Nov to mid-Feb daily 11–3
Explore 100 acres of beautiful woodland with walks, trails and glades. One of the finest private collections of trees and shrubs in the North, it provides interest all year round and has a Birds of Prey and Mammal Centre and a tea room.

PLAY A ROUND
Bedale Golf Club
bedalegolfclub.com
Leyburn Road, DL8 1EZ
01677 422451 (secretary)
Open daily all year
Founded in 1894, this is one of North Yorkshire's most picturesque and interesting courses. It is set in parkland with tree-lined fairways and receptive greens protected by bunkers providing a good golfing test.

EAT AND DRINK
The Castle Arms Inn
Meadow Lane, Snape, nr Bedale, DL8 2TB | 01677 470270
In the sleepy village of Snape, this family-run 18th-century pub is a good starting point for walking and cycling, and visiting local stately homes, castles and film locations. The homely interior has exposed beams, flagstoned floors and real fires in the bar, which is home to real ales from the Marston's Brewery. A meal in the restaurant selected from the ever-changing menu might feature a pub classic or something more cosmopolitan from the Italian chef. Afterwards, there is a range of home-made desserts and liqueur coffees on offer to tempt you.

▲ Bempton Cliffs from Thornwick Bay

▶ **Bempton Cliffs** MAP REF 331 F1

One of the most important nesting bird sites on the east coast, these towering, sheer 400-foot chalk cliffs offer seasonal accommodation to more than 200,000 breeding seabirds including puffins, guillemots, razorbills, kittiwakes and fulmars. It is one of the country's most significant breeding sites for Britain's largest seabird, the gannet, with several thousand nests.

Until conservation laws intervened in the 1950s, the cliffs were worked by 'climmers' – intrepid locals who abseiled on ropes to gather hundreds of thousands of eggs each year; some of the ledges and pillars are still named after them.

One of the best coastal walks in the area leads east from here round the spectacular cliffs of Flamborough Head.

MEET THE WILDLIFE
RSPB Nature Reserve
rspb.org.uk
YO15 1JF | 01262 422212
Visitor Centre open daily Mar–Oct
9.30–5, Nov–Feb 9.30–4

The RSPB runs six safe viewing points and a visitor centre here, with screens showing live images from the cliffs. Watch out for grey seals and puffins in early summer.

▶ Beverley MAP REF P332 B2

Beverley is one of the best-looking old market towns in the north of England, and has often been voted among the top places to live in the UK. Discover a great range of boutique stores and the medieval market.

Dating back to around the 700s, the town was founded by John – later St John – of Beverley, whose first building project was a monastery. He became known as a bit of a miracle-worker, pilgrims came to see, and Beverley grew to become one of the most important Christian centres in the North.

Today one of the town's main attractions is the architecture. It has streets lined with mostly 18th- and 19th-century houses, two market places and the North Bar of 1409 – a brick gateway. Beverley Minster – a large, long building with twin towers and an interior full of light and elaborate carving – is very impressive, but don't miss out on the smaller St Mary's Church at the other end of the town, which is also rather special. The carving of a rabbit in St Michael's Chapel, with a pilgrim's staff and pouch, is reputedly the inspiration for the White Rabbit in Lewis Carroll's *Alice's Adventures in Wonderland* (1865).

Beverley also has quite a reputation for music, with music festivals throughout the year attracting visitors from far and wide.

Horseracing has been a part of life in the town since the 16th century, and the course at Beverley is well known for its racing on the flat, and for its family-friendly events.

TAKE IN SOME HISTORY
Beverley Minster, St John
beverleyminster.org.uk
Minster Yard North, HU17 0DN
01482 868540 | Open Mar–Apr
9–5, May–Sep 9–5.30, Oct 9–5,
Nov–Feb 9–4

There's no doubt Beverley Minster is one of the finest Gothic churches in Europe and is equal to the greatest of British cathedrals. Its twin towers are the town's landmark. The current church was built between 1220 and 1425, embracing and blending the elements Early English, Decorated and Perpendicular architectural styles. The central tower holds an unusual treadwheel crane – originally a donkey would have walked in it, raising a platform to roof-height for building repairs. Inside you can see a 13th-century double staircase to a lost chapter house in the north choir aisle, a 14th-century altar screen and the huge east window – the only surviving medieval window here. Don't miss the lively misericords, or the Saxon Frith Stool, where sanctuary could be claimed in times past by sitting on it.

Beverley Guildhall

museums.eastriding.gov.uk
Register Square, HU17 9XX
01482 392783 | Open every Fri,
10–4; phone for guided tours at
other times

A fantastic Grade I listed building, this has an equally fascinating history, with parts dating back to a private dwelling of 1320. The Guildhall has been the seat of civic governance in Beverley for over 500 years and is now a museum – don't miss the Georgian courtroom.

GET ON THE WATER

Beverley Boat Hire

beverleyboathire.co.uk
316 Hull Bridge Road, HU17 9RT
07726 491390

Why not experience the Beverley area by hiring a boat, with either a rowing or motor launch along the River Hull? Available by the hour, half or full days.

GO TO THE RACES

Beverley Racecourse

beverley-racecourse.co.uk
York Road, HU17 8QZ
01482 867488

With the first Grandstand for the course built way back in 1767, you could rightly say horseracing is a big part of Beverley. The course has two prestigious races: the Hilary Needler Trophy in May and Beverley Bullet Sprint in August. A range of special events unconnected to racing take place throught the year.

▶ PLACES NEARBY

The impressive windmill at Skidby is a short drive away, and there are several good pubs in the area.

Skidby Windmill

www.museums.eastriding.gov.uk
Skidby, Cottingham, HU16 5TF
Open Sat–Thu 10–5, Fri 10–4.30

This handsome five-storey windmill to the south of Beverley still grinds wheat to make flour on a weekly basis, and its four white sails are a noted landmark for miles around. The Museum of East Riding Rural Life is located in the buildings at its feet. You can buy the flour on the spot, and there's also a cafe.

The Ferguson Fawsitt Arms & Country Lodge

fergusonfawsitt.com
East End, Walkington HU17 8RX
01482 882665

Three miles from Beverley in the picturesque village of Walkington, there is a timeless quality to this Victorian pub named after two important local families. Parts of the pub used to form the village blacksmith's shop where carriage wheels were repaired. Open fires, dark-wood panelling, carved settles, beams and some decent tiling to the floor welcome those set on sampling a pint of Black Sheep, or diners intent on a good Sunday roast, home-made steak pie from the carvery or a traditional pub meal from the bar food menu.

The Pipe and Glass Inn 🏅🏅
pipeandglass.co.uk
West End, South Dalton, HU17 7PN
01430 810246

With its neat, creamy paint job and red pantiles the 15th-century Pipe and Glass has been well cared for by its current owners and prepped to meet the demands of the discerning 21st-century visitor. It's still very much a pub – something the local community must be very grateful for – but it's also a dining destination in its own right, with a deserved reputation for contemporary British cuisine. The rustic bar has a smart finish with Chesterfield chairs and sofas, and a wood-burning stove, while the restaurant is dominated by horse-themed prints and chunky wooden tables. The industrious and creative team in the kitchen deliver arresting options such as a starter cheesecake made with Yellison goats' cheese and partnered with beetroot macaroon, golden beets and candied walnuts. It all seems entirely in keeping with the setting and chimes with the times. The wine list is a cracker, too.

▶ Bilsdale MAP REF 337 E4

The long valley of Bilsdale extends all the way along the B1257 from Helmsley in the south towards Stokesley in the north – and is farmed up to the moorland tops, just as it was centuries ago by the monks of Rievaulx Abbey (see page 231). The monastic connection is recalled by names such as Crossholme and Low Crosses Farm. Scattered farmsteads punctuate the valley, but today the only village is tiny Chop Gate. Pronounce it 'Chop Yat' to sound like a local.

The River Seph is ever-present in the valley bottom – the B1257 accompanies it almost from its source to where it joins the River Rye to the north of Rievaulx. On the roadside about 8 miles north of Helmsley is the Sun Inn. Just yards away from the pub is a much earlier thatched building, of cruck-frame construction, that dates back to the 16th century. This was the original Sun Inn – also known as Spout House – which was a favourite watering-hole from first receiving its licence in 1714 until 1914.

When the licence transferred to the new Sun Inn, the older building fell into disrepair, until the National Park Authority rescued and renovated this delightful example of vernacular architecture. Now it is considered to be the best cruck-framed house in the National Park – not counting those in Ryedale Folk Museum of course (see page 146) – and one of the oldest. Take a look inside, for the interior has been restored to how it might have looked more than three centuries ago. A witch post still stands near the inglenook fireplace, to ward off the 'evil eye'. Up narrow stairs are tiny rooms, open to the thatch and fitted out with wooden box beds. Downstairs are the diminutive bar and snugs of the original pub layout, and the beer cellar.

Five miles north of Helmsley on the B1257, just before you enter Bilsdale, is Newgate Bank, a vantage point with a picnic site from where you can enjoy views of the valley and the Hambleton Hills. Chop Gate also has a picnic site and a car park.

SADDLE UP
Bilsdale Riding Centre
bilsdaleridingcentre.co.uk
Hawnby, Helmsley YO62 5LT
01439 798225
The centre has a large number of horses and ponies to suit all standards of riding experience, from the forward-going to the bomb-proof variety. Less experienced and novice riders will get plenty of encouragement, help and support to improve riding skills.

▶ Bingley MAP REF 327 E5

Sitting astride the River Aire and the Leeds and Liverpool Canal, in a steep-sided valley, Bingley is a typical West Yorkshire town. Ancient and modern sit side-by-side in Bingley, with some rather unlovely structures from more recent times. The old butter cross, stocks and market hall have been relocated from the main road to just outside the modern Arts Centre. Don't miss a stroll down to the magnificent staircase of locks on the canal here, known as the Five Rise Locks.

With its locks, wharves and plethora of mills, the town grew in size and importance during the 19th century as the textile trades expanded. But Bingley's pre-eminence did not begin with the Industrial Revolution – it's actually one of Yorkshire's oldest settlements, with its market charter being granted by King John – who may have stayed at the Old White Horse coaching inn, if legend is to be believed – as far back as 1212.

TAKE IN A SHOW
Bingley Arts Centre
bingleyartscentre.co.uk
Main Street, Bingley | BD16 2LZ
A lovely 350-seat theatre in the heart of the town, with a wide range of events and shows throughout the year. The centre is home to 'Bingley Little Theatre' (BLT), who present eight plays each year, along with a programme of Studio activities.

PLAY A ROUND
Shipley Golf Club
shipleygolfclub.com
Beckfoot Lane | BD16 1LX

01274 568652 (secretary)
Open Sun–Mon, Wed–Fri, Tue pm
Laid out by the renowned golf course architect, Alister MacKenzie, this parkland course is set in a beautiful wooded valley on the outskirts of Bingley.

EAT AND DRINK

Five Rise Locks Hotel and Restaurant
five-rise-locks.co.uk
Beck Lane, BD16 4DD
01274 565296
This one-time mill-owner's family home is now a family-run hotel on a pleasingly intimate scale – just nine bedrooms, with a restaurant that's worth knowing about. On the menu, you'll find some appealing modern British dishes.

▶ PLACES NEARBY
The town of Shipley is just two stops east by train, from where you can switch to the Tramway. The Dick Hudsons is popular with walkers on the moors.

The Dick Hudsons
vintageinn.co.uk
Otley Road, High Eldwick,
BD16 3BA | 01274 552121
On the edge of Rombald's Moor, north of Bingley, this is a famous old inn serving a range of modern pub food favourites as well as a good selection of beer and wine. Some people just come for the view though, which spans West Yorkshire all the way to Emley Moor. The pub is named after a 19th-century landlord.

▲ The Leeds and Liverpool Canal at Bingley

Shipley Glen Cable Tramway
shipleyglentramway.co.uk
Tramway Office Prod Lane, Baildon, Shipley, BD17 5BN | 01274 589010
Open Sat–Sun, staff permitting
Take a ride on the oldest working cable tramway in Great Britain – if you exclude cliff lifts. Dating from 1895, the line was built to serve the local beauty spot of Shipley Glen. At nearly a quarter-mile in length, the woodland ride provides a pleasant alternative to the steep path.

Shipley lies on the edge of Bradford, and the Glen was a popular Edwardian pleasure garden. On busy days, as many as 17,000 people would take the tramway up to the Japanese gardens and boating lake. The attractions are now gone, but you can still ride on the tramway – which runs on Sunday afternoons throughout the year in good weather. There is a souvenir shop at the top, while the bottom station houses a small museum and replica Edwardian shop.

▶ Bolton Abbey   MAP REF 327 E3

boltonabbey.com
Skipton, BD23 6EX | 01756 718000 | Car parks open daily Jun–Aug 9–9,
mid-Mar–May & Sep–Oct 9–7, Nov–mid-Mar 9–6; Strid car park
daily 9.30–4

The Bolton Abbey Estate, owned by the Duke of Devonshire, is
an enjoyable amalgamation of recreational, historical and
geographical features – and you can stay at The Devonshire
Arms to enjoy the comforts of one of the best hotels in the
country and one of the region's best restaurants (see page
7170). For most people, though, Bolton Abbey is just a great
day out, within easy reach of the cities of Bradford (see page
73) and Leeds (see page 170), offering ample parking and
plenty to see and do.

Some of the first people to enjoy the site were the
Augustinian monks who moved here from Embsay in 1154 to
found a new priory by the banks of the River Wharfe. It was
finished by the following century – but now lies in evocative
ruins in a meadow, an area of great beauty and serenity. The
high altar, topped by the imposing east window, was raised on
a step that spanned the entire width of the building. Now this
step is covered in grass, a mute witness to the majestic church
that once stood here.

The adjoining priory church of St Mary and St Cuthbert is
one of the finest in the Dales. It was first built in 1220, and
escaped the destruction of the Dissolution only to fall victim to
dwindling congregations in the 1970s. It's been restored, and
you can look inside to see the breathtaking stained-glass and
superb wall paintings.

▼ River Wharfe and Bolton Abbey

▲ Bolton Abbey ruins

Day tickets allow you to drive between the several car parks across the vast Bolton Abbey estate. If you drive along the B6160 you'll pass under a narrow stone archway – part of an aqueduct that once carried water to the mill, of which little now remains. Shops on the estate sell Bolton Abbey-branded goods, and there are restaurants and a pub in the village of Bolton Abbey, which grew up beside the priory.

You can enjoy great walks in the area, including marked nature trails near the river and through Strid Wood, which is a Site of Special Scientific Interest – you'll get a leaflet showing the colour-coded walks handed to you at the car park entrance. There are more than 60 different varieties of plants, and about 40 species of birds nest on the estate every year. Spring brings snowdrops and later whole rivers of bluebells, and in summer the air is thick with dragonflies, butterflies and bees. Local nature groups post notices to tell you what you're likely to see at any given time.

As the River Wharfe flows through the Bolton Abbey grounds, in one place it thunders through a narrow ravine called The Strid which is just a few feet across – little more than a stride, or 'strid'. Please resist any desires to jump across, as several people have been killed over the years as they slipped on the rocks and fell into the fast-flowing river, which is up to 30 feet deep in places.

Bolton Abbey is part of the steam railway link to Embsay, near Skipton (see page 264).

SEE A LOCAL CHURCH

St Mary and St Cuthbert

boltonpriory.org.uk
Bolton Abbey, Skipton, BD23 6AL
01756 710238

The Priory Church of St Mary and St Cuthbert stands above a wide curve in the River Wharfe amid the ruins of Bolton Priory. The original priory was established here by a group of black-robed Augustinian priests in a sheltered spot protected from the cruel winter weather by the surrounding hills. All but the 13th-century nave now lies in ruins – which is now the Priory Church of St Mary and St Cuthbert.

Its Tudor roof is embellished with gilded bosses, including the face of a Green Man, whose visage is framed by a leaf twisting from an eye and another from one side of the mouth.

Most of the remaining church is in the Gothic style, but more work was done in the Victorian era. The unfinished west tower, begun in 1520 and now roofed in, forms a magnificent entrance. Six Victorian stained-glass windows in the south wall by A W N Pugin tell the life of Christ in 36 scenes. Set in the west wall is a tiny stained-glass window of St Cuthbert, who the church is named after.

EAT AND DRINK

Cavendish Pavilion

cavendishpavilion.co.uk
Bolton Abbey, Skipton, BD23 6AN
01756 710245

Bolton Abbey has a number of teashops but this one has the best setting, down by the river between the priory ruins and The Strid.

The Burlington Restaurant

burlingtonrestaurant.co.uk
BD23 6AJ | 01756 718111

A handsome spa hotel on the northern edge of the Duke of Devonshire's Bolton Abbey estate, The Devonshire Arms makes the most of its glorious surroundings and is home to the Burlington Restaurant. Inside, a lively decorative tone banishes all thought of bland anonymity, and recent new investment has seen the upgrading of the spa and some of the guestrooms. Staff are classically trained, and understand that a careful balance of correct attention to detail and easy-going warmth is what impresses most.

The principal dining room is the chandeliered Burlington, with its conservatory extension. Here, against panoramic views over the countryside and the River Wharfe, Adam Smith pulls out all the stops for dynamic contemporary Yorkshire cooking full of innovation and intensity. A kitchen garden supplying vegetables, herbs, fruits and edible flowers is at the core of the operation (do pop in and have a look when you've a moment), and much else comes from the surrounding estate and from Dales growers and producers.

▲ Bolton Abbey

The Devonshire Brasserie & Bar ◉

devonshirebrasserie.co.uk
BD23 6AJ | 01756 710710

This is the informal brasserie within The Devonshire Arms – a room marked out by bright vibrant colours, contemporary artwork, comfortable seating, informal service, and a buzz in the air. The menu runs along modern British brasserie lines and is very crowd pleasing, especially after a busy day around the estate.

▶ **PLACES NEARBY**

To the west of Bolton Abbey is Hesketh Farm Park.

Hesketh Farm Park

heskethfarmpark.co.uk
BD23 6HA | 01756 710444
Open mid-Feb to mid-Oct; check website for opening times

This working farm has more than 1,000 animals, including cattle, sheep and pigs, and some you might not expect to see in the Yorkshire Dales, including giant tortoises.

▶ Bolton Castle MAP REF 335 E4

boltoncastle.co.uk

Leyburn, DL8 4ET | 01969 623981 | Open Apr–Oct daily 10–5;
castle may close early on some Saturdays due to weddings, please
check website

This solid square fortress is a medieval masterpiece, commissioned by Sir Richard Scrope – an MP and Chancellor of the Exchequer – as an impressive residence rather than for any defensive purposes. Fascinating documents about the construction still survive – they include the licence to crenellate, dated 1379, and a builders' contract from 1378 that refers to the construction of the 'Privees'. You'll be pleased to know there's been some improvement of the facilities since those days. Beneath the massive walls there are archery and falconry displays, a herb garden and vineyard, and a tea room too – plenty to keep everyone occupied.

The magnificent four corner towers that rise to 100 feet give only a small indication of the grandeur of the original building – there were eight halls, each independent household units inside the castle. Climb to the top of the turrets for splendid views over Wensleydale, and as you look out, try to imagine the vast tracts of forest that covered the region in medieval times.

Bolton Castle's most notable – if unwilling – resident was Mary, Queen of Scots, who was imprisoned here in July 1568 for six months. You can see the bedchamber in which she is thought to have stayed, decorated in appropriate style. There are tapestries, arms and armour to see, and tableaux give a vivid impression of life in the castle over the years – including a rather scary oubliette dungeon, a hole in the ground into which prisoners were dropped and then forgotten about. An arm bone was found down there, still held by an iron manacle.

On the ground floor, just off the courtyard, you'll find the brew house, the bake house, the meal house, the forge and the threshing floor. On the first floor is the ruined great hall, with the state chamber and guest hall – keep going upwards to find a chapel and some monks' cells.

◀ Bolton Castle

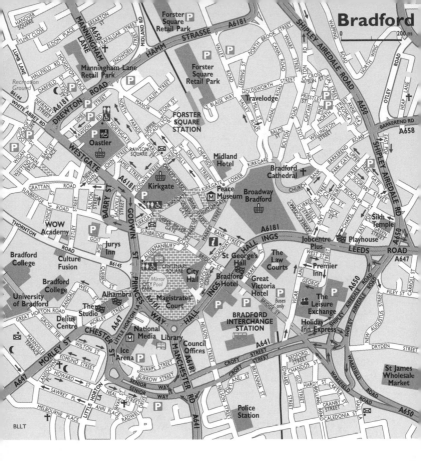

▶ Bradford MAP REF 327 F6

One of the three largest cities in Yorkshire, Bradford is the stone to nearby Leeds' brick. Once vital cogs in the engine room of the Industrial Revolution, these twin cities are being revitalised for the 21st century. Thanks to the location of the National Science and Media Museum in the city, Bradford has an entirely new claim to world fame: it's the world's first UNESCO City of Film – recognising the rich heritage in film productions and television series. Quite a coup.

Bradford was a Saxon settlement that grew up around a shallow river crossing, and began to develop as a manufacturing town in the 16th century. Soft water for processing raw wool and easy access to coal to fuel the machinery of the mills were key ingredients in Bradford's success. The Industrial Revolution led to its rapid growth, based on the weaving of high-quality woollen worsted cloth. Its status as the wool capital of the world was reflected in civic building on a grand scale, which you can still see clearly today – the Italianate town hall is echoed in the magnificent chimney of Lister's Mill, a city landmark. With the textile and manufacturing industries came acute air pollution, but that is well in the past – blackened buildings have been scrubbed back to their golden Yorkshire stone, and the old commercial quarter of Little Germany is a delight to explore. Waves of immigration from Pakistan, India and Bangladesh since the 1950s have given Bradford a strong British Asian culture, celebrated in the vibrant annual Mela festival in the City Park.

Bradford's industrial story is vividly told at the Industrial Museum and Horses at Work, set in a former spinning mill in Eccleshill – you'll see working machinery, horse-drawn rides, textile workers' cottages and the mill-owner's house.

VISIT THE MUSEUMS AND GALLERIES

National Science and Media Museum

scienceandmediamuseum.org.uk
BD1 1NQ | 0844 856 3797
Previously the National Media Museum, a new chapter opened in March 2017 as the museum became the National Science and Media Museum. If you're a fan of the moving image, then the seven floors of galleries with permanent exhibitions focusing on photography, television, animation, videogaming, the Internet and the scientific principles behind light and colour should be right up your street. And the added focus on 'science' promises a new dimension to the visiting exhibitions too.

Bradford Industrial Museum and Horses at Work

bradfordmuseums.org
Moorside Mills, Moorside Road,
Eccleshill, BD2 3HP | 01274 435900
Open Tue–Fri 10–4, Sat–Sun 11–4
Moorside Mills is an original spinning mill, now part of a museum that brings vividly to life the story of Bradford's woollen industry. There is the machinery that once converted raw wool into cloth, and the mill yard rings with the sound of iron on stone as Shire horses pull trams, haul buses and give rides. Daily demonstrations and changing exhibitions take place.

Cartwright Hall Art Gallery

bradfordmuseums.org
Lister Park, BD9 4NS
01274 431212 | Open Tue–Fri 10–4,
Sat–Sun 11–4
Built in dramatic Baroque style in 1904, Bradford's civic art gallery has permanent collections of 19th- and 20th-century British art, contemporary prints, and older works by British and European masters. Look out for works by William Blake and Walter Sickert, Andy Warhol, Roy Lichtenstein, Richard Hamilton and David Hockney.

Bolling Hall

bradfordmuseums.org
Bowling Hall Road, BD4 7LP
01274 431814 | Open Wed–Fri
11–4, Sat 10–5, Sun 12–5

A classic West Yorkshire manor house, complete with galleried 'housebody' (hall), Bolling Hall dates mainly from the 17th century but has medieval and 18th-century sections. You'll see panelled rooms, plasterwork in original colours, heraldic glass and a rare Chippendale bed.

CATCH A PERFORMANCE

Alhambra Theatre

bradford-theatres.co.uk
Morley Street, BD7 1AJ
01274 432000

One of the north's premier theatres, the Alhambra offers a fantastic range of entertainment from ballet and opera to variety and comedy, musicals, drama and Yorkshire's biggest Christmas pantomime.

St George's Hall

bradford-theatres.co.uk
Bridge Street, BD1 1JT
01274 432000

If you're lucky, you'll catch a big classical concert by the resident Hallé Orchestra, or perhaps something with local Queensbury-based Black Dyke Mills Band, one of the oldest and best-loved championship brass bands. Lots of household-name bands and entertainers also appear at this premier venue.

EAT AND DRINK

New Beehive Inn

newbeehiveinn.co.uk
171 Westgate, BD1 3AA
01274 721784

Dating from 1901 and centrally located with many tourist attractions nearby, this classic Edwardian hotel retains its period Arts and Crafts atmosphere, with five separate bars and gas lighting. No surprise, then, that it's on the national inventory list of historic pubs. Outside, with a complete change of mood, you can relax in the Mediterranean-style courtyard. The pub offers a good range of unusual real ales, such as Salamander Mudpuppy and Abbeydale Moonshine, and over 100 malt whiskies, served alongside some simple bar snacks. Music fans should attend the cellar bar, which is open at weekends and features regular live bands.

Prashad ◉◉

prashad.co.uk
137 Whitehall Road, Drighlington, BD11 1AT | 0113 285 2037

When it comes to pukka Indian cooking, the competition in Bradford is strong – but Mrs Kaushy Patel's take on the vegetarian repertoire ensures that a zealous local following beats a path to her door. The venue goes for a bright and cheerful look, with one wall taken up by a huge mural of a tumultuous Indian street scene. The all-in-one thali platter is a splendid way into the vegetarian cuisine of the Gujarat, or you could head south for a spicy uttapam or masala dosa pancake served with spicy lentil soup and coconut chutney.

> ## Bransdale   MAP REF 337 F4

The unspoiled valley of Bransdale drives deep into the moors, but most visitors pass it by. If you're leaving Helmsley along the A170 towards Kirkbymoorside, you should look out on the left for a signpost to Carlton for a delightful little drive. The road loops around Bransdale and then returns to the A170 about 5 miles further east at Kirkbymoorside.

Beyond the houses that comprise the village of Carlton, the views open up dramatically. To the left is unenclosed heather moorland; to the right the valley bottom is divided up by neat drystone walls either side of Hodge Beck. This pattern is punctuated by a handful of scattered farmsteads. The moors, with barely a tree to be seen, echo to the evocative calls of the curlew, red grouse and lapwing, while sheep graze the grassy verges and wander idly across the road. Unenclosed for most of the way, the road heads north – inscribed milestones at the roadside mark the way.

The Church of St Nicholas sits on a hillock overlooking the valley. Dating from 1886, the building is a typical moorland church – tiny and rather undemonstrative, but with a real sense of spirituality that grander churches so often lack.

The road then makes a broad sweep to the right, before continuing the circuit of Bransdale. Here sturdy farmsteads with fanciful names – Cow Sike, Toad Hole and Spout House – gaze down into the bottom of the valley.

Before arriving in Kirkbymoorside, you get the chance to visit Gillamoor and Fadmoor, a pair of pretty and unspoiled moorland villages barely half a mile apart. The houses of both are grouped around their village greens, but Gillamoor has an extra surprise in store. St Aidan's Church stands on its own at the end of the village – you are almost upon it before you see that it is sited on the edge of a steep precipice which commands breathtaking views across lower Farndale, the River Dove and on to the purple heather moors beyond. You'll also see a very unusual sundial in front of Dial House Farm in Gillamoor: a central column is mounted on top of a stepped base and on top is a stone globe mounted on an inscribed cube, with a dial face on four of its sides.

> ## Bridlington   MAP REF 331 E2

Breezy Bridlington is a pleasant seaside resort, with a good prom and a reputation for bracing sea air – the town's Latin motto, *Signum Salutis Semper*, translates as 'always the bringer of good health'. It lies in the curved bay to the south of Flamborough Head, on a bit of coast that is notoriously unstable, constantly shifting and changing – groynes help to hold the fine golden sands in place, and a sea wall protects the town from the worst of the North Sea winter storms.

For the mill workers of West Yorkshire, Bridlington was a popular holiday destination, and perhaps inevitably it now feels more like a retirement dormitory – but the three main parks give it a green and open feel, and local fishing boats still land shellfish at the quay. The town was thrown a lifeline when the handsome old Spa Pavilion dance and concert hall was restored to glory at the start of the 21st century, attracting big names like the Kaiser Chiefs and Kasabian for a younger clientele.

Bridlington's two beaches offer traditional seaside fun for families. The North Beach is made up of sand and shingle surrounded by wide promenades backed against the impressive Flamborough cliffs, whereas the South Beach is a mainly sandy affair.

Artist David Hockney still has a modest home in the town – many of his acclaimed recent works have featured the landscape of the Wolds.

ENTERTAIN THE FAMILY
Sewerby Hall and Gardens
eastriding.gov.uk/sewerby
Church Lane, YO15 1EA
01262 673769 | Estate open daily dawn–dusk; hall open Easter–Sep
The Georgian mansion, set in 50 acres of parkland overlooking Bridlington Bay, dates back to 1715. You can see the 19th-century Orangery, art galleries, archaeological displays and a room dedicated to pioneer aviator and local star, Amy Johnson (1903–1941), with a collection of her trophies and mementoes. The grounds include magnificent walled gardens and rose gardens and host many events throughout the year. Families should head for the Children's Zoo and play areas, and the woodland and clifftop walks.

SEE A LOCAL CHURCH
Bridlington Priory Church
bridlingtonpriory.co.uk
YO16 7JX | 01262 672221
A grand landmark in the town, the priory church celebrated 900 years of existence in 2013. It was refurbished in Victorian times by the great George Gilbert Scott, and its uneven twin towers feature in the charming tapestry which tells its history, worked by local women in 1995. Catch an organ recital here if you can – the 4,212 pipes of this magnificent instrument

were overhauled in 2006, and it's well worth hearing.

CATCH A PERFORMANCE
The Spa
bridspa.com
South Marine Drive, YO15 3JH
01262 678258
Bridlington's much-loved variety palace was built in 1896 to entertain hordes of Victorian tourists, and once included a theatre, concert hall, bandstand and refreshment rooms. The theatre burned down in 1906, so the current Spa Theatre and Opera House was built in 1907. Magnificently refurbished in the 21st century, today it hosts a wide range of public performances, concerts, theatre, opera and public dances.

EAT AND DRINK
Harbour Fisheries
9 Harbour Road, YO15 2NR
01262 603071
Yes, you've got to have fish and chips when you're at the seaside. It's the law – well, almost. And this is possibly Bridlington's best.

▶ Brimham Rocks MAP REF 327 F2

nationaltrust.org.uk
Summerbridge, HG3 4DW | 01423 780688 | Open daily until dusk

One of the most fantastic collections of natural standing rocks anywhere lies jumbled on Nidderdale's moorland. Brimham Rocks are just off the B6265, four miles east of Pateley Bridge (see page 213), and should not be missed. Nowhere will you see a sight quite like them: blocks and boulders of dark millstone grit 20 feet and more in height, weathered simply by natural forces – wind, rain, frost and ice – into strange and surreal shapes.

Brimham Rocks have attracted tourists since the 18th century, and over the years some have acquired quirky names, such as the Blacksmith and Anvil, the Indian Turban, the Sphinx, and the Dancing Bear. So odd are these shapes that it is hard to believe they were not created by a team of talented sculptors. One in particular, known as the Idol, is enormous and seems to be improbably balanced on a rock scarcely the size of a dinner plate. There is also a Kissing Chair and the inevitable Lover's Leap.

The car park at the entrance to the site is big, and there's a choice of several walks through the area, which extends for 387 acres around the rocks themselves. An easy central path leads to Brimham House, converted into an information centre with refreshment facilities and a shop attached.

▶ Druid's Writing Desk, Brimham Rocks

▶ **Brompton** MAP REF 339 D5

When you're driving on the A170, you could pass straight through Brompton and miss a gem; many do in their haste to get to the Yorkshire coast. The pretty little village is set around a small lake, into which the church doors were thrown during the Civil War – they were later recovered and re-hung. The poet William Wordsworth took the time to get to know Brompton, for he courted Mary Hutchinson, a local girl who lived at Gallows Hill Farm, and they married in the 14th-century church here in 1802. The wedding ceremony was recorded in her diary by his sister, Dorothy – she even joined the happy couple on their honeymoon in Grasmere, in the Lake District.

The village has a unique – if little-known – place in the history of aeronautics. Wilbur and Orville Wright may have made the history books with the first manned and powered flight in their flimsy craft in 1903, yet 50 years before that, an unsung squire of Brompton Hall had quietly set about building a flying machine.

Brompton Hall had been the home of the Cayley family since Stuart times, and Sir George Cayley (1771–1857) developed an unquenchable scientific curiosity. This was an age when enthusiastic amateurs, especially those blessed with private incomes, could indulge their whims in the arts and sciences. Sir George, however, was no mere dabbler; his inventions included caterpillar tracks and a new form of artificial limb, prompted by an accident to one of his estate workers. Seeing how the River Derwent regularly flooded the flat countryside, to the chagrin of local farmers, he designed and constructed a sea cut to divert flood waters straight into the North Sea near Scarborough.

But the prospect of flight remained Sir George's passion. Even before the 18th century was out he was designing gliders – continuing to refine the craft's aerodynamics until he had a controllable machine that could carry a man. He had already experimented with propellers, abandoning them merely because the internal combustion engine was not even on the horizon. His various experiments proved that a contoured wing could provide much greater lift than a wing with a flat profile.

Although an inscription in the porch of All Saints Church acknowledges Sir George as the 'Father of Aeronautics', his pioneering efforts are largely overlooked. Facing the main road through the village you can see the six-sided building, the summerhouse – now boarded up – where Sir George worked on his flying machines.

Sir George volunteered his understandably reluctant coachman to make the first manned flight. On a still day in 1853, the glider made a short 55-yard hop across Brompton Dale. The coachman, relieved to have survived, but unwilling to entertain thoughts of another death-defying flight, resigned on the spot, telling Sir George that he was paid to drive, not to fly.

▶ **PLACES NEARBY**

You can take to the saddle at Snainton Riding Centre, west of Brompton.

Snainton Riding Centre
snaintonridingcentre.co.uk

Station Road, Snainton, YO13 9AP
01723 859218
Qualified, friendly instructors offer a wide range of lessons from beginner to advanced, and pony days for kids in the summer holidays.

▶ Burton Agnes Hall   MAP REF 331 E2

burtonagnes.com
YO25 4ND | 01262 490324 | Hall and gardens open Apr–Oct, mid-Nov to 23 Dec daily 11–5; gardens only early Feb–early Mar

It's pretty unusual for the same family to own a property since it was built, over 400 years ago, but that's the deal with this fabulous Tudor mansion. That it's never been put up for sale means it's stuffed with family treasures, too.

The original builder was Sir Henry Griffith, who employed Robert Smithson, master mason to Queen Elizabeth I, as his architect. Uniquely, his plans have been preserved, revealing not only the unity of the design but also how little has changed.

You'll find a turreted gatehouse is a foretaste of the glories to come. The perfect symmetry of the red-brick mansion, three storeys high, with two square and two compass bays, is preserved by having the entrance door at the side of one of the bays. Inside you'll see vivid biblical, allegorical and mythological figures carved into the astonishing Elizabethan screen and massive chimneypiece, almost the height of the wall in the Great Hall. The Red Drawing Room is an incredible example of brilliantly painted and gilded Elizabethan panelling, with another outstanding carved chimneypiece depicting the Dance of Death.

Burton Agnes has a ghost – of Anne, youngest daughter of Sir Henry Griffin. Fatally wounded by robbers, Anne declared she could never rest unless part of her remained at Burton Agnes. When they ignored her wishes and buried her in the churchyard, her ghost walked until her family fulfilled their promise and moved her to the site – and it walks again if ever she is disturbed.

As well as the house, you can enjoy a woodland walk, children's play area and picnic area. Throughout the year, diverse artists are in residence – you can view their artwork in the summer house and in the hall.

TAKE IN SOME HISTORY
Burton Agnes Manor House
www.english-heritage.org.uk
Maypole Hill, YO25 4ND
0370 333 1181 | Open Apr–Oct
This is a rare and well-preserved example of a Norman house. Some interesting Norman architectural features can still be seen, including the vaulted undercroft, but the building was remodelled and encased in brick during the 17th and 18th centuries, giving it a rather forbidding appearance. The house is next door to Burton Agnes Hall.

▶ Castleton   MAP REF 338 A2

Once upon a time there was a castle in Castleton, but now only the name and a mound to the north of the village remain. It seems also lots of the stone from the ruined castle was probably recycled and used to build Danby Castle (see page 92). Castleton also used to have regular markets and a goods yard on the railway; the markets have gone, but the village still has its station on the Esk Valley Line.

Despite its small size, Castleton is a centre for walking, birding and other outdoor pursuits.

The pleasant 35-mile long Esk Valley Walk runs through the village, ending at Whitby.

▶ Clapham MAP REF 326 A2

Clapham is one of the prettiest little villages that anyone could wish to find; it is almost as if it was planned with the picture postcard in mind. Clapham Beck runs through its centre, crossed by old stone bridges, and matching old stone cottages line its narrow lanes. It is much more wooded than most villages in the Dales, which possibly adds to its appeal, and with several guest houses and cafes, a pub, a nature trail and a couple of shops for essential supplies, it would make an excellent base for exploring the southern part of this area.

The Ingleborough Estate Nature Trail celebrates one of Clapham's well-known sons, Reginald Farrer, who spent his time collecting plant species from all around the world and cultivating them here on the family estate. He died in 1920, before he was 40, but by that time he had become one of Britain's leading botanical experts and earned himself the moniker, 'the father of English rock gardening'. The trail leads to Ingleborough Cave, where you can take an hour-long tour into the network of caves below Ingleborough (see page 152) to see what is said to be the longest stalactite in the country, at 16 feet and 5 inches.

Follow the bridleway between Clapham and Austwick and you will see a signpost to the Norber Boulders. This scattering of boulders, with each on its own little pedestal of rock, looks at first glance as if it ought to be of some human significance, but in fact it's a completely natural occurrence. The boulders, also called the Norber Erratics, are several hundred million years old and were dropped here by the actions of a glacier about 25,000 years ago. They are formed of Silurian gritstone, a type of rock found in Crummack Dale about half a mile to the north.

Dame Alice Ketyll, a Clapham inhabitant in the mid-15th century, was an unusual witch in that she was actually very popular with the villagers, using her strange powers for their benefit wherever possible. Predictably, she was less popular with the Church – an ecclesiastical court tried her for witchcraft and punished her by demanding that she line the roof of the village church with lead. Dame Alice could not afford to buy the lead, so she took a party of clerics and workmen to Ingleborough where they found both lead and silver. The silver paid for the men to take the lead and line the church roof, and Dame Alice's reward for this ingenuity was that she could be buried in the churchyard.

◀ Danby Dale from Castleton Rigg

GO UNDERGROUND
Ingleborough Cave
ingleboroughcave.co.uk
LA22 8EE | 01524 251242
Open daily mid-Feb to Oct; tours
every half hour from 10–4
Concrete walkways lead
through spectacular limestone
chambers, dripping with calcite
– safe for the family dog on a
lead, and even pushchairs, but
be prepared to duck.

Floodlighting is reflected in
the pools. Expert guides help
you make the most of your tour.

EAT AND DRINK
The New Inn
newinn-clapham.co.uk
Old Road, LA2 8HH | 01524 251203
The New Inn, an 18th-century
coaching inn in the heart of the
Yorkshire Dales, is well known
among walkers, cavers and
cyclists. The menu, using
locally sourced ingredients, has
a faintly Mediterranean/Asian
twist, but the beers are from
Yorkshire – including Copper
Dragon ales – and from across
the border in Lancashire.

▶ Cleckheaton MAP REF 323 D1

Cleckheaton is a small bustling town on the River Spen, with a
commercial heart as yet undepleted by out-of-town shopping
centres. Clustered around the junction of the A643
Huddersfield/Morley and A638 Wakefield/Bradford roads, it
feels as though it should be busier than it is. The M62 has
relieved the town of much of its choking traffic, however, and
life in Cleckheaton progresses at an affable pace.

Once a thriving textile town, Cleckheaton specialised in
carding – the process by which clumps of raw materials
such as wool or cotton are combed into straight fibres,
ready to be spun. By 1838 there were at least 11 carding mills
in and around the town, and 50 years later its output won
it an undisputed reputation as the carding capital of the world.

East of the town, at Gomersal, is the Grade I listed Oakwell
Hall, a fine Tudor manor, set in an extensive country park.

TAKE IN SOME HISTORY
Oakwell Hall
kirklees.gov.uk
Nutter Lane, Birstall, WF17 9LG
01924 326240 | Open Tue–Thu
11–4, Sat–Sun 12–5 (winter 12–4)
Explore the moated Elizabethan
manor house, built by John Batt
in 1583 and furnished as it
might have looked in the 1690s.
Charlotte Brontë visited, and
Oakwell was the inspiration for
Fieldhead in her novel *Shirley*.
You can also let off some steam
in the 110-acre country park,
with its visitor information
centre, period gardens,
nature trails, arboretum and
children's playground.

TAKE IN A SHOW
Cleckheaton Town Hall
kirklees.gov.uk
Bradford Road, Cleckheaton,

BD19 3RH | 01274 335030
Tue–Thu 11–4, Sat–Sun 12–4
The 500-seat Cleckheaton
Town Hall is a lively venue to
see a wide range of
performances, including local amateur dramatics, dance and drama. The theatre dates back to 1892 and is is also home to the Cleckheaton Folk Festival, which takes place every July.

▶ The Cleveland Hills   MAP REF 337 E4

You can't really miss the Cleveland Hills – the magnificent range which marks the northwestern boundary of the North York Moors National Park. They're a major geological boundary, too.

The rocks forming the hills date back to the Middle Jurassic period – some 161 million years ago – but the rest of the North York Moors are formed from Lower Jurassic age stone. The hard gritty rocks of the moorland are gradually being worn away from the north and west by springs, rain and rivers, and because the later rocks beneath them are fairly soft, a steep escarpment is formed along the eroding edge – so if you wondered why the Cleveland Hills have a steady slope to the south and a steep drop to the north and west, now you know.

On top of Hasty Bank, the northern escarpment of the Cleveland Hills, you can see the Wainstones, the largest outcrop of rocks in the National Park and a favourite with climbers. Another set of rocks can be found on Nab End Moor, in Bilsdale (see page 65). These are just one of a number of formations on the moors that are known as the Bridestones. Others – the remains of ancient stone circles – can be found near Grosmont. The best-known Bridestones are in the hands of the National Trust on Bridestones Moor – reach them via the Dalby Forest Drive. Weathered into strange shapes, these rocks make a surreal moorland landmark.

The Cleveland Way (see below) runs along the hills, as does part of Alfred Wainwright's celebrated Coast to Coast walk.

▶ Cleveland Way   MAP REF 337 E4, 339 D3

After the Pennine Way (see page 216) opened in 1965 – with a good section travelling through Yorkshire – the county was the natural choice for the second National Trail. Opened in 1969, the Cleveland Way is a more manageable 110-mile walk. Its name comes from the Cleveland Hills, which it does pass through – but only for a short section, and actually most of the walk is within the North York Moors National Park.

The walk is a roughly horseshoe-shaped route and breaks into two distinct sections. From the starting point at Helmsley, it meanders through the moorland scenery of the Hambleton and Cleveland Hills. The highest point of the trail comes when you cross Urra Moor. Once you can spot the North Sea at Saltburn-by-the-Sea, you follow the coastal path down to the finishing point at Filey Brigg.

It's possible to break the walk up into sections that offer a single day's hike, with each part ending at a point where budget accommodation is available.

An extra segment of the Cleveland Way, known as the Missing Link, has been developed to allow you to make a complete loop from Scarborough back to Helmsley. This longer circular walk is about 180 miles long, and means you can now start and finish at any convenient point on the route.

▶ Coxwold MAP REF 329 D1

Coxwold is one of Yorkshire's prettiest villages, and you'll find it about three miles south of Kilburn. Cottages straggle down either side of the broad main street, overlooked by the distinctive octagonal tower of the 15th-century church. Almshouses here date back to the reign of Charles II, and there's a wonderful old hostelry that's worth stopping off at: The Fauconberg Arms Inn.

The slightly tipsy-looking 15th-century Shandy Hall lies opposite St Michael's Church, and was once the home of Laurence Sterne (1713–68). As a writer Sterne was a relatively late developer, not picking up his quill until the ripe old age of 46. The publication of his picaresque novel, *The Life and Opinions of Tristram Shandy, Gentleman*, coincided with his becoming the vicar of Coxwold in 1760. Literary success was immediate, and Sterne was able to indulge his taste for high living. When he died in 1768, after contracting pleurisy, his skull was buried in Coxwold churchyard.

Northeast of the village is ruined Byland Abbey. To the south of Coxwold is Newburgh Priory, which was built as an Augustinian house in 1145. After the Dissolution, Henry VIII rewarded his chaplain, Anthony Bellasis, by giving him the site. He – and the owners who followed him – transformed the priory into a fine country house, which is still owned by the Wombwell family.

▶ Byland Abbey

TAKE IN SOME HISTORY
Byland Abbey
english-heritage.org.uk
YO61 4BD | 01347 868204
Open Apr–Jun Wed–Mon, 11–6,
Jul–Aug daily 11–6, Sep Wed–Sun
10–6, Oct–Mar Sat–Sun 10–4

A hauntingly beautiful monastic ruin dating back to 1177, set in meadows in the shadow of the Hambleton Hills. Marvel at the collection of medieval floor tiles still in their original setting. The dramatic west facade, with its 26-foot diameter window, still stands almost to its full height, and gives an impression of just how huge the nave used to be.

Newburgh Priory
newburghpriory.co.uk
YO61 4AS | 01347 868372
Open Apr–Jun Wed and Sun
2.30–4.45

It's said that Oliver Cromwell, Lord Protector during England's brief republican era, was buried here, after his daughter married into the family. Some of the house reflects its Tudor origins, but it was remodelled in the 18th century. Newburgh is still lived in today by its current owners, and there are extensive gardens to explore.

EAT AND DRINK
Coxwold Tearooms
coxwoldtearooms.co.uk
School House, YO61 4AD
01347 868077

You can eat in either of the two rooms – one very cosy and the other airy – or outside in the tea garden. Why not treat yourself to afternoon tea with home-baking, or sample the delights of Yorkshire ham and eggs?

▶ Cropton Forest   MAP REF 338 B4

Cropton Forest occupies a large area of the North Riding Forest Park between Rosedale in the west and Newtondale to the east. The moors in Yorkshire never stand still, and this woodland is one of the most dramatic changes made in the 20th century to the landscape.

The Forestry Commission began planting in the 1920s, and now the area makes up one of the most extensive man-made forests in the country. The woodlands are now reaching maturity, and upwards of 120,000 tonnes of timber are felled every year to meet consumer demand for softwoods. More recently, greater care has been taken to ensure that plantings harmonise with their surroundings. Areas of broadleaved and mixed woods provide a more varied habitat for wildlife, and are easier on the eye than vast conifer plantations.

The recreational possibilities of Cropton Forest are now being realised. On any summer weekend you will see mountain bikers tackling the forest trails, walkers following well-waymarked footpaths and families enjoying themselves at the many picnic sites and adventure playgrounds. Those who prefer their nature 'red in tooth and claw' will head for the solitude of the breezy moor-tops. The Newtondale Horse Trail offers 37.5 miles of bracing, traffic-free riding. Local riding stables hire out horses by the hour or day. Cropton Forest also has a campsite, forest cabins and educational outdoor activity centres set out amid the trees. The North Yorkshire Moors Railway passes through the eastern edge of the forest, and stations at Levisham and Newtondale give you easy access to the woodland.

Roman roads are not hard to find – on the map at least. The Roman road – commonly known as Wade's Causeway – across Wheeldale Moor, immediately to the north of Cropton Forest, is still that rare thing – a Roman road which is still visible on the ground (see page 290). You can see more Roman remains at Cawthorn Camp, which is believed to have been used as a training camp – these earthworks are signposted from the minor road between the villages of Cropton and Newton-on-Rawcliffe. From the purpose-built car park, the waymarked path, no more than a mile long, guides you around the well-preserved earthworks revealing a camp, two forts and an annexe wedged side by side on a plateau, with panoramic views to the north across Cropton Forest to the moors beyond. By the year AD 122, when the Emperor Hadrian was constructing his famous wall to the north, Cawthorn Camp had been abandoned.

▼ Steam train, Cropton Forest

EAT AND DRINK

The New Inn

newinncropton.co.uk

YO18 8HH | 01751 417330

It's quite an advantage when making your pub distinctive to have an acclaimed microbrewery at the bottom of the garden. The Great Yorkshire Brewery ensures this family-run free house is popular with locals and visitors alike. Ale lovers especially flock to the annual beer festivals in May and November. A great Yorkshire menu is served in the restored village bar and in the elegant Victorian restaurant, with a lunchtime sandwich option.

▶ **Danby** MAP REF 338 A2

The lovely village of Danby lies on a crossroads – don't go too fast or you'll miss it. All around are signs of prehistoric settlement, known about today thanks to the efforts of John Atkinson, who came here in 1847 as minister of the parish. He was passionate about these moors, with their burial mounds, standing stones and wayside crosses, and did much to publicise their existence and preserve them. There are a number of interesting features in the immediate vicinity, and the easiest way to see them is to stop off at the National Park Visitor Centre, a former shooting lodge by the River Esk just half a mile from the village on the road to Lealholm.

At the centre you can discover what makes the North York Moors so special and the unique habitats that the moors support. The evolution of the moorland landscape is explained, there's an outdoor play area and indoor climbing wall. Those whose needs extend no further than a mug of tea and a slice of cake are equally well catered for. Waymarked walks explore the riverbank and immediate environs; longer walks start from the car park.

Just a little way downstream from Danby is the intriguingly named Duck Bridge. This superb late 14th-century arched packhorse bridge is a tangible reminder of

▼ Little Fryup Dale, north from Danby Rigg

a time when sturdy ponies, laden down with twin pannier bags, were the main means by which goods and sundries were transported.

The packhorse trail leads towards Danby Castle, a fortified house of distinction – though most of the medieval stonework has since been incorporated into a farmhouse, and there is only limited public access. The castle, built in the 14th century, was once the home of Catherine Parr, the sixth wife of Henry VIII, who fared better than his other wives and, indeed, survived him. Past Danby Castle Farm the road goes through a minor but famously picturesque valley, Little Fryup Dale.

The minor roads between Castleton, Danby and Lealholm in the Esk Valley are ideal for cycling as they are quiet and the valley floor level. With a little help from a good map, you can avoid most of the steep gradients on the roads out of the valley.

GET OUTDOORS
The Moors National Park Centre
northyorkmoors.org.uk
Lodge Lane, YO21 2NB
01439 772737 | Open daily, Feb half-term–Mar 10.30–4, Apr–Jul & Sep–Oct, 10–5, Aug 9.30–5.30, Nov–Feb 10.30–4
This centre is the ideal place to start exploring the North York Moors National Park. See the exhibition about the area as well as the continuous exhibition of arts, events, videos and local walks.

SEE A LOCAL CHURCH
St Hilda's Church
moorland-parishes.webplus.net
Off Tofts Lane, YO21 2NH
Check website for details
The present church was built in the 15th century, but the first church was built on this spot between 1089 and 1141, when Robert de Brus II of Castleton Castle died. It was de Brus who gave the church and rights to the Prior of Guisborough – but there is evidence of an earlier Saxon building here, if you look. A number of restorations have taken place and today the church has a calm, early English appearance, and is well worth a study.

EAT AND DRINK
Stonehouse Bakery and Tea Shop
stonehousebakery.co.uk
3 Briar Hill, YO21 2LZ
01287 660006
This traditional bakery in the village centre produces fabulous bread, including sun-dried tomato and olive breads and ciabatta. They also make the delicious sandwiches that are available in the adjoining tea shop. Cakes, too, come from the bakery's ovens, and their scones are perfect with jam and cream in a traditional cream tea.

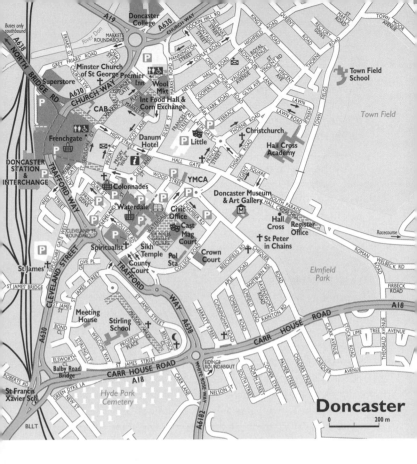

▶ Doncaster   MAP REF 324 C3

Doncaster is a lively town, where modern shopping and service industries have left the old industrial manufacturing and coal-mining heritage behind. Public transport today brings you straight into the Frenchgate shopping centre. Historically, 'Donny' owes its existence to three Rs – Romans, racing and the railway.

Doncaster's imposing Victorian Gothic minster church, St George's, was built by architect George Gilbert Scott, and is a symbol of the town's prosperity in the 19th century. It reflects a major boost to the town's fortunes with the arrival of the railways, and the decision by the Great Northern Railway to move its engine works from Boston to Doncaster – which eventually became the largest employer in the area. Through the years, many steam, diesel and electric locomotives were built in the town, including the famous record-breaker *Mallard* (see page 309).

Evidence has been found that this spot on the River Don was inhabited way back in the Palaeolithic era – with flint blades dating back to 10,000 BC. The Romans arrived in AD 71, establishing a fort which they called Danum. The location was key, for it lay on a direct line between Lindum (Lincoln) and Eboracum (York). When the Romans shipped out in AD 407 a village had already formed around the fort, and this grew into a thriving market town. It was well protected with ditches and ramparts of earth, interrupted by four main gateways, two of which survive.

By the 18th century, Doncaster was an important coaching stop, with the Great North Road passing through the centre of the town. The splendid gilded Mansion House and the theatre both date from this period, and the St Leger horserace – which is the oldest of the classics – was held on the racecourse for the first time in 1776.

TAKE IN SOME HISTORY
Mansion House
doncaster.gov.uk
High Street, DN1 1BN
01302 734032
Doncaster's civic Mansion House is one of only three in the country. Built by the architect James Paine in the Palladian style, it was officially opened in April 1749 – making it one of the oldest buildings still standing in the town. For many years it housed the Council Chambers, but since the council meetings moved to the new Civic Building, the Mansion House has taken on a leisurely mantle, and has become a focus of civic pride once again. Afternoon tea and tea dances take place throughout the year, as do regular open days.

VISIT THE MUSEUMS AND GALLERIES
Doncaster Museum and Art Gallery
doncaster.gov.uk
Chequer Road, DN1 2AE
01302 734293 | Open Wed–Fri 10–4.30, Sat–Sun 10.30–4.15

Learn about the history of Doncaster through the ages in this town-centre museum, with an interesting look at its place in railway history. Upstairs hosts a wide-ranging collection of fine and decorative art, ceramics, glass, silver and sculpture. The historical collection of the Kings Own Yorkshire Light Infantry is housed here, together with temporary exhibitions.

Cusworth Hall, Museum and Park Hall
doncaster.gov.uk
Cusworth Lane, DN5 7TU
01302 782342 | Open Mon–Wed 10–4.30, Sat–Sun 10.30–4.15; park open 24hrs
As an 18th-century country house set in a landscaped park, Cusworth Hall is a perfect location for The Museum of South Yorkshire – which illustrates the way local people lived, worked and entertained themselves here over the last 200 years. Recent extensive refurbishment has revealed much more of this exquisite

building. Walk in the park for great views of the metropolis of Doncaster. Make sure to pause at the tea room.

GO ROUND THE GARDENS
Brodsworth Hall and Gardens
english-heritage.org.uk
Brodsworth, DN5 7XJ
01302 722598 | House open Apr–Sep daily 11–5; gardens & servants' wing open Apr–Oct Tue–Sun 10–5.30, Nov–Mar Sat–Sun 10–4

When in the 1860s Charles Thellusson built a mansion on his 8,000-acre South Yorkshire estate, northwest of Doncaster, the gardens were laid out in a 'high Victorian' formal Italianate style to complement the architecture of the house. In recent years they've been restored to their full glory. Clipped box, yew and holly were established to form domed, pyramidal and cubic shapes, hedges and edges, and a marble fountain and a wealth of Italian statues were installed. Flights of steps leading from the terrace down to the extensive lawn were designed with extreme formality, with shallow urns at the head and marble greyhounds at the foot. Symmetrical flower beds, in keeping with the overall geometry of the design, are cut out of the turf – look out for the three-tier Italian marble dolphin fountain, like an elaborate cake-stand.

In February and March you can enjoy the sight of some 500,000 snowdrops and over 30 varieties of daffodil, many of them growing naturally in long grass. In April the floral tapestry changes as up to 5,000 tulips take over, and in summer the rose garden and wild flower meadows attract the most attention. The woodland walks become more vibrant as autumn progresses, and then in winter the original garden design, with its sculptural topiary, becomes all-important.

In contrast to all this primping in the gardens, Brodsworth Hall has been left as it was when the last owner died in 1988 – a state of genteel neglect. It plays host to many special events throughout the year, and during the summer months on a Sunday often has live music playing in the gardens.

GET OUTDOORS
Potteric Carr Nature Reserve
ywt.org.uk
Mallard Way, DN4 8DB
01302 325736 | Open daily Apr–Oct 9–5.30, Oct–Mar 9–5

This extensive nature reserve contains a mixture of habitats, from open water and marsh, wet woodland and scrub, and is maintained by the Yorkshire Wildlife Trust. Explore five miles of paths – accessible to wheelchairs – and the 14 well-constructed viewing hides. Around 100 species of birds breed here, and 28 species of butterfly have been spotted too. The Kingfisher Tearooms cafe provides a great spot to stop and refresh yourself.

CATCH A PERFORMANCE
Cast
castindoncaster.com
Waterdale, DN1 3BU
01302 303959

Doncaster's new performance venue, opened in 2013, replaces the smaller Civic Theatre. It boasts five performance spaces, with the 620-seat Main Space the big area, and it's already providing a varied programme of music, dance, drama, theatre, comedy and children's shows.

GO TO THE RACES
Doncaster Racecourse
doncaster-racecourse.co.uk
Leger Way, DN2 6BB
01302 304200

Doncaster is one of the oldest established centres for horseracing in Britain, with records of the first race in the 16th century. The course was first mapped out in 1614, and Doncaster now holds the distinction of opening and closing the flat season. The world famous St Leger Festival is held in September and is a major occasion, with a fair and other events across the town.

PLAY A ROUND
Doncaster has five notable golf courses. Doncaster Golf Club is located on the southern outskirts of the town and is an undulating heathland course with wooded surroundings. It's constructed on sandy subsoil which drains well, allowing play all year. Doncaster Town Moor Golf Club is situated in the centre of the racecourse and has easy walking, but is a testing, heathland course with good true greens. The notable hole is the 11th (with a par 4). Wheatley Golf Club is a fairly flat well-bunkered, lake-holed, parkland course. It's well-drained and is in excellent condition all year round.

A flat, easy-walking course surrounded by woodland – that's the Owston Park Golf Course, with a lot of mature trees and a few ditches in play. Thornhurst Park Golf Club is surrounded by Owston Wood, and this delightfully scenic parkland course has numerous strategically placed bunkers, and a lake which comes into play at the seventh and eighth holes.

Doncaster Golf Club
doncastergolfclub.co.uk
278 Bawtry Road, Bessacarr,
DN4 7PD | 01302 865632
Open Tue–Sun

Doncaster Town Moor Golf Club
doncastertownmoorgolfclub.co.uk
Bawtry Road, Belle Vue, DN4 5HU
01302 533167 | Open Mon–Sat

Wheatley Golf Club
wheatleygolfclub.co.uk
Armthorpe Road, DN2 5QB
01302 831655 | Open Mon–Fri

Owston Park Golf Course
owstonparkgolfcourse.co.uk
Owston Lane, Owston, DN6 8EF
01302 330821 | Open daily

Thornhurst Park Golf Club
thornhurstmanor.co.uk
Holme Lane, Owston, DN5 0LR
01302 337799 | Open daily

EAT AND DRINK
The Cadeby Pub & Restaurant
cadebyinn.co.uk
Main Street, Cadeby, Doncaster,
DN5 7SW | 01709 864009
Just outside Doncaster, The
Cadeby serves Yorkshire-
brewed real ales, while Old
Rosie is on cider duty. Snacks
and light meals are available at
lunchtime, as well as an
evening à la carte menu.

▶ **PLACES NEARBY**
Yorkshire Wildlife Park (see
page 98) is near Doncaster,
as is Conisbrough Castle.

Conisbrough Castle
english-heritage.org.uk
Castle Hill, Conisbrough
DN12 3BU | 01709 863329
Open end Mar–Sep daily 10–6, Oct
10–5, Nov–Mar Sat–Sun 10–4
To the west of the town is this
spectacular and formidable
ruin, the inspiration for Sir

10 castles in Yorkshire

Walter Scott's classic novel
Ivanhoe (1820). Its magnesian
limestone keep stands up to
97 feet high. The roof has been
restored, and a visitor centre
opened in 2014.

▼ Conisbrough Castle

▶ Yorkshire Wildlife Park

MAP REF 324 C4

yorkshirewildlifepark.com
DN4 6TB | 01302 535057 | Open mid-Mar to Oct 10–6,
Nov to mid-Mar 10.30–4

Since opening in 2009, the park has established itself as one of
Yorkshire's top attractions. Walk around between the landscaped
enclosures – the pride of lions, rescued from neglect in a
Romanian zoo, get nine acres to themselves – to see tigers,
leopards and giraffes at a respectful distance. In the 'African
Plains' field, zebras, antelopes, ankole cattle and ostriches mix and
roam free. There are also walk-though areas where you can get
really close to some of the animals – including Lemur Woods,
Wallaby Walkabout and South America Viva. Meerkats are another
favourite, and there's a herd of Bactrian camels. Big favourites are
the four polar bears – Victor, Pixel, Nissan and Nobby. Regional
food is served at the Wild Cafe, and children love the dropslides
and astraslides in the Jungle Play Barn. Top tip – leave your pet
dog at home: they're not allowed on the site.

▶ Egton Bridge   MAP REF 338 B3

Egton Bridge and Egton are two villages to the west of Scarborough separated by the River Esk – and they have nothing to do with eggs. An early settlement here appeared in the Domesday Book as Egetune, meaning 'the town of the oak trees'. The oaks are gone, as are the annual hiring fairs, when farmers would look to employ farm labourers for the forthcoming year. Even the weekly markets are no longer held, but the village is important as the venue for one of the area's largest agricultural shows, which takes place each year in August.

Egton Bridge was the birthplace in 1599 of Father Nicholas Postgate, who cared for his Catholic flock at great risk to himself in an age when baptising a child into the Catholic faith was a crime. Father Postgate was sent for trial at York in 1678, where he was found guilty and was hung, drawn and quartered. One of the pubs in the village is named in his honour.

EAT AND DRINK

Horseshoe Hotel

egtonbridgehotel.co.uk
YO21 1XE | 01947 895245

The Horseshoe is an 18th-century country house set in beautiful grounds by the River Esk. It's a great base as a hotel – handy for visiting Whitby, Robin Hood's Bay, the North Yorkshire Moors Railway and TV's *Heartbeat* country. Inside the welcoming bar are oak settles and tables, local artists' paintings, and plates around the picture rails. Along with some great beers, such as Durham Brewery ale, local ingredients are used to create the varied menu.

The Postgate

postgateinn.com
YO21 1UX | 01947 895241

Set in the Esk Valley within a stone's throw of the river, The Postgate is a typical North York Moors country inn, and played the part of The Black Dog in TV's *Heartbeat*. Being on the Coast to Coast trail, and becoming known as a food destination, the pub is popular with walkers who chat amiably with locals in the bar over their pints of Black Sheep.

The Wheatsheaf Inn

wheatsheafegton.com
YO21 1TZ | 01947 895271

This modest old pub is very popular with fishermen, as the River Esk is at the foot of the hill. The pub sits back from the wide main road and it would be easy to drive past it. But don't miss out – the welcoming main bar is cosy and traditional, with low beams, dark green walls and comfy settles, while the menu offers sandwiches, soup and hot focaccia rolls at lunchtime, as well as a range of light lunches, and the evening menu has a great feel too.

▶ Filey MAP REF 339 F5

Set on its own sandy bay between Bridlington and Scarborough, Filey is a genteel little holiday resort, protected to the north by the lump of land known as Filey Brigg. The Romans built a signal station there in the fourth century to watch out for invaders, but now it's left to the birders. Butlins holiday camp was a feature here for many years – but fashions change, and it's been converted to a block of new housing called The Bay. Today Filey's still known as a quiet place, its Victorian and Edwardian buildings giving it a certain grace and style.

Filey grew first as a fishing town, but started to change in the 18th century, when folk who found the resort at Scarborough too brash moved here for a quieter life. Charlotte Brontë visited twice, and Bradford-born composer Frederick Delius (1862–1934) also holidayed here, staying with his family in the posh Royal Crescent, and no doubt strolling along the promenade above the beautiful beach. Walk it yourself and you'll encounter some interesting sculptures – the giant lobster is a real winner.

Inland the freshwater marsh of Filey Dams is a nature reserve favoured by some 20 species of butterfly, not to mention great crested newts. Entry is free, and you can watch for interesting migrant birds from two hides.

VISIT THE MUSEUM
Filey Museum
fileymuseum.co.uk
8–10 Queen Street, YO14 9HB
01723 515013 | Open Easter–Oct
Sun–Fri 11–5, Sat 2–5
The museum is in an old fisherman's cottage – the oldest building in the town apart from the church, with its roots in 1696. It's a great little place, manned by local enthusiasts. One unusual display relates to the fishermen's knitted jumpers, called 'ganzeys'; in the seashore room you can make your own rubbings of various natural forms and learn about the fossils found along this coastline.

HIT THE BEACH
Filey Beach
It's often overlooked, but Filey has a well-deserved local reputation for a long sandy beach set in a wide bay. Head slightly north, and Filey Brigg is renowned for the wildlife living in the many rock pools.

▶ Flamborough Head MAP REF 331 F2

The most northerly outcrop of chalk in Britain is at Flamborough Head. Here the chalky hills of the Yorkshire Wolds meet the North Sea to form a large headland, with Filey Bay to the north and Bridlington to the south. Near the tip of this windswept headland you'll find two white lighthouses, one still working and dating from 1806 and the other an octagonal chalk tower, constructed in 1674 to bear a beacon of burning coal.

The headland is equidistant between Land's End and John o'Groats: a toposcope points out the directions. This useful instrument also commemorates the Battle of Flamborough Head in 1779, during the American War of Independence, when a Franco-American squadron clashed with two Royal Navy vessels just offshore – both sides claimed victory.

The vertical 400-foot cliffs at Bempton (see page 62) on the northern side are the dramatic location of one of the largest seabird nesting sites in Europe. Caves along this rocky shoreline are said to have been used by smugglers in the 18th and 19th centuries to hide their contraband sneaked over from France and Holland – brandy, lace, silks and tobacco.

TAKE IN SOME HISTORY
Flamborough Lighthouse
trinityhouse.co.uk
01262 673769
Enjoy a fascinating trip inside the 1806 working lighthouse – but check opening times first.

PLAY A ROUND
Flamborough Head Golf Club
flamboroughheadgolfclub.co.uk
Lighthouse Road, YO15 1AR
01262 850333
This east coast links course moulds itself around the contours of the cliffs which form part of the famous Flamborough Head, and has spectacular panoramic sea views.

EAT AND DRINK
The Seabirds Inn
theseabirds.com
Tower Street, YO15 1PD
01262 850242
This 200-year-old village pub lies just west of the famous

chalk promontory of Flamborough Head and its equally famed lighthouse. With the North Sea so close it's no surprise to fine plenty of fish on offer. The extensive specials menu changes with the seasons and there are guest ales on tap in the bar.

▼ Flamborough Lighthouse

▶ Fountains Abbey & Studley Royal   MAP REF 328 A2

nationaltrust.org.uk

HG4 3DY | 01765 608888 | Open Apr–Sep daily 10–5, Oct and Feb–Mar 10–4, Nov–Jan Sat–Thu 10–5; deer park 7–9

Fountains Abbey, and its surrounding parkland, was designated a UNESCO World Heritage Site in 1986, and is one of the most extensive monastic ruins in Europe. Yet to refer to Fountains as a ruin does it a disservice, and even the term 'remains' does not prepare you for the awesome and graceful sight of the best-preserved Cistercian abbey in Britain. It looks as if it may have been only a few years ago that the monks finally moved out.

The abbey was founded in 1132 by a group of so-called 'black monks' who broke away from a Benedictine abbey in York because the order was not strict enough for them. They sought to return to a more simple way of life. The buildings you see today were mostly constructed in the years from 1150 to 1250, though the north tower, which looms up into the sky, is a 16th-century addition. This is called Huby's Tower, named for Marmaduke Huby, the abbot who had it built not long before the Dissolution.

In medieval times Fountains Abbey was the richest abbey in Britain – it owned a great deal of the land in the Yorkshire Dales, and used it for grazing large herds of cattle and sheep. As you travel around the Dales today you will come across constant references to land that once belonged to the abbey, and buildings that were once its granges or outlying farms. Sheep-rearing and the resultant meat, cheese and wool were a massive source of revenue for the monks – you can only try to imagine the wealth that would ensue if a single landowner or estate farmed the same area of land today.

A visitor centre was added in 1992 amid some controversy and fears that it would intrude on the beauty of the abbey itself, but it's hidden well away. The centre caters well for the 300,000 people who come here each year, and its design ensures that while Huby's Tower can be seen from the visitor centre, the centre can't be seen while you're walking around the abbey estate. The centre incorporates an auditorium, a restaurant, and the largest National Trust shop in Britain. You can also see the beautifully restored monastic mill, and a handful of rooms in Fountains Hall, the 17th-century home of the subsequent owners of the abbey.

The adjoining parkland of Studley Royal was created in the 18th century and then merged with Fountains Abbey in 1768. They were the lifetime's work of John Aislabie, and then his son, William. John Aislabie inherited the Studley Royal estate in 1699 when he was Treasurer of the Exchequer, but involvement in the disastrous South Sea Bubble left him free to spend more time with his garden. The landscaping took 14 years, then another decade for the construction of the buildings. You can follow several paths around the gardens, through which the River Skell flows, and acquiring a map is probably a good idea as there is a great deal to see here including elegant temples and water cascades. St Mary's Church, built by William Burges in the 19th century, is the focal point of the 400-acre deer park, home to herds of red, fallow and Manchurian sika deer, about 350 in total.

▼ Fountains Abbey

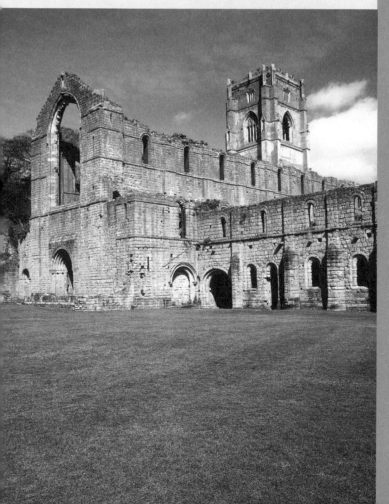

▲ Deer in the grounds of Studley Royal

ENTERTAIN THE FAMILY

If you've got young children, you might like to know that the Easter Monday egg-rolling tradition was revived at Fountains Abbey in the 1980s, at the suggestion of an estate worker who recalled the tradition from his own childhood. Hard-boiled eggs are thrown or rolled down a hill, a prize being given to the one that goes the furthest before disintegrating completely. In some areas children would decorate their eggs and put them on display before rolling them down the nearest slope, and finally eating any eggs that remained edible.

▶ Goathland   MAP REF 338 C3

High on the North York Moors, this pleasant village has achieved fame by proxy as the location for the popular television series *Heartbeat*. On the small screen Goathland was transformed into fictional Aidensfield, where the local police constable trod his rural beat, stuck forever in the 1960s. Episodes were filmed throughout the moors, but the village of Goathland will be especially familiar to the fans. Its relatively new-found fame brings its own problems and Goathland does get very busy at bank holiday weekends.

Goathland was popular with visitors long before the television series began, and though by no means the prettiest village on the moors, it's certainly well worth visiting in its own right. The broad grass verges, closely cropped by the loose sheep, lead directly on to the heather and bracken of the moors. Those black-faced moorland sheep are everywhere – local farmers enjoy grazing rights throughout the village, so the sheep roam where they will. They keep the grass closely cropped, but beware: they have only the most rudimentary road sense.

The church, just a century old, but on a site of Christian worship for a thousand years, was furnished by Robert Thompson of Kilburn. Look for the little carved mice that were the craftsman's trademark. Near the church is a pinfold – a small, square paddock enclosed by stone walls, where stray beasts could be kept until claimed by their owners.

A brief look around reveals several notable waterfalls. The best known is the 70-foot Mallyan Spout, easily reached via a footpath beside the Mallyan Spout Hotel. The hotel's Victorian architecture is a reminder that the first influx of visitors came with the building of the railway in the 1830s. Before that, Goathland's moorland setting kept it in relative isolation. It's still a popular stopping-off point for tourists on the North Yorkshire Moors Railway (see page 206).

The village also makes an excellent centre for exploring the surrounding moorland and the stretch of Roman road known as Wade's Causeway, on Wheeldale Moor (see page 290).

Leave Goathland in any direction and you will soon find yourself on expansive heather moorland. Though blackened in winter (hence an old name for the moors: Blackamore) the heather bursts into life during July, August and September, when miles of tiny flowers paint the uplands in glorious purple. The bell heather has deep purple flowers, while those of the cross-leaved heather have a pinker hue. The scene is made even more colourful during late summer by the blue-black bilberries and the rich rusty-brown bracken.

EAT AND DRINK

Goathland Tea Rooms & Gift Shop

goathlandtearooms.co.uk
West Mount, Goathland, YO22 5AL
01947 896446

Located right in the heart of Goathland, the Tea Rooms are housed in a former doctor's surgery, and afternoon tea here is just what the doctor ordered. Choose either a proper Yorkshire cup of tea or one of their speciality coffees, and you'll be refreshed and ready for more sightseeing.

▶ **PLACES NEARBY**

Beck Hole is a tiny hamlet of nine cottages and a pub hidden in the steep Murk Esk Valley, north of Goathland.

Birch Hall Inn

beckhole.info
Beck Hole, YO22 5LE
01947 896245

This charming little free house has just two tiny rooms, and no more than 30 people plus two small dogs have ever fitted inside with the door closed. So, think cosy here beside an open fire in winter, with a pint of the pub's house ale, Beckwatter. In warm weather, food and drink can be enjoyed in the large garden, which has peaceful countryside views. The food is simple fare and features the local butcher's pies and old-fashioned flatcakes filled with ham, cheese, corned beef or farmhouse pâté.

▶ Goole MAP REF 325 D1

Goole's a place today with a confused state of identity. It's a major international port – but located some 45 miles from the sea. Historically, it has always been part of the huge West Riding of Yorkshire. Then in 1974, it was divided into the new county of Humberside – but when Humberside was abolished, Goole found itself in the new East Riding. The flat surrounding land means that its twin water towers, nicknamed 'the salt and pepper pots', are a local landmark.

Goole as a port is as important today as it ever has been, handling nearly three million tonnes of cargo every year – making it one of the most important in northeast England. It owes its status to the work of the Dutch engineer, Cornelius Vermuyden, who diverted the River Don to drain the marshland of Hatfield Chase in South Yorkshire for Charles I. This made the lower Don viable for barges and linked it with the River Ouse – and the port of Goole sprung from that, becoming the UK's furthest inland port. A canal link to Leeds in 1826 ensured its continued prosperity, bringing in coal to fuel the Industrial Revolution and transporting manufactured goods to the markets of the European continent.

VISIT THE MUSEUM
The Yorkshire
Waterways Museum
waterwaysmuseum.org.uk
Dutch River Side, DN14 5TB
01405 768730 | Open Mon–Fri 9–4,
Mar–Nov Sat–Sun 10–4
Discover the story of the Aire
and Calder Navigation and the
growth of Goole and its busy
port. Find out how to sail and, in
the interactive gallery, see how
wooden boats were built. Enjoy
the unique 'Tom Pudding' story,
brought to life through the
vessels on the canal and the
boat hoist in South Dock. You
can rediscover the Humber
keels and sloops, and Goole's
shipbuilding history through the
objects, photos and memories
of Goole people.

▶ Grassington MAP REF 327 D2

Appearances can be deceptive. Grassington may look
as if it has always been a small and sleepy Wharfedale village,
but the discovery of large and valuable lead deposits on the
surrounding moors saw it develop into a thriving industrial
mecca between the 17th and 19th centuries. In fact, by the
early 1800s it was noted for drunkenness and violence – but the
arrival of Methodism did much to improve the locals' behaviour.

Today there's nothing like that to ruffle the genteel feathers,
as Grassington is now the major tourist centre in Upper
Wharfedale, with guest houses, shops and eating places
around its famous cobbled market square. It also has a
National Park Centre, near the middle, and the Upper
Wharfedale Folk Museum – a tiny but enjoyable collection
housed in two 18th-century former lead-miners' cottages,
which explores the history of mining in the area.

The town embraces several festivals through the year, none
more popular than the Dickensian extravaganza in December,
when everybody dresses up and joins in the fun.

VISIT THE MUSEUM
Grassington
Folk Museum
grassingtonfolkmuseum.org.uk
6 The Square, BD23 5AQ
01756 753287
Exhibits relating to Upper
Wharfedale are displayed
in 18th-century lead-miners'
cottages. The museum
is run by volunteers, so
check the opening times
before visiting.

GET OUTDOORS
Grassington National
Park Centre
yorkshiredales.org.uk
Hebden Road, BD23 5LB
01756 751690 | Open Apr–Oct
daily 10–5, Nov–Mar Sat–Sun 10–5,
last week Dec, Feb half term
The centre, on the edge of
Grassington, provides a useful
introduction to the area, with
maps, guides and local
information. Check out the

guided walks particularly. There is also a 24-hour public access information service and a full tourist information service, and you can learn more about the effects of agriculture and climate change in the region.

EAT AND DRINK

Grassington House ◉◉
grassingtonhousehotel.co.uk
5 The Square, BD23 5AQ
01756 752406
The stone-built Georgian house overlooks its cobbled village square amid the limestone hills of Wharfedale. Inside, the place has been subjected to all the tender loving care its architectural heritage requires, with a high level of elegance and comfort throughout. The crimson-toned No 5 dining room is the nerve-centre, extending into a conservatory space, and there's an outdoor terrace to capitalise on the surroundings. A new state-of-the-art, eco-friendly kitchen produces modern food with the accent on sharply etched flavours. Daily fish specials are listed separately to the main menu.

▷ **PLACES NEARBY**

To the east of Grassington you will find Parcevall Hall Gardens, and a couple of good places to stop and refresh yourself.

Parcevall Hall Gardens
parcevallhallgardens.co.uk
Skyreholme, BD23 6DE
01756 720311 | Open Apr–Oct 10–6

Enjoying a hillside setting east of Grassington, these beautiful gardens surround a Grade II-listed house which is used as the Bradford Diocesan Retreat House (not open to the public). The terraced formal gardens are superb, including a rose garden, and Chinese and Himalayan species are a speciality here. Explore further on the woodland trails.

The Craven Arms
craven-cruckbarn.co.uk
Appletreewick, BD23 6DA
01756 720270
Originally part of a farm, this 16th-century Dales pub has spectacular views of Wharefdale. The building retains its original beams, flagstone floors, gas lighting and magnificent fireplace; the village stocks are still outside. Traditional real ales are served, and there's a beer festival every October. The blackboard menu changes daily and offers plenty of choice. A heather-thatched cruck barn to the rear provides additional dining space.

Wharfe View Tearooms
The Green, Burnsall, BD23 6BS
01756 720237
Facing the Green, and beyond it the River Wharfe in the centre of the delightful village of Burnsall, the Wharfe View is a favourite stopping place for walkers and motorists alike. Choose from a scrummy menu of cakes and sandwiches, then sit in the front garden and watch the world go by.

▶ **Great Ayton** MAP REF 337 F2

Great Ayton village is split by the River Leven, whose clear waters seem almost to deny that the industrial heartland of Middlesbrough is just a short drive away. Behind Great Ayton is the famous profile of Roseberry Topping, the conical peak – 1,056 feet/322m and a distinctive landmark for miles around.

Great Ayton has two churches that lie almost side by side. The first is All Saints – a delightful building dating back to the 12th century, though additions have been made in every succeeding century. The interior is quite simple, with walls of rough-hewn stone, and enough original architectural detail to keep most lovers of old churches engrossed. The population of Great Ayton grew to the point where the congregation could no longer squeeze into this atmospheric building – so Christ Church was consecrated as the new parish church in 1877. Fortunately the old church escaped the fate of so many redundant churches, and is now open for you to have a look around during the summer months.

▼ The Cleveland Hills, seen from Cliff Ridge

Captain James Cook's mother and five of his brothers and sisters are buried in the churchyard. The great navigator and explorer lived here as a boy, and a statue of him as a child stands on the green. Don't bother looking for his house, however – that was dismantled and shipped to Australia in 1934.

VISIT THE MUSEUM
Captain Cook Schoolroom Museum
captaincookschoolroom
museum.co.uk
101 High Street, TS9 6NB
01642 724296 | Open Jul–Aug daily
11–4, Apr–Jun & Sep–Oct 1–4

The museum is in a building once used as a charity school, founded in 1704 by Michael Postgate, a local landowner. It was here, between 1736 and 1740, that James Cook received his early education. Although small, the museum has been entirely refreshed and modernised and features a reconstruction of a schoolroom of the early 18th century, when teaching methods were very different from today. Interactive displays about James Cook's early life and education, and his later achievements provide enjoyment for the whole family.

Grosmont MAP REF 338 C3

Built largely to house those who worked on the Pickering–Whitby railway line that splits the village in two, Grosmont was originally – and unimaginatively – called Tunnel. With its terraced houses and mining spoil, Grosmont presents a more industrial face to the world than the other villages of the Esk Valley. Indeed, it was while excavating the Pickering–Whitby line in 1835 that the richest ironstone deposits were first discovered. Once completed, the railway was a convenient method of getting that ironstone to ships in Whitby harbour. By the middle of the 19th century, Grosmont was a major supplier of ironstone to the ironmasters' furnaces on the rivers Tyne and Tees.

The name 'Grosmont' recalls the 13th-century Grandmontine Priory, founded here by French monks. The priory is long gone, its place taken by Priory Farm and its stonework salvaged for secular buildings.

The Pickering–Whitby line was built in 1836 after consulting with George Stephenson, who came to the project straight from the triumphant success of his Stockton–Darlington railway. Closed in 1965, a victim of Beeching's notorious axe, the line was reborn eight years later – thanks to massive support from amateur railway enthusiasts – as the North Yorkshire Moors Railway, manned by volunteers (see page 206). Railway buffs can spend some time admiring the gleaming old locomotives at Grosmont Station, which has been convincingly restored to how it may have looked in the 1950s; you can also see the engine sheds. Uber-fans can rent the station cottage and live the dream of steam.

The Rail Trail walking route extends from Grosmont to Goathland, so you could combine it with a trip along this most scenic of railway lines – the Rail Trail booklet suggests the train journey to Goathland followed by a walk back to Grosmont. The three-mile footpath follows the route of the original section of line between the two villages, via Beck Hole, as laid in 1836.

TAKE A TRAIN RIDE
Grosmont Station
nymr.co.uk
YO22 5QE | 01947 895359

For information about the North York Moors routes, see page 206. The Esk Valley line also goes through to Whitby.

▶ Guisborough   MAP REF 337 F2

Guisborough is one of Yorkshire's lost and found towns – having been in the North Riding of Yorkshire until 1974, it was stripped of its Yorkshire status until 1996. It's now firmly back in North Yorkshire, and the broad main street and cobbled verges show that markets have been held here for centuries. Today the market traders put up their stalls on Thursdays and Saturdays, drawing their customers from many of the villages on the edge of the moors.

Beyond the main street is the largely 15th-century Church of St Nicholas, where a cenotaph reinforces the links between the local de Brus family and the Bruces of Scotland. Robert the Bruce's grandfather is buried nearby at Gisborough Priory. Nearby is Gisborough Hall, originally built by Sir Thomas Chaloner, and now a luxury hotel sitting in beautiful wooded surroundings.

TAKE IN SOME HISTORY
Gisborough Priory
english-heritage.org.uk
TS14 6HG | 01287 633801
Open Mar–Oct Wed–Sun 10–4
The spectacular east window of the ruined priory still stands to its full height of nearly 71 feet, gazing out across farmland. A priory was founded here in 1119 for the Augustinian order by Robert de Brus, a relative of the Scottish King Robert the Bruce. Today, the gatehouse is the only part of the original building left standing, thanks partly to a fire in 1289 and partly to the destruction wrought during the Dissolution of the Monasteries in 1540. The

Chaloner family acquired the site in 1550 and still own it today, with English Heritage responsible for maintenance.

EAT AND DRINK
Gisborough Hall ◉◉
gisborough-hall.co.uk
Whitby Lane, TS14 6PT
01287 611500

On the edge of the North York Moors, the hall is an imposing Victorian-built, creeper-covered country-house hotel within well-kept grounds. Chaloner's restaurant is in what used to be the billiard room, a large space with pillars, a fireplace, white-patterned burgundy-coloured carpet and white upholstered seats at wooden-topped tables. The kitchen works around the abundance of Yorkshire's produce and the dishes never seem overdone. The kitchen clearly has an understanding of the balance of textures and flavours.

▶ PLACES NEARBY
Just a mile out of Guisborough, on the A173 in the direction of Skelton, is Tocketts Watermill.

Tocketts Watermill
www.tockettsmill.co.uk
Tocketts Mill Country Park, Skelton Road, TS14 6QA | 01287 639120
Check website for opening times, which are quite short and sporadic

The water of Tocketts Beck still turns the waterwheel of this old flour-mill, and on certain milling days – usually Sundays in summer – you can see one of the most complete working water mills in England in action. Wheat, rye, beans, peas and oats were brought to be ground here, using millstones with evocative names such as bluestones, French burrs and Derbyshire greys. In addition, the lower floor of the mill was used as a buttery. The mill and house have been fully restored.

▶ Hackness MAP REF 339 D4

Steep-sided, wooded valleys fan out from the lovely picturesque village of Hackness, which was established at the point where Lowdale Beck meets the River Derwent. It's hard to believe this unspoilt, secluded spot is only three miles from the outskirts of Scarborough.

While Hackness hides in its valley, you can enjoy panoramic views by taking the minor roads to the hilltop villages of Broxa and Silpho. Immediately to the south is the Forge Valley, a beautiful wooded dale created at the end of the Ice Age by glacial meltwater. Forge Valley takes its name from the iron forges, thought to have been worked by the monks of Rievaulx Abbey in the 14th century, which were fuelled by timber from this ancient woodland. Today the Forge Valley is a beauty spot and a haven for wildlife. The woods on either side of the river feature native species including oak, ash, elm and willow –

▲ The River Derwent

making an appealing contrast to the fairly regimented conifer plantations elsewhere. Woodpeckers drum insistently; wagtails search for food along the riverbank; tiny warblers fill the woods with song each summer – this is a most relaxing place. The walking is excellent during any season, and a wheelchair-friendly boardwalk follows the river for a mile.

St Hilda, Abbess of Whitby Abbey, established a nunnery here in AD 680, but Vikings and Henry VIII finished it off between them. Hackness Hall occupies the site where the nunnery once stood – a handsome Georgian house built in 1791 (not open to the public).

The Ghost of Hackness was the invention of a local 18th-century vicar's daughter when she found herself a little short of money: she reported seeing a spectral figure that intimated a sum of £50 would allow his soul to be put at rest...

▶ PLACES NEARBY

Yew Tree Café and Bistro
yewtreescalby.co.uk
Scalby, YO13 0PT
01723 367989
A short drive back to Scarborough is the small village of Scalby, complete with this gem of a cafe. Traditionally a firm favourite for lunches and a popular choice for a cuppa, in the last few years the Yew Tree has carved a reputation for being an excellent evening eatery too. Don't miss the wide range on the specials board.

▶ Halifax   MAP REF 322 C1

In the heart of the Pennine Hills, Halifax became a powerhouse of the textile industry during the Industrial Revolution. The town's wealth in the 19th century came from cotton, wool and carpet manufacture. The landmark of the mighty Dean Clough Mill was built in the 1840s for a carpet maker and become one of the largest carpet factories in the world – it is now a Grade II listed building. Trading took place in the magnificent Italianate arcaded Piece Hall of 1779, which later became a public market – here hand-loom weavers of the district would offer their wares, or 'pieces', for sale to the cloth merchants, and now you can shop to your heart's content in a range of independent boutiques. Other significant buildings in the town include the town hall – designed by the Houses of Parliament architect, Charles Barry, in 1863 – and the Wainhouse Tower, a late-Victorian folly. The steep cobbled thoroughfare up Beacon Hill is known as the Magna Via, and was once the main route into the town from the east – pity the poor packhorses who staggered up and down it.

Unlike most Yorkshire towns, Halifax wasn't listed in the Domesday Book, so its early life is very difficult to piece together – but by the 12th century, the town was growing, and lawlessness was starting to be a problem. The solution? The Halifax Gibbet – a guillotine, which beheaded some 63 felons between 1286 and 1650. If you want to see the original blade, it's on display in the Bankfield Museum.

VISIT THE MUSEUMS AND GALLERIES

Bankfield Museum
museums.calderdale.gov.uk
Boothtown Road, Akroyd Park,
HX3 6HG | 01422 354823
Open Tue–Sat 10–4
Built by Edward Akroyd in the 1860s, this Renaissance-style building is set on a hill overlooking the town. You'll find an outstanding collection of costumes and textiles, including one gallery featuring East European textiles. There is also a section on toys, and the museum of the Duke of Wellington's Regiment is housed here. Temporary exhibitions are held and there is a lively programme of events, workshops and activities.

Eureka! The National Children's Museum
eureka.org.uk
Discovery Road, HX1 2NE
01422 330069 | Open daily 10–5 during school hols; term time Tue–Fri 10–4, Sat–Sun 10–5
Eureka! is a place where children play to learn and grown-ups learn to play, a place designed to inspire children to find out about themselves and the world around them. With over 400 'must touch' exhibits,

interactive activities and challenges spread through six main gallery spaces, you can find out how your body and senses work, discover the realities of daily life, and experiment with creating your own sounds and music.

TAKE IN SOME HISTORY
Shibden Hall
museums.calderdale.gov.uk
Lister's Road, HX3 6XG
01422 352246 | Open Mar–Oct
Mon–Thu 10–5, Sat–Sun 11–5,
Nov–Dec Mon–Thu 10–4, Sat–Sun
11–4, Jan–Feb Sat–Sun 11–4
Take a fascinating journey through the lives of the four wealthy families who owned this 15th-century timber-framed manor house – its rooms have been laid out to illustrate life in different periods of its history. Craft weekends, featuring more than 30 craftworkers demonstrating historic skills, are held throughout the year. The hall is surrounded by beautifully restored gardens.

GO SHOPPING
The Piece Hall
thepiecehall.co.uk
Blackledge, Halifax, HX1 1RE
01422 525217
The sole survivor of the great 18th-century northern cloth halls, The Piece Hall reopened in 2017 after a £19 million conservation programme. Built in 1779 for the trading of 'pieces' of cloth, it is one of Britain's most outstanding Georgian buildings, and is now a hub of heritage, shopping, eating and drinking.

PLAY A ROUND
The town has two top golf clubs: Halifax Golf Club is a moorland course crossed by streams and natural hazards, while Lightcliffe Golf Club is a parkland course where the signature hole is a dog-leg with the second shot over a deep ravine.

Halifax Golf Club
halifaxgolfclub.co.uk
Union Lane, Ogden, HX2 8XR
01422 244171 | Open Mon–Fri

Lightcliffe Golf Club
lightcliffegolfclub.co.uk
Knowle Top Road, Lightcliffe,
HX3 8SW | 01422 202459
Open Mon–Tue, Thu–Fri, Sun

▼ Eureka! The National
Children's Museum

▶ **PLACES NEARBY**

There are a number of places to visit around Halifax, including an exciting adventure centre in Ogden, the Smith Art Gallery in Brighouse and a couple of great places to eat and drink in Holmfield and Shibden.

Another World Adventure Centre

anotherworldadventurecentre.co.uk
Moss Farm, Keighley Road, Ogden, Halifax HX2 8YB
01422 240700

Fancy snowboarding without the snow? Well, at the original Mountain Boarding Centre you can do just that. It's similar to surfing and snowboarding but can be done on any surface, at any time of the year, in any weather. No board? No worries, you can hire one. There are lots of other activities on offer, too, including archery, gokarting and grass sledging.

Smith Art Gallery

museums.calderdale.gov.uk
Halifax Road, Brighouse, HD6 2AF
01422 352334 | Open Mon, Fri 10–5, Tue, Thu 10–4, Sat 10–3.30

Surrounded by a park and beautiful gardens, this purpose-built art gallery and public library, known as 'The Rydings', is host to a range of works from artists including Thomas Sydney Cooper, Marcus Stone and Atkinson Grimshaw. The rear of the gallery has a changeable display covering photography, mixed media and sculpture, so there's always something different to enjoy.

Holdsworth House Hotel 👁️👁️

holdsworthhouse.co.uk
Holdsworth Road, Holmfield, HX2 9TG | 01422 240024

Built during the reign of Charles I, Holdsworth House looks fit for a king with its handsome creeper-covered façade and charming period interior. There's nothing dated about the elegant public spaces, sporting stylish furniture and luxurious fabrics, while the restaurant is the embodiment of sophistication with its burnished oak-panelled walls, oil paintings and mullioned windows. There are other delights, including a romantic listed gazebo and a pretty walled courtyard. The kitchen is in tune with the rest of the operation, delivering food that is rooted in British (and Yorkshire) tradition but has a bit of style about it.

Shibden Mill Inn 👁️👁️

shibdenmillinn.com
Shibden Mill Fold, HX3 7UL
01422 365840

This 17th-century inn, once a mill (the millstream, Red Beck, runs past it and is part of the garden), is an atmospheric old place with nooks and crannies, open fires, low beams, rustic-looking furniture and friendly but professional staff, all creating an inviting and hospitable environment, helped along by candlelight in the evenings. The kitchen puts its shoulder to the wheel, turning out some inspired dishes that show a degree of complexity.

▶ Hardraw   MAP REF 334 C4

Hardraw is a hamlet that would probably be visited only by those passing through on the Pennine Way if it was not for the existence of Hardraw Force. At just shy of 100 feet, it has the longest free drop of any waterfall in England – above ground, at least – and was notably painted by J M W Turner on his travels through the Yorkshire Dales in the early 19th century. Unusually, to reach the waterfall you must pass through the Green Dragon pub, paying a small entrance fee as you do so.

The volume of water from the fall is not great, so it's best visited after heavy rain. Those who do not mind a slight splashing can walk round behind the fall, although take care on the wet rocks as they are slippery. In 1739 and 1881 the falls froze completely to produce an impressive 100-foot icicle.

The village is the home of the Hardraw Scar Brass Band Contest, held in September. It was founded in 1881 and is reputed to be the second oldest brass band competition in the world. Bands from across the north – and beyond – compete in the championship.

EAT AND DRINK

The Green Dragon Inn
DL8 3LZ | 01969 667392
Entering the bar parlour of the Green Dragon is like stepping into a Tudor film-set, although parts of the inn are much older – 13th century, in fact. Gravestones, forming part of the floor, were washed away from the neighbouring churchyard during floods. The choice of real ales and ciders is good, and pub food includes home-made steak and kidney pie; lamb shank, mash and veg; and a seasonal dish of pheasant bourguignon with horseradish mash and creamed cabbage. Beer festivals in June and July, a third with cider in October, and regular live folk music are all big draws.

The Moorcock Inn
moorcockinn.com
Garsdale Head, LA10 5PU
01969 667488
West of Hawes on the Sedburgh road, this 18th-century inn stands alone in open countryside at the tip of Wensleydale, although it is only three-quarters of a mile from Garsdale Station. Inside is a traditional blend of original stonework, bright colours and comfortable sofas. Savour a glass of local real ale from the Tirril Brewery, draught lager or one of the 50 malt whiskies, and enjoy the spectacular views from the garden. Home-cooked lunches include jacket potatoes, sandwiches and pub classics – and there's a wide menu for dinner, too.

▶ Harewood House & Bird Garden   MAP REF 328 B4

harewood.org

Leeds, LS17 9LG | 0113 218 1010 | Open daily Apr–Oct, grounds 10–6; house 12–4

The first glimpse of Harewood House is intimidating, soaring above the level parkland, with neither buildings nor trees to soften the approach. You cannot fail to be impressed by the sheer size and magnificence of the north facade of this stately home. The entrance is dominated by a classical pediment and pillars. The entrance hall itself is equally stern and cold, its walls and ceilings covered with roundels depicting stories from classical myths – even the alabaster figure of *Adam*, by Jacob Epstein, which stands sentinel here, is of heroic masculine proportions – and modern art is given its place in this remarkable mansion.

This is the treasure house and home of the Lascelles family, and Regency furniture, coronation chairs and Chippendale pieces give way to comfortable sofas; Lascelles and Canning portraits by Reynolds and Gainsborough mingle with modern family photos. There are works of wonder to be seen everywhere: superb Sèvres pieces in the China Room, including a tea service given to Marie Antoinette in 1779, and delightful views of Harewood House by Turner, Girtin and Richmond. The gallery holds Chinese porcelain and Italian pictures including a Tintoretto and a Titian.

The first Lascelles came over to England with William the Conqueror. Later Colonel Francis Lascelles fought for Parliament in the Civil War and went on to become MP for the North Riding, beginning a long family tradition of parliamentary service. The Lascelles' fortune came from sugar plantations in the West Indies, which enabled Francis's grandson, Henry, to buy Gawthorpe and Harewood, and his great-grandson, Edwin Lascelles (1735–1795), to realise his dream of building a grand new house on the hill.

John Carr of York was charged with building the house, a farm and model village. Lascelles then contacted the up-and-coming Scottish architect Robert Adam, who changed little of the Palladian exterior of the house, but put his stamp firmly on the interior. This resulted in a glorious series of state rooms with delicate and elaborate plasterwork designs. Adam selected all the carpets and commissioned Thomas Chippendale, born only a few miles away at Otley (see page 211), to provide all the furniture and furnishings – a task that he performed with both flair and sympathy. The simple elegance and understated opulence of his inlaid and gilded pieces are the perfect complement to Adam's room schemes.

The foundation stone was laid in January 1759, but it was not until 12 years later that the house became habitable. The following year, Lancelot 'Capability' Brown submitted his plans for landscaping the park, creating a 'natural' undulating vista from the house down to the artificial lake. Planting woodland and altering the lie of the land took nine years and cost £6,000, but created an idyllic and supremely English setting for this gem of a country house.

The Bird Garden is a bonus: see lots of exotic species, including penguins, macaws and cranes – in aviaries and garden settings. The penguins are fed daily at 2pm – book your place early.

◀ Harewood House

▶ Harrogate MAP REF 328 B3

Harrogate lies on the fringe of the Yorkshire Dales, and is a magnet for anyone with serious shopping in mind. It's an attractive and lively town with theatres, cinemas and good restaurants, and a load of new hotels and conference centres created by the busy hospitality industry. But Harrogate has not lost its charm, and the spa town that developed after the discovery of a spring in 1571 is still plainly visible.

You'll be struck by the amount of lush greenery around, especially the wide swathes of grass and flowerbeds known as The Stray. These 200 acres are protected under an ancient law, which ensures that residents and visitors alike are entitled to enjoy them. There are more pretty flowers as well as a boating pond, playground, crazy golf and other activities in the Valley Gardens, Harrogate's main park. Its entrance is close to the Royal Pump Room Museum.

Harrogate's origins can be traced in the octagonal Royal Pump Room Museum, which was originally built in 1842 in order to enclose the old sulphur well on this site. In addition to serving up local history, the museum serves up cups of the pungent spa water that first made the town so famous. It claims to be the strongest sulphur water in Europe, so some visitors may prefer Perrier, or to refresh the palate with a visit to one of the famous Bettys tea rooms, a real Yorkshire institution, which offer delicious cream cakes and Yorkshire fat rascals – a fruity scone.

Not quite a Yorkshire institution is a visit to a Turkish baths, so perhaps it is just a coincidence that the entrance to the baths is a short stroll down Cambridge Road from Bettys. Harrogate is one of the few places where you can enjoy a Turkish bath in all its original 19th-century splendour, in the Royal Baths Assembly Rooms. Its original Victorian exterior masks a beautifully renovated tiled interior, which includes a cold plunge bath, several hot rooms, a steam room, massage room and a relaxing rest room for when the ordeal is over. There are both mixed and 'ladies only' sessions, so check first if you are thinking of going.

You can glimpse a snapshot of Victorian life here through the paintings of William Powell Frith. The son of a Harrogate hotelier, Frith specialised in narrative painting in a very traditional style. The municipal Mercer Art Gallery on Swan Road has many of his pieces.

A final treat is Farrah's Original Harrogate Toffee, dating back to 1840 – a brittle butterscotch type sweet, lightly flavoured with lemon and packaged in distinctive blue and silver tins, and still cooked up in copper pans. You'll find it

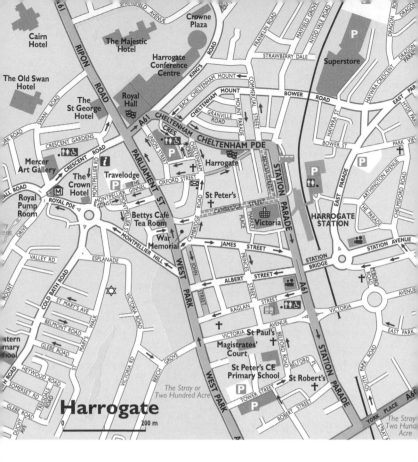

Harrogate

0   200 m

everywhere, but notably at Farrah's own shop on Montpellier Parade, which also has a wealth of other local goodies, including cheeses and Voakes's pork pies.

VISIT THE MUSEUMS AND GALLERIES
The Royal Pump Room Museum
harrogate.gov.uk
Crown Place, HG1 2RY
01423 556188 | Open Mon–Sat 10.30–5, Sun 2–5 (closes 4pm Nov–Mar)
Housed in the pump room, the museum tells the glory of Harrogate's Spa heyday and its connection to Russian royalty. Also see the stunning Egyptian collection and temporary exhibitions of social history.

Mercer Art Gallery
harrogate.gov.uk
Swan Road, HG1 2SA
01423 556188 | Open Tue–Sat 10–5, Sun 2–5 (4 Nov–Mar)
This is where the Harrogate district's collection of fine art resides – with some 2,000 pieces from the 19th and 20th centuries, including Atkinson Grimshaw, Dame Laura Knight, Alan Davie, Sir Edward Burne-Jones and many more. There's always something different to see – together with the regular touring exhibitions.

GO ROUND THE GARDENS
RHS Garden
Harlow Carr
rhs.org.uk
Crag Lane, HG3 1UE (satnav friendly postcode) | 01423 565418 | Open 9.30–6, Nov–Feb 9.30–4

Botanical enthusiasts will want to visit this Royal Horticultural Society Garden on the outskirts of the town, off the B6162. With 68 impressive acres, Harlow Carr has a lovely mix of the formal and informal, with a gardening museum, plant and gift shops, and places for refreshments. Courses, demonstrations and practical workshops are held in the Study Centre, and there is even a branch of Bettys, the famous Yorkshire tea rooms.

SEE A LOCAL CHURCH
St Wilfrid Church
stwilfrid.org
Duchy Road, HG1 2EY
01423 504629

This beautiful church is Gothic Revival at its best and is true to the reforms of the Anglo-Catholic Oxford Movement, which sought to reinstate lost traditions into the Anglican Church. It's also probably the finest building of the distinguished architect Temple Moore, with its lovely exterior stonework in honey-coloured Tadcaster limestone. Work on the church began in 1904, but Moore died suddenly in 1920, leaving his son-in-law to complete it in 1935. Inside, the solid-looking church is surprisingly spacious and light.

RELAX
Harrogate Turkish Baths
and Health Spa
turkishbathsharrogate.co.uk
Parliament Street, HG1 2WH
01423 556746

Choose your treatment and unwind in this extraordinary tiled edifice. Basic bathing will take you from the steam room through various levels of hot rooms to the heat-fest that is the Laconium, before you cool off in the plunge pool and chill out in the Frigidarium – the whole process takes around 90 minutes, and you'll need a swimming costume for modesty. Sessions are split for 'ladies' and 'mixed', and numbers are limited so book ahead.

GO SHOPPING
Farrah's Food Hall
farrahs.com
29 Montpellier Parade, HG1 2TG
01423 525266 | Open Mon–Sat 9–5.30, Sun 10–5

Toffee and other sweets, of course – but also a great deli with savoury treats, and there's the Palm Court Café upstairs.

PLAY A ROUND
Harrogate has two notable courses. The Harrogate Golf Club is on fairly flat terrain with MacKenzie-style greens and tree-lined fairways. While it's not a long course, the layout penalises the golfer who strays off the fairway. Subtly placed bunkers and copses of trees require you to adopt careful

thought and accuracy if par is to be bettered. The last six holes include five par 4s, of which four exceed 400 yards. The Oakdale Golf Club is a pleasant undulating parkland course which provides a good test of golf for the low handicap player without intimidating the less proficient. A special feature is an attractive stream which comes in to play on four holes.

Harrogate Golf Club
harrogate-gc.co.uk
Forest Lane Head, Starbeck, HG2 7TF
01423 862999 | Open Mon,
Wed–Fri, Sun, Tue pm only

Oakdale Golf Club
oakdalegolfclub.co.uk
Oakdale Glen, HG1 2LN
01423 567162 | Open daily

EAT AND DRINK
Bettys Cafe Tea Rooms
bettys.co.uk
1 Parliament Square, HG1 2QU
01423 814070
When young confectioner Frederick Belmont travelled from Switzerland to find his fortune he came to Harrogate accidentally – by catching the wrong train. He liked the place well enough to stay, married a local lass and opened the first Bettys tea room. Today's unique Swiss–Yorkshire fusion menu continues to reflect the heritage of the family business. Sister company, Taylor's of Harrogate, imports and blends all the excellent teas served, and each of the tea rooms has a shop selling teas, coffees, speciality breads, cakes, pastries and chocolates, all handmade at Bettys Craft Bakery. If you like you can take a cookery course too at Bettys Cookery School, also in Harrogate. You'll find more branches in York, Ilkley and Northallerton.

Bettys At RHS Garden Harlow Carr
bettys.co.uk
Crag Lane, HG3 1QB
01423 505604

▼ Bettys Cafe Tea Rooms

This is Bettys' sixth tea room, and the first new one to open for more than 30 years. And what a great location – the Royal Horticultural Society's 58-acre Harlow Carr Garden. An existing building was transformed with Lloyd Loom chairs, marble-topped tables, palm trees, and a terrace overlooking the garden. There is also a tea house in the middle of the gardens, plus a Bettys shop and deli.

Hotel du Vin & Bistro Harrogate ◉

hotelduvin.com
Prospect Place, HG1 1LB
01423 856800
The senses have always been well catered for by the tea shops and Victorian spa in Harrogate, a tradition continued 21st-century-style by the local outpost of the HdV chain in a luxuriously converted terrace of eight Georgian town houses opposite the 200-acre Stray Common. As its name suggests, the Hotel du Vin brand takes a serious approach to the grape, so a snifter of one of the impressive array of wines available by the glass in the bar is a good move before settling into the slick Gallic-style bistro.

Studley Hotel ◉◉

orchidrestaurant.co.uk
28 Swan Road, HG1 2SE
01423 560425
In the Studley Hotel's Orchid restaurant, a multinational brigade of chefs delivers authentic regional flavours in an eclectic Pan-Asian melting pot of cuisines from China, Indonesia, Japan, Korea, Malaysia, the Philippines, Thailand and Vietnam. Mango and darkwood interiors divided by Japanese lattice-style screens make for a classy contemporary setting, with a large TV screen providing a live video feed of the action in the kitchen. Express lunch menus offer stonking value. Key ingredients are flown in regularly from Asia.

White Hart Hotel ◉

whitehart.net
2 Cold Bath Road, HG2 0NF
01423 505681
The White Hart is quite a Harrogate landmark, having been a comfortable resort of the discerning traveller since the Georgian era. The old dining room is now a trendy pub called the Fat Badger, while the main eating space is called the Brasserie, with a quality menu to match.

▶ **PLACES NEARBY**

Knaresborough (see page 164) is just a short 15-minute drive away, and there is a luxurious spa in Follifoot.

Rudding Park Hotel, Spa & Golf ◉◉

ruddingpark.co.uk
Follifoot, HG3 1JH | 01423 871350
When you're ready for the whole country-house pampering package, Rudding Park fits the bill. It has its own golf course, glossy spa, and food that's

worth a detour in the Clocktower Restaurant. The interior offers vibrant, colourful spaces, from the long limestone bar, to the grand conservatory with a 400-year- old Catalonian olive tree, and the dining room with its eye-catching pink glass chandelier and elegantly understated contemporary looks.

▶ Hawes MAP REF 334 C4

It's nice when family businesses still make up most of the shops in a town's main street – and that's the case in Hawes, the main town of Upper Wensleydale. It is certainly the place to stock up on good local produce, especially on the busy Tuesday market day when stalls line the streets and farmers conduct their business at the livestock market along the Leyburn road – even if you're not intending to buy a cow, do look in for a flavour of farming life in the Dales.

To sample Wensleydale cheese, and for the chance to watch it being made, you should head for the Wensleydale Creamery. Cheese has been made in the farm kitchens of Wensleydale since French monks introduced the skill in the 12th century. This factory, built in 1897 by a local corn merchant, has a visitor centre, which includes a museum, video display, licensed

▼ St Margaret's, Hawes

restaurant, shop, free cheese-tasting and viewing platforms into the works. A more conventional museum is the fascinating Dales Countryside Museum, in the Station Yard. The arrival of a railway link in 1877 boosted Hawes' fortunes, but the trains no longer run. The museum – which also contains a tourist information centre and a National Park Centre – has first-class displays on life in the Dales, particularly on small local industries such as knitting and peat-cutting.

Just across from the Station Yard is the entrance to Outhwaite and Son, rope-makers, where you can see how the rope is produced as well as buy rope products, gardening items and gifts in the shop.

VISIT THE MUSEUM
Dales Countryside Museum and National Park Centre
dalescountrysidemuseum.org.uk
Station Yard, DL8 3NT
01969 666210 | Open daily
Feb–Dec 10–5
It's a fascinating museum telling the story of the people and landscape of the Yorkshire Dales, with a static steam loco and carriages with displays.

Added features include hands-on interactive displays for children, a Research Room, temporary exhibitions and special events. There's a family exhibition every summer with activities for visitors of all ages, and an outdoor sculpture trail to follow. Its collection is enhanced by the inclusion of material donated by the local authors and historians, Marie Hartley and Joan Ingilby.

LEARN ABOUT CHEESE
Wensleydale Creamery Visitor Centre
wensleydale.co.uk
Gayle Lane, DL8 3RN
01969 667664 | Open daily 10–4
The home of the delicious cheese made famous by Wallace and Gromit offers a fantastic interactive family experience. As well as having fun driving the children's milk tankers and playing the cheese truckle roll game, there's some education sneaked in too, such as how a cow makes milk. You can also watch the Yorkshire Wensleydale cheese being made in the new creamery.

▼ Wensleydale cheese, made only in Wensleydale

▲ On the Brontë Way

▶ Haworth MAP REF 327 D5

If the Reverend Patrick Brontë had not produced the literary offspring that he did, Haworth today would still be a very appealing but possibly quiet village. It might be noted for a steep cobbled street that leads up to its parish church, but no more. As it is, the Brontë Parsonage Museum, just beyond the church, is thronged with visitors from all round the world, while beyond on the moorland, footpath signs in several languages direct thousands to the sites that inspired *Wuthering Heights*. The area around has been dubbed Brontë Country, and the appeal shows no signs of waning.

The one-time home of Patrick Brontë and his surviving children – Emily, Charlotte, Anne and Branwell – is now a museum in which you can study their lives and literary and artistic works in detail. Manuscripts and paintings attract as much attention as their living rooms, furnished accurately with many of the family's own possessions. Marvel at the miniature books they created for their toy soldiers, and at the touching mementos of their short lives, including Charlotte's tiny boots, and Aunt Branwell's doom-laden teapot. It is a fascinating place to visit for anyone who has ever read *Wuthering Heights* or *Jane Eyre*, but you'd be advised to avoid bank holidays and summer weekends when coach parties crowd the narrow corridors. There's more space to browse in the modern extension, which houses most of the literary artefacts and enlightening temporary exhibitions.

Outside the parsonage is the parish church, surrounded by tombstones, where all the family except Anne are buried in the crypt (Anne died in and is buried at Scarborough, see page 250). Aside from its Brontë connections, it's a striking church with appealing stained-glass windows and statuary.

An earlier influence on the religious life of Haworth was John Wesley. He was a frequent visitor, and crowds would travel from as far away as Leeds to hear him preach. Sermons would start at dawn and last all day, his chapel overflowing. Wesley inspired William Grimshaw, who went on to spend the next 20 or so years as a Methodist minister in Haworth. By the time of his death in 1763 he was a household name.

Haworth is bulging with tea rooms and souvenir shops, and the tourist industry has meant that other visitor attractions have grown up, including the Brontë Weaving Shed, a reflection of the importance of wool in industrial West Yorkshire. You can buy samples of the local Brontë tweed in the mill shop.

At the bottom of the very steep Main Street is Haworth's railway station on the Keighley and Worth Valley line, which is run by enthusiasts. Some of the line's old steam engines are on display here.

TAKE IN SOME HISTORY
Brontë Parsonage Museum
see highlight panel opposite

GO WALKING
No visit to Haworth is really complete without a walk on the moors to see the landscape which inspired the Brontës. The moors they knew best are west beyond the Brontë Parsonage to what is now called the Brontë Waterfalls and Ponden Kirk.

EAT AND DRINK
Cobbles and Clay
cobblesandclay.co.uk
70–72 Main Street, BD22 8DP
01535 958961
At the top of Haworth's cobbled Main Street, this colourful cafe combines with a pottery gift shop. Sit outside in the cobbled hubbub, retreat inside or go through to the balconied seating area at the rear with views across the Worth Valley.

The Fleece Inn
fleeceinnhaworth.co.uk
67 Main Street, BD22 8DA
01535 642172
Solidly planted on the steep cobbled road in Haworth's old town, this gritstone inn dates from the days when the Brontë sisters were writing their novels in the village vicarage. The enticing pub is owned by the Timothy Taylor Brewery; their award-winning Yorkshire beers are as reliable as the steam trains on the famous heritage railway at the foot of the hill. Escape the hurly-burly and indulge in one of the pub's renowned home-made pies or maybe a fish butty: no-

▶ Brontë Parsonage Museum

MAP REF 327 D5

bronte.org.uk
Church Street, BD22 8DR | 01535 642323 | Open daily Apr–Oct
10–5.30, Nov–Mar 10–5

Haworth Parsonage was the lifelong family home of the Brontës.
An intensely close-knit family, the Brontës saw the parsonage as
the heart of their world, and the moorland setting provided them
with inspiration for their writing. It's a poignant place to visit, full of
items that belonged to the family. Look out for lively changing
exhibits in the museum part at the back.

nonsense, filling fare (with some interesting starters) is the staple here. Each Monday evening the town's celebrated brass band practises upstairs.

No.10 The Coffee House

10thecoffeehouse.co.uk
10 Main Street, BD22 8DA
01535 644694

Escape from the bustle of Haworth's Main Street to quiet rooms, where freshly brewed Fairtrade tea and coffee are served with a range of delicious home-baked cakes and Italian biscuits.

The Old White Lion Hotel

oldwhitelionhotel.com
Main Street, BD22 8DU
01535 642313

This 300-year-old coaching inn looks down onto the famous cobbled Main Street of Haworth. In the charming bar the ceiling beams are supported by timber posts, and locals appreciatively quaff their pints of guest ale. Food is taken seriously and 'dispensed with hospitality and good measure' with some great meals in the Gimmerton Restaurant, where vegetarians are also well catered for.

▶ PLACES NEARBY

You can visit the Keighley and Worth Valley Railway (see page 157) and its railway buffet at Oxenhope Station, or the Old Silent Inn at Stanbury.

Old Silent Inn

oldsilentinnhowarth.co.uk
Hob Lane, Stanbury, BD22 0HW
01535 647437

In a dip in the moors beyond Haworth, the Old Silent is a characterful 17th-century watering hole and restaurant. The name derives from a legend of Bonnie Prince Charlie seeking refuge here and the silence of the locals when questioned on the subject.

Oxenhope Station Buffet

kwvr.co.uk
Oxenhope Station, BD22 9LD

A short drive away, or more aptly a steam train ride away, is the Keighley and Worth Valley Railway's railway buffet – and it is exactly that, a buffet car parked by the platform at Oxenhope Station. Especially good if you like trains, and parking is free. There are plans for a new cafe building to replace the buffet car.

▶ Hebden Bridge MAP REF 322 B1

An appealing little industrial town built in a steep-sided valley, Hebden Bridge has successfully reinvented itself as the capital of Upper Calderdale in recent years. It's known for its excellent walking country, its bohemian population, interesting independent shops, narrowboat trips along the Rochdale Canal, and its very popular summer arts festival.

At one time more than 30 textile mills here belched thick smoke into the Calder Valley, the fug only lifting during Wakes

Week, the mill-hands' traditional holiday. With Hebden Bridge being hemmed in by hills and the mills occupying much of the available land on the valley bottom, the workers' houses had to be built up the steep slopes, hence the 'over and under' houses which are a local feature, with one dwelling built directly on top of another.

VISIT THE WORKSHOP
Walkley Clogs

clogs.co.uk
Unit 10, Mount Pleasant Mills, Midgley Road, Mytholmroyd
HX7 5LR | 01422 885757
Open Tue–Fri 10–5, Sat 10–4

Wooden-soled clogs were traditionally the shoes of the poor workers. Now they're upgraded to chic, and their practical functionality is celebrated in this workshop, where you can see them being carved and constructed, and talk to the master cobblers who make them in around 40 different styles. Perhaps you might be tempted to buy a pair of their new wacky clogs.

▶ Helmsley MAP REF 337 F6

It may be only the size of a large village, but the handsome market town of Helmsley has the purposeful, bustling, reassuring air of a county town. It is especially busy on Friday – market day. The old market cross on its stepped base is still in place, though the square is dominated by a more elaborate monument, designed by Sir Gilbert Scott to commemorate the second Lord Feversham. The buildings around it are characterised by their sturdy rubble stone walls and orange pantile roofs, softened by pretty floral window boxes and hanging baskets.

A number of roads converge here and at one time this was an important halt on stagecoach routes. There was even a regular service to London from the Black Swan Inn – an establishment that advertises its presence with a large wooden swan in place of the name on the inn's sign.

These days more adventurous souls arrive with walking boots, cagoule and rucksack, for Helmsley is the starting point of the Cleveland Way. If you're walking the Cleveland, you follow the acorn waymarkers up Castlegate to get an excellent view of the castle standing head and shoulders above the little town, before descending into Ryedale and the atmospheric ruins of Rievaulx Abbey (see page 231).

Helmsley is where the National Park Authority has its administrative headquarters – so perhaps it's not too much of a surprise that there's also a well-stocked tourist information centre where you can browse for books, brochures and maps

TAKE IN SOME HISTORY
Helmsley Castle
english-heritage.org.uk
Castlegate, YO62 5AB
01439 770442 | Open Apr–Sep daily
10–6, Oct daily 10–5, Nov–Mar
Sat–Sun 10–4

This is an atmospheric ruin
with formidable double
earthworks. The castle was
built for defence rather than
show – although it didn't see
any military action until the
Civil War. It was here that the
troops of Colonel Jordan
Crossland, a loyal supporter
of Charles I, were besieged by
the Parliamentarian army of
Sir Thomas Fairfax, which
numbered a thousand troops.
The siege lasted three months.
It might have lasted longer,
but Royalist reinforcements
were intercepted, and
provisions confiscated.

▼ Castlegate and All Saints
Church, Helmsley

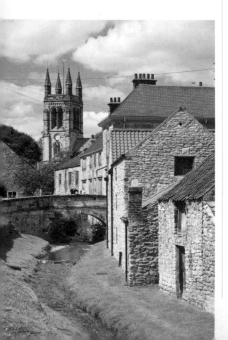

Crossland, forced to
surrender, marched out of
the castle on 22 November
1644, 'with colours flying and
drums beating'. While the
Parliamentarians accepted
this amicable surrender, they
dismantled enough of the castle
to ensure that it could never
again be used by any side in a
conflict. They failed in their
attempts to blow up the
Norman keep, however, and the
eastern wall still stands to its
full height of 97 feet, giving you
an idea of what an impressive
fortification it once was.

GO ROUND THE GARDENS
Helmsley Walled Garden
helmsleywalledgarden.org.uk
Cleveland Way, YO62 5AH
01439 771427 | Open Mar–Oct
daily 10–5

Run by the local community for
the local community, this is a
very special place. There are
long borders and extensive
glasshouses to admire, and
an important collection of
Yorkshire apple trees – with a
different variety for each month
of the year. Its setting is the old
walled kitchen garden of nearby
Duncombe Park, abandoned in
the 1920s and gradually
restored in the 1990s.

EAT AND DRINK
Black Swan Hotel ◉◉◉
blackswan-helmsley.co.uk
Market Place, YO62 5BJ
01439 770466

Set in a trio of ancient houses
spanning the centuries from
Elizabethan to Georgian to

Victorian, the Black Swan is still right at the heart of this lovely little market town, albeit with a rather neat boutique look these days to go with the old-world charm of its open fires and antiques. The Gallery restaurant (it doubles up as a daytime gallery showcasing original artworks for sale) is where Patrick Bardoulet gets to show off his high level of skill and creative flair, sourcing the finest Yorkshire ingredients and turning them into dishes that wow with their clearly defined flavours and beautiful presentation. It's a comfortable place to stay, too.

Feversham Arms Hotel & Verbena Spa ⊚⊚
fevershamarmshotel.com
1–8 High Street, YO62 5AG
01439 770766
The Feversham Arms gets its name from the earl who rebuilt an old coaching inn in 1855. He wouldn't recognise the distinctive hotel today, complete with lovely gardens, spa and all-year heated outdoor swimming pool. There's oodles of contemporary style behind the old stone frontage, with a restaurant of dark walls under its vaulted atrium and banquettes, and designer-style seating at correctly set tables an appropriate setting for sharp and sophisticated cooking built on fine regional ingredients.

Scotts Fish and Chips
scottsfishandchips.co.uk
6 Bridge Street, YO62 5BG
01439 772465
There's often a queue down Bridge Street outside Scotts and that's because they are award-winning fish and chips – Scotts was awarded Fish and Chip Shop of the Year in 2013 and in the National Fish and Chip Awards 2014. You can take away or eat in.

▶ Hole of Horcum   MAP REF 338 C4

This remarkable landform, sometimes known as the Devil's Punchbowl, is a huge natural amphitheatre seemingly scooped out of Levisham Moor. The valley bottom is primarily pastureland, while the steep slopes support woods and moorland. If you're driving on the A169 Pickering–Whitby road you'll skirt the rim of the Hole of Horcum – stop a while to gaze in wonderment. If you decide to follow some of the good paths in the area, there's a large car park provided.

Many stories account for the origin of the Hole of Horcum, and you can take your pick between the factual and the fanciful. Legend tells that Wade, a local giant, scooped up a handful of earth to throw at his wife, Bell, thus creating the huge landform. Apparently he missed her and the clod of earth landed to form Blakey Topping, little more than a mile away. To judge from the plethora of folk tales, Wade and his wife spent much of their time tossing missiles at one another. The factual origin of the Hole of Horcum is more prosaic – it was scoured out over millennia by glacial meltwater.

Just beyond a steep hairpin bend is the former Saltersgate Inn, one of the many solitary inns on the North York Moors. They were generally sited on junctions of well-used tracks, catering to people on the move – as many still do today. This one takes its name from an old salt route. From Anglo-Saxon times on, salt had been valued for its use in curing meat and fish, and it was so valuable as a preservative that a special tax was levied on it. The River Tees was the site of important salt pans, where tidal waters were evaporated to leave their salt solution, and salt roads – known as saltersgates – led across the North. The people who stood at the bar of this pub in its heyday were most likely to have been hauliers leading trains of heavily laden packhorses across the moors, as the inn lay on an old salt road linking Whitby with the market town of Pickering. Later it catered to stagecoach traffic, and was the site of a tollbooth when the road became a turnpike. Its exposed location meant that it was regularly cut off by snow and buried in deep drifts. After centuries of serving beer and providing shelter to all-comers, the Saltersgate Inn finally closed its doors in 2006.

▶ Hornsea MAP REF 331 F4

A small seaside resort to the south of Bridlington, Hornsea is famous as the home of Hornsea Pottery. The factory closed in 2000, but you can see a large display of the distinctive and stylish tableware, synonymous with the 1960s and 1970s, in the Hornsea Museum. The promenade in the town is small, but well-formed, and the Blue Flag-winning beach is rarely full – a tip to remember on a sunny summer's day.

Away from the sea, Hornsea is home to Yorkshire's largest freshwater lake – Hornsea Mere – with some 250 species of birds and a raftfull of activities for you to explore. For walkers and cyclists, the town is well known as being one end of the Trans Pennine Trail, the epic 207-mile multi-user route which passes across Yorkshire.

VISIT THE MUSEUM
Hornsea Museum
hornseamuseum.com
11 Newbegin, HU18 1AB
01964 533443 | Open Easter–Oct
Mon–Fri 11–5, Sat 10–4, Sun 1–4

The former farmhouse illustrates local life and history. There are 19th-century period rooms and a dairy, plus craft tools and farming implements. You'll find photographs, local personalities and industries featured along with the display of Hornsea Pottery wares.

HIT THE BEACH
Hornsea Beach

There's a long promenade to stroll along in this classic seaside resort, with easy access to the town, and the recently landscaped gardens make Hornsea's seafront a top spot. Beachwise there's tons of sand and shingle – and plenty of parking too.

GET ON THE WATER
Hornsea Mere

hornseamere.com
Hornsea HU18 1AX | 01964 533277
Open 8.30, closing times seasonal; contact for details

Whether you want to go birdwatching or enjoy boating on the lake, Hornsea Mere has something for everyone. If you fancy the water, but don't want to row, take one of the motorboat trips. The licensed Mere Café retains loads of old-fashioned charm.

▶ Horton-in-Ribblesdale MAP REF 326 B1

This straggling village along the River Ribble is easily missed – but Horton-in-Ribblesdale is a practical centre for many visitors to North Yorkshire. It's surrounded by the so-called Three Peaks – Pen-y-Ghent, Whernside and Ingleborough – and the gruelling annual Three Peaks Challenge Race starts and ends here. The Pen-y-Ghent Cafe has become an important centre for hikers, particularly for the very efficient safety system it operates, allowing walkers to clock out and clock back in again at the end of the day. Walkers can attempt their own Three Peaks Challenge, which was first completed in 1887. That very first walk took 10 hours. Today, if you finish the 25-mile route in under 12 hours, you're eligible for membership of the Three Peaks of Yorkshire Club. If an average speed of only 2 mph doesn't seem very fast, remember that the total height of the Three Peaks, each of which is ascended on the walk, is over 7,000 feet. No small challenge.

The Pennine Way long distance trail (see page 216) weaves its way through Horton in Ribblesdale, which is also a stop on the Settle–Carlisle railway line. One of the big attractions nearby is the Ribblehead Viaduct, a triumph of engineering, with 24 vast arches rising to 165 feet above the valley floor (see page 226).

GO CAVING AND CLIMBING
Yorkshire Dales Guides

yorkshiredalesguides.co.uk
Hornby Laithre, Stainforth, Settle, BD24 9PB | 01729 824455

There are innumerable opportunities for climbing and caving throughout the area, and this long-established company offers expert guided instruction.

EAT AND DRINK
Pen-y-Ghent Cafe

horton-in-ribblesdale.com
BD24 0HE | 01729 860333

An institution among walkers, cyclists and runners who take up the Three Peaks Challenge, this is more than just a place for a mug of tea and a piece of home-made cake (though it is excellent for that, too). The weekend safety service ensures walkers can log in when they start the walk and log out again when their day is completed. Should you not complete the walk or not return to the cafe, it's important to ring to prevent a search party!

▶ Hovingham Hall   MAP REF 329 E1

hovingham.co.uk
YO62 4LX | 01653 628771 | Open June, contact for details

Hovingham, on the edge of the Howardian Hills, is a pretty village threaded by the stream of Marrs Beck. The Worsley family have been here since the mid-16th century, and their attractive Palladian mansion was constructed in the 18th century. Thomas Worsley, its builder, was a descendant of Oliver Cromwell. He was a man whose passion was horses, and he designed it so that the stable block and indoor riding school (where he reputedly taught the future King George III to ride) faced on to the village green. You have to pass through it to reach the main entrance to the house. Hovingham Hall is still the home of the Worsleys, but along with its gardens it's open to the public in June for guided tours. The house has a wonderful collection of pictures and furniture.

EAT AND DRINK
Hovingham Bakery
Spa Tea Room

hovingham.org.uk
Brookside, Hovingham, YO62 4LG
01653 628898

The bakery provides delicious fresh bread and cakes, and serves them in its little tea room by the beck – you can sit outside on summer days. The hearty sandwiches using home-baked bread are a meal in themselves, and there are excellent cream teas – the fruit scones are a particular favourite with many visitors.

The Worsley Arms Hotel ◉◉

worsleyarms.co.uk
Main Street, Hovingham ,YO62 4LA
01653 628234

This village hotel and pub form part of the Worsley family's historic Hovingham Hall Estate, Hambleton Stallion from nearby Thirsk, and Black Sheep from Masham are on tap in the Cricketers' Bar. You can eat here at the bar or in the restaurant; lunch and afternoon tea are also served in the large walled garden. The pub hosts regular wine evenings and a supper club.

▶ Hubberholme MAP REF 335 D5

With its riverside setting, surrounded by trees in the valley
floor, there are fewer more picturesque villages to be found
than Hubberholme. So agreed the Bradford-born writer,
J B Priestley (1894–1984), who described this venerable
stone settlement at the confluence of Langstrothdale and
Wharfedale as the 'smallest, pleasantest place in the world'.
He drank in the village pub, and a plaque in the church
commemorates his great affection for the tiny village where his
ashes are buried.

The Church of St Michael and All Angels is a major
attraction, with a rood loft dating from 1558. In 1571 an
edict was issued from York to destroy all rood lofts in the
region, and Hubberholme's was one of only two in Yorkshire
to escape destruction – perhaps because of the village's
comparative isolation.

The church has suffered in the past from flooding, and it is
claimed that this was once so bad that fish were to be seen
swimming in the nave. Look out for Robert Thompson of
Kilburn's mice – carved and definitely not swimming – on
the oak furnishings.

EAT AND DRINK

The George Inn

thegeorge-inn.co.uk

BD23 5JE | 01756 760223

Stunningly located beside
the River Wharfe, this pub
was built in the 1600s as a
farmstead and still has
flagstone floors, stone walls,
mullioned windows and an
open fire. Beers are local,
coming from the Black
Sheep and Yorkshire Dales
breweries, and you can
enjoy your pint on the terrace
in the summer months.
For lunch there's soup,
sandwiches and baskets of
chips; but the traditional
choices for an evening meal
are based on locally sourced
produce. A tip – to check if the
bar is open, look for a lit candle
in the window.

▼ The Church of St Michael
and All Angels, Hubberholme

▶ **Huddersfield** MAP REF 322 C2

Huddersfield is an attractive town midway between Leeds and Manchester, featuring some fine Victorian architecture. In fact, it has the third highest number of listed buildings of any town or city in the whole of the UK, and there's a great town trail leading from the tourist office which will take you around. The handsome town hall of 1881 is typical – stone-built and sturdy looking. The Gothic Ramsden Building, now part of the university, is rather more playful. The George Hotel has the air of an elegant Italian mansion – and is where the game of rugby league was formalised in 1895. But by far the best is the uber-grand Railway Station, with its vast classical facade, once described as 'a stately home with trains in it' – and it's all true.

The town's location near to the joining of the rivers Colne and Holme made Huddersfield an ideal centre for textile production in the industrial boom – despite attempts by the Luddites in the early 19th century to halt the mechanised wheels of progress – and to this day, Huddersfield produces record amounts of woollen products. Today, Huddersfield's largest employer is the town's university, which can trace its history back to a science and mechanical institute founded in 1825. Famous sons of Huddersfield include no fewer than two prime ministers – Herbert Asquith (1852–1928) and Harold Wilson (1916–95).

Yorkshire has a great tradition of shared amateur music-making. Huddersfield Choral Society is the leading choir of its kind, with an international reputation. Catch them in concert in the town hall if you can – their annual performances of Handel's *Messiah*, in December, are usually sold out well in advance. If you can get a ticket, be prepared to stand for the 'Hallelujah Chorus' – it's a Yorkshire tradition.

There's been a settlement here for over 4,000 years. Castle Hill, a local landmark topped off with the solid, four-square Victoria Tower in honour of that queen's Diamond Jubilee, was unsurprisingly the site of an Iron Age hill fort, and the remains of a Roman fort were unearthed just west of the town.

VISIT THE MUSEUMS AND GALLERIES

Tolson Museum
kirklees.gov.uk
Ravensknowle Park, Wakefield Road,
HD5 8DJ | 01484 223830
Open Mar–Oct Tue–Fri 11–5, Sat–
Sun 12–5, Nov–Feb Tue–Thu 11–4,
Sat–Sun 12–4

Here you'll find displays on the development of the cloth industry and a collection of historic horse-drawn vehicles, along with archaeology, Roman finds, natural history, toys and folk exhibits. There is a full programme of events and temporary exhibitions.

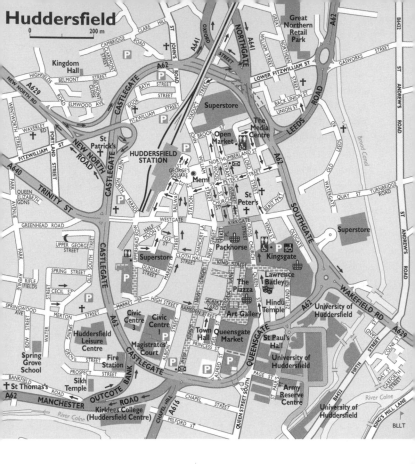

Huddersfield

Huddersfield Art Gallery
kirklees.gov.uk
Princess Alexandra Walk, HD1 2SU
01484 221964 | Open Tue, Wed, Fri,
Sat 11–4, Thu 11–7
Right in the centre of the town,
this gallery exhibits a rotating
display of Kirklees Council's
collection of paintings and
sculptures – with notable
examples from Francis Bacon,
L S Lowry and Henry Moore.

TAKE A TRAIN RIDE
Kirklees Light Railway
kirkleeslightrailway.co.uk
Park Mill Way, Clayton West,
HD8 9XJ | 01484 865727
This wonderful three-and-a-
half-mile narrow gauge railway
runs on the trackbed of the old
Lancashire and Yorkshire
Railway's branch line to the
village of Clayton West. The
railway hosts a range of special
events throughout the year,
including a very good
Halloween Ghost Train.

CATCH A PERFORMANCE
Huddersfield Town Hall
kirklees.gov.uk
Ramsden Street, HD1 2TA
01484 223200
This imposing Victorian hall
in the town centre hosts
classical concerts and comedy
events. Hear a brass band,
or perhaps the famous
Huddersfield Choral Society.

PLAY A ROUND

Huddersfield has three top clubs: Bradley Park Golf Course is a parkland course with fairways lined with mature trees; the Huddersfield Golf Club is a testing heathland course of championship standard, laid out in 1891; and Longley Park Golf Club is a lowland course, surrounded by mature woodland.

Bradley Park Golf Course

bradleyparkgolf.co.uk
Off Bradley Road, HD2 1PZ
01484 223772 | Open daily

Huddersfield Golf Club

huddersfield-golf.co.uk
Fixby Hall, Lightridge Road,
Fixby, HD2 2EP | 01484 426203
Open Mon–Fri, Sun

Longley Park Golf Club

longleyparkgolfclub.com
Maple Street, Aspley, HD5 9AX
01484 422304 | Open Mon–Wed,
Fri, Sun

▼ Victoria Jubilee Tower at Castle Hill, Huddersfield

EAT AND DRINK

315 Bar and Restaurant ◉◉

315barandrestaurant.co.uk
315 Wakefield Road, Lepton,
HD8 0LX | 01484 602613
This place brings a touch of metropolitan chic to Huddersfield. There's a buzz in the air throughout, with a sleek bar, a restaurant done out in restful neutral tones, with upholstered seats at correctly set tables and contemporary lighting, and a conservatory extension with vivid yellow-striped pillars. The menu bursts with bright, modern ideas. There's also a casual dining area for a more relaxed setting, which is next to the bar.

▶ PLACES NEARBY

To the north of Huddersfield are the villages of Brighouse and Rastrick, which face each other across the River Calder. They are home of one of Yorkshire's finest brass bands. The quality of its music is world-class but its hard-working members are amateurs who play in their spare time and the band is self-supporting. The Brighouse and Rastrick started in 1881 as a temperance band, and came to wide public prominence in 1977 with their pop-chart hit version of *The Floral Dance*. Today they're in demand to play all over the country, of course, but to catch a concert in the local area, check the band's website: brighouseandrastrickband.com.

▶ Hull   MAP REF 332 C3

There were more than a few people sniggering at the announcement that Hull was to be the UK City of Culture in 2017. Well, all of those doubters have been silenced, as Hull dazzled with a year of events to make any city proud. And the punters loved it – hotel bookings were up some 80 per cent between July and September, as the world finally realised what Yorkshire people have always known – Hull is a pretty cool place.

Hull has few architectural gems to offer – it was second only to London in terms of bomb-damage and devastation in World War II, and postwar reconstruction was achingly slow. Its wealth was built on the back of Arctic fishery, its location, where the River Hull pours into the estuary of the Humber, giving it unparalleled access to the network of waterways that led into the industrial heart of northern England. You can learn more about the city's glory days as the East Coast's premier white fish port in the super Maritime Museum. With the decline of heavy industry in the North, and fishing quotas slowly strangling the once-proud deep-sea trawler fishing fleet, by the end of the 20th century things were looking grim for Hull. Now things are looking up. Today's Hull is a vibrant place, with extensive new building for retail, commerce and housing, and a very popular university. Disused docks have been revitalised as shopping centres, offices, museums and leisure marinas.

It was Edward I who named the original settlement 'Kings Town upon Hull', when he granted it its royal charter back in 1293. In those early days, export and import trade was based on wool and wine. The population grew massively during the 18th century, and new docks were opened to cope with the demand of a booming maritime trade. It was then that local MP William Wilberforce began his crusade in Parliament opposing slavery. His campaigning led to the abolition of the slave trade within the British Empire in 1807, and of slavery as an institution in 1833.

The coming of the railways in 1840 led to the most productive time in Hull, which continued up until World War I. Major civic buildings were built and Hull was granted city status in 1897. In 1902 it got its own telephone system, memorialised in the unique cream-coloured phone boxes.

Notable engineering projects around the city include the ultra-practical Tidal Surge Barrier, designed to protect the surrounding low-level landscape from the dangers of flooding; and upstream at Hessle, the elegant Humber Bridge – the world's longest single-span suspension bridge when it opened in 1981.

Hull can offer a string of famous sons and daughters, from Amy Johnson, the first woman to fly solo from London to Australia, to cinema magnate J Arthur Rank, and poet Philip Larkin, who was born in the Midlands but made Hull his home (find his statue at the railway station). Top comedian Lucy Beaumont also hails from here.

MEET THE SEALIFE
The Deep
see highlight panel opposite

VISIT THE MUSEUMS AND GALLERIES
Maritime Museum
hullcc.gov.uk
Queen Victoria Square, HU1 3DX
01482 300300 | Open Mon–Wed, Fri & Sat 10–5, Thu 10–7.30, Sun 11–4.30
Hull's maritime history is illustrated here, with displays on whales and whaling, ships and shipping – it's a fascinating collection of national significance.

Wilberforce House
hullcc.gov.uk
23–25 High Street, HU1 1NE
01482 300300 | Open Mon–Sat 10–5, Sun 11–4.30
The 17th-century merchant's house was the birthplace of William Wilberforce, a leading campaigner against the slave trade. Displays tell the story of slavery and abolition, and explore modern issues surrounding slavery.

Ferens Art Gallery
hullcc.gov.uk
Queen Victoria Square, HU1 3RA
01482 300300 | Open Mon–Wed, Thu 10–7.30, Fri–Sat 10–5, Sun 11–4.30

Regional art rubs shoulders with international names at this excellent art gallery – and it's free. Look out for the maritime paintings of John Ward, works by Old Masters and modern pieces by the likes of Stanley Spencer, Gillian Wearing and David Hockney. A special hands-on gallery is dedicated to young artists of the future, aged six to ten.

Streetlife – Hull Museum of Transport
hullcc.gov.uk
High Street, HU1 1PS
01482 300300 | Open Mon–Sat 10–5, Sun 11–4.30
This purpose-built museum traces 200 years of transport history, all brought to life with a vehicle collection of national importance, displays and authentic scenarios. The mail coach ride recreates a Victorian journey by four-in-hand.

Museums Quarter
Hull's city museums are all free, and four of them are found together here in the historic old town. First, journey back 235 million years to encounter sea monsters and a life-sized woolly mammoth at the Hull and East Riding Museum of Archaeology. Then there's the Streetlife Museum of Transport

▶ The Deep MAP REF 332 C3

thedeep.co.uk
Tower Street, HU1 4DP (satnav HU9 1TU) | 01482 381000
Open daily 10–6

The Deep is one of the deepest and most spectacular aquariums in the world. It is a unique blend of stunning marine life, fun interactives and audio-visual presentations, which together tell the dramatic story of the world's oceans. Discover the thrilling underwater world as you've never seen it before – complete with alien and weird life forms including giant Japanese spider crabs, giant Pacific octopus, wolf eels and flashlight fish. Highlights include more than 3,500 fish, spectacular sharks and rays, Europe's deepest viewing tunnel and a glass lift ride through a 30-foot-deep tank. The Deep has an annual programme of special events, all available to book online.

and the birthplace of William Wilberforce (see both on page 142). Finally you can explore the hazardous life of Britain's deep-sea fishermen aboard the city's last sidewinder trawler, the *Arctic Corsair*.

CATCH A PERFORMANCE
Hull New Theatre
hulltheatres.co.uk
Kingston Square, HU1 3HF
01482 300306
Hull New Theatre is one of the best regional theatres in the country, with a varied programme throughout the year. The annual Christmas pantomime is a legend in itself.

PLAY A ROUND
Ganstead Park Golf Club is an easy walking parkland course with many water features and Hull Golf Club is an attractive mature parkland course.

10 singers & bands from Yorkshire

▶ **Arctic Monkeys** – Sheffield
▶ **The Beautiful South** – Hull
▶ **Melanie Brown** (Mel B or Scary Spice) – Leeds
▶ **Joe Cocker** – Sheffield
▶ **Lesley Garrett** – Doncaster
▶ **Kaiser Chiefs** – Leeds
▶ **Pulp** – Sheffield
▶ **Chris Rea** – Middlesbrough
▶ **Kate Rusby** – Penistone, Barnsley
▶ **Shed Seven** – York

Ganstead Park Golf Club
gansteadpark.co.uk
Longdales Lane, Coniston, HU11 4LB
01482 817754 | Open daily

Hull Golf Club
hullgolfclub.co.uk
The Hall, 27 Packman Lane, HU10 7TJ | 01482 660970
Open Mon–Tue, Thu– Fri, Sun

▶ **PLACES NEARBY**
Burton Constable Hall is some 11 miles northeast of Hull.

Burton Constable Hall
burtonconstable.com
HU11 4LN | 01964 562400
There has been a building here since at least the Middle Ages, and a medieval manor house survives as part of the present building. The house owes much to a sensitive remodelling that took place under William Constable in the late 18th century. He kept most of the original exterior, but employed some of the most illustrious craftsmen of the day to transform the interior into a series of elegant Georgian rooms. Robert Adam, James Wyatt and John Carr all contributed designs for the interior, Timothy Lightoler added the new stable block and Thomas Atkinson the orangery. The exterior is graceful and imposing – three storeys high, built of red brick, with stone mullioned and oriel windows and castellated towers. Thomas Chippendale supplied the chairs, sofas, firescreens and side tables in the ballroom.

▶ Hutton-le-Hole MAP REF 338 A4

It is to Hutton-le-Hole's benefit that it lies just off the main A170 between Thirsk and Scarborough – for, unlike its larger neighbours, the village has managed to maintain its distinct personality instead of giving way to tourism. One of Yorkshire's most picturesque villages, its houses are set back from Hutton Beck, a sparkling watercourse spanned by a succession of pretty little bridges. The village green is the size of a meadow, but the grass is cropped short by sheep, which wander wherever they choose – as likely as not in the middle of the road. The houses of discreet grey stone, with the red-tiled roofs so typical of the moors area, give the village a timeless air. The tiny church has some very fine oak furniture made by Robert Thompson of Kilburn (see page 161); look closely to find the trademark carved mouse that can be found on all his work.

Once you have admired the village, don't miss a visit to the outstanding Ryedale Folk Museum, where some 20 historic buildings from around the area have been painstakingly moved and rebuilt on one site as a working village-cum-open-air-museum.

The dales are rich in folklore and one local legend tells of Kitty Garthwaite – 'Sarkless Kitty' – from the nearby village of Lowna Bridge. It was 1787, and young Kitty was walking out with Willie Dixon of Hutton-le-Hole when she learned of the rumour that her beau was seeing another lass. A lovers' tiff by the River Dove followed, and later Kitty was found drowned, wearing only her sark, or petticoat. After their argument, Willie had ridden to York to get a marriage licence. On his return his horse stumbled and Willie drowned in the same pool where Kitty had earlier been found. The ghost of Kitty, naked but carrying her sark over her arm, began to haunt the riverside spot where the lovers kept their trysts.

▼ Hutton Beck, Hutton-le-Hole

VISIT THE MUSEUM
Ryedale Folk Museum
ryedalefolkmuseum.co.uk
YO62 6UA | 01751 417367
Open Apr–Sep daily 10–5,
Feb–Mar, Oct–Dec daily 10–4

Don't miss this super outdoor museum. Exhibits include a 500-year-old thatched and cruck-framed farmhouse from Danby, moved to the museum's five-acre site in 1967. The tall 16th-century manor house is a huge hall open to the roof beams. This was once the meeting place of the Manor Court, where disputes were settled and common rights safeguarded. Other museum buildings house a primitive 16th-century glass furnace, a photographer's studio, and a row of shops recreated as they would have looked more than a hundred years ago. At the heart of the museum is a fascinating collection of everyday items dating to before the 1950s, collected and preserved by brothers Edward and Richard Harrison. There are historical vehicles and bygones, working craft days and rare farm breeds – something for everybody, in fact.

The cruck-framed house contains one of the rare examples of a witch post to have survived – most of which are found in the north of England. This post, of mountain ash, is elaborately carved with a cross and other, more ambiguous, symbols. It stands by the fireplace, so it would be passed by anyone who came into the living area, and also had the practical purpose of supporting the beam across the inglenook. It was designed, of course, to ward off evil spirits and protect those who sat here enjoying the fire's warmth.

▶ Ilkley   MAP REF 327 E4

Ilkley is quite an elegant place, as former spa towns tend to be. Classy antiques shops rub shoulders with expensive independent clothes shops, which attract smart customers from all over the country – and in The Box Tree it has one of the top restaurants in the north.

Ilkley's situation is great, with the Yorkshire Dales to the north, easy access to Harrogate to the northeast, and Leeds to the southeast. The River Wharfe runs through the town, and above it looms Ilkley Moor (see page 150), where the original spa was located. This was at White Wells, cottages built in 1756 by the landowner, Squire Middleton, to provide plunge baths for visitors. Ilkley's growth began with the discovery of these mineral springs, whose particularly cold nature was believed to enhance their curative effects. Today, the cottages contain a small museum, with displays about the Victorian spas as well as local wildlife and walks.

As the railway reached Ilkley in 1865, it brought regular visitors to such an extent that by the end of the century there were no fewer than 15 springs open to the public. Wealthy industrialists from Bradford and Leeds, keen to find somewhere more pleasant to live away from the sooty cities, built large houses here and, as a result, Ilkley now boasts some handsome Victorian architecture, with arcades of shops as well as more modern shopping precincts.

In the centre of town is All Saints Church, which is well worth a visit for its Anglo-Saxon crosses, two Roman altars and fine stained glass, some of which was designed by the William Morris Gallery. Arts and Crafts fans will also find a window by Burne-Jones in St Margaret's Church in Queens Road. Look in the gardens opposite to see the Panorama Stone, the most accessible of the several prehistoric carved rocks in and around the town. Next door to All Saints is the Manor House Museum. This is believed to stand on the site of the Roman fort of Olicana, possibly dating back to AD 79.

In 1859 Charles Darwin published his radical scientific theories of evolution in *On the Origin of Species* – and took refuge in the spa facilities at Ilkley as the inevitable repercussions began to materialise. Initially staying in Wells House, he was joined by his family and they moved to North View House, now incorporated into the large building on the left at the top of Wells Road. To celebrate Ilkley's connections with the pioneering evolutionist, the former pleasure gardens across the road have been transformed into a Millennium Green or community space known as Darwin Gardens, with a maze, picnic sites, several mosaics and other interesting features, and rejuvenated paths and woodland.

VISIT THE MUSEUMS
White Wells Spa Cottage
visitbradford.com
Access on foot only from Wells Road, Ilkley | 01943 608035
Open weekends during school holidays and whenever flag is flying
This is a museum based within the original spa, where you can see the chilly stone plunge pool and displays on Victorian ailments and cures. Bring your swimming costume and towel if you fancy a dip.

Ilkley Toy Museum
ilkleytoymuseum.co.uk
Whitton Croft Road, Ilkley
LS29 9HR | 01943 603855
The phrase most heard at the Ilkley Toy Museum is "I used to have one of those...". Exhibits ranging from dolls, dolls houses, teddy bears, tin plate toys, lead figures and a selection of games, together with wooden and paper toys – all dating from 350 BC to the present day. Bring your memories...

SEE A LOCAL CHURCH
St Margaret's Church
stmargaretsilkley.org
Queens Road, LS29 9QL
01943 607015
Built in 1879 in the Perpendicular style, St Margaret's has broad east and west windows, and a nave with a handsome open-beam wooden roof, and a low arch with a wooden screen to the chancel. Although Sir John Betjeman rather dismissively described it in his guide as 'spa suburban', the church possesses many fine points. These include a sumptuous carved reredos, a Burne-Jones stained-glass window and a remarkable baptistry painting of the *Madonna and Child with St Margaret and St John*, also known simply as *The Madonna of the Moors*, by the well-respected local artist, Graeme Willson, dating from 2004.

GO SWIMMING
Ilkley Lido
bradford.gov.uk
Denton Road, LS29 0BZ
01943 600453
Dating from the 1930s, this art deco open-air pool enjoys lovely views of the surrounding moors – and there's a heated indoor pool next door if things get too cold. There's a cafe and bowling green on the site too – perfect in summer.

GO ORIENTEERING
Ilkley Tourist Information Centre
visitilkley.com
Station Road, LS29 8HA
01943 602319
There are a number of permanent orienteering courses located on Ilkley Moor and in Middleton Woods. For further information, contact the tourist information centre.

▼ All Saints Church, Ilkley

PLAY A ROUND

Ben Rhydding Golf Club

benrhyddinggolfclub.com
High Wood, Ben Rhydding,
LS29 8SB | 01943 608759
Open daily all year

Ben Rhydding Golf Club is a compact but testing course through moorland and parkland with splendid views over the Wharfe Valley.

Ilkley Golf Club

ilkleygolfclub.co.uk
Nesfield Road, Myddleton,
LS29 0BE | 01943 600214
Open daily all year

Ilkley Golf Club is a beautiful parkland course in Wharfedale. The Wharfe itself is actually a hazard on the first seven holes – in fact, the third is laid out entirely on an island in the river.

EAT AND DRINK

Bettys Café Tea Rooms

bettys.co.uk
32–34 The Grove, LS29 9EE
01943 608029

One of the six famous Bettys (the original is in Harrogate, see page 123), the Ilkley version has a wrought-iron canopy and an extensive tea and coffee counter stacked with antique tea caddies. Of particular interest are the specially commissioned stained-glass windows, depicting wild flowers from Ilkley Moor, a large marquetry picture showing a medieval hunting scene made entirely of unstained wood veneers and the large teapot collection. The tea room is a favourite with ramblers, tired, hungry and thirsty from a tramp across the moors, as well as the more genteel local clientele. The guiding principle of Bettys' founder, Frederick Belmont, was that 'if we want things just right we have to do it ourselves', and Bettys Bakery still makes all the cakes, pastries, chocolates, breads and scones served in the tea rooms.

Box Tree ◉◉◉

theboxtree.co.uk
35–37 Church Street, LS29 9DR
01943 608484

It feels only right that the Box Tree, one of northern England's destination venues under successive owners since the early 1960s, should be housed in one of Ilkley's oldest buildings. Decorated throughout to a very high standard, it has a particularly attractive lounge, with opulently upholstered furniture and portraits and seascapes on the walls. In November 2014, an extra dining room was opened on the first floor. Simon Gueller maintains the Box Tree's stellar reputation for cutting-edge food that utilises some of the advanced technical means that today's chefs love, but in a style that continues to make sense to aficionados of old-school haute cuisine. Every plate looks artfully composed and is often quite complex, but flavours shine forth, and every last ingredient is given its due.

The Crescent Inn

thecrescentinn.co.uk

Brook Street, LS29 8DG

01943 811250

Part of a hotel dating back to 1861, The Crescent is a landmark building in the centre of Ilkley, sharing the site with its sister restaurant next door. The pub blends original Victorian features, such as an open fire, with contemporary interiors including handcrafted furniture upholstered in local cloth. Choose from an ever-changing range of real ales from local breweries such as Saltaire, or pick one of the 15 wines by the glass. The menu features unpretentious and enjoyable dishes.

Ilkley Moor Vaults

ilkleymoorvaults.co.uk

Stockeld Road, LS29 9HD

01943 607012

Known locally as The Taps, it sits at the start of the Dales Way above the old packhorse bridge across the River Wharfe. A popular and stylish establishment, it is equally good for a pint of real ale or a classic dish of pub food. Everything is made from scratch in the kitchen from the bread to the pickles. There's an ever-changing specials board, full gluten-free menu, impressive children's menu and early bird deals. A large function room caters for weddings and private parties.

▶ Ilkley Moor MAP REF 327 E4

Ilkley Moor is a long ridge of millstone grit, immediately to the south of Ilkley. Part of the wider Rombalds Moor, it's a great area for walking. Its most famous feature is the group of boulders, large and small, known as the Cow and Calf Rocks – climbers use them and the quarry behind for practice most weekends. There are tremendous views from here over Wharfedale and Ilkley town (see page 146). As you explore, you'll find lots of indications that prehistoric people used these moors too – odd carvings in the scattered rocks of the moor include neolithic cup-and-ring marks, and a looped swastika pattern believed to date back to the Bronze Age. The Twelve Apostles is a Bronze Age ring of standing stones – none higher that 3 feet – located at the junction of two ancient routes across the moor. Much of the area is a dedicated Site of Special Scientific Interest, protected as upland habitat for ground-nesting birds, so be sensitive and keep dogs under control when you visit.

Ilkley Moor is celebrated in the popular Yorkshire dialect song, 'On Ilkla Moor baht 'at', a darkly humorous anthem which warns of the perilous consequences of walking on the moor without a hat.

▶ Graffiti old-style on Ilkley Moor

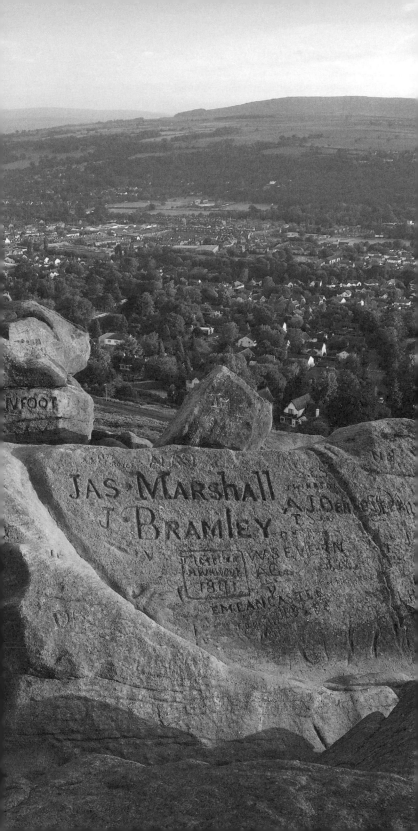

▶ Ingleborough MAP REF 334 B6

There are several ways you could approach the flat-topped
Ingleborough on foot: from Clapham, Ingleton, Horton in
Ribblesdale or Chapel-le-Dale – and each is an energetic but
rewarding climb to the top of the 2,372-foot peak. Until
accurate measurement of hills became possible, Ingleborough
was believed to be the highest point in Yorkshire, but we now
know that it is surpassed by neighbouring Whernside.
Ingleborough is one of Yorkshire's famous three peaks – along
with Whernside and Pen-y-Ghent – and in April each year fell
runners compete to run to the tops of all three. At its top is a
wide plateau, with a triangulation point and a stone windbreak,

▼ Limestone pavement, Ingleborough

and of course grand views all around. An Iron Age hill fort once stood here, and horseraces have been run in more recent memory, with bonfire beacons still lit occasionally for special celebrations.

The path up from Chapel-le-Dale is the shortest and steepest approach, giving a daunting impression of the challenge to come as you look up at Ingleborough's imposing heights. From Clapham the walk is about four miles, passing Ingleborough Cave (see page 84) on the way. Ingleborough's slopes have a great number of potholes, so you need to take care if you stray from the path. Anywhere that is fenced off will be like that for a purpose, so don't let curiosity get the better of you.

South of the summit of Ingleborough you'll see the Gaping Gill pothole – though to describe it as a pothole is like calling Westminster Abbey a parish church. In fact, you could probably fit the abbey inside Gaping Gill: some mathematician has already worked out that you can fit York Minster inside the main cavern. This is about 120 feet high and 500 feet long, and from the surface the stream of Fell Beck plunges down into it, making this one of the highest waterfalls in Britain at a total of 364 feet.

The breathtaking sight of the interior of Gaping Gill is normally reserved for experienced potholers, but twice a year, on spring and summer bank holidays, local caving clubs set up a rope winch and bosun's chair and allow ordinary mortals to share the joy, lowering them down.

⸺

▶ **Ingleton** MAP REF 334 A6

Ingleton, on the edge of the Yorkshire Dales National Park, has too much modern sprawl to be called a pretty village – but it has an attractive centre with steep winding streets going down to the gorge where its celebrated Waterfalls Walk starts. Before the arrival of the railway in the late 19th century, bringing the visitors and walkers who heralded much of the new development, Ingleton relied on its woollen and cotton spinning industries, and before that coal mining and stone quarrying. Now instead of mill-workers' cottages there are guest houses, shops and several pubs – though the rock quarry is still one of the largest in the Dales.

The Church of St Mary the Virgin is in a dominating position in the village, and has been rebuilt several times over the centuries. Its oldest feature is a Norman font, carved with figures from the life of Christ, which was rediscovered in 1830, having been hidden in the river below for safe-keeping during times of religious persecution. The church has a rare copy of what is known as the Vinegar Bible, so-called because of a misprint in 1717 in what should have been the Parable of the Vineyards.

On the B6255 to the northeast of Ingleton is the White Scar Cave, the best show cave in the Dales. With rivers and waterfalls, it makes for exhilarating subterranean guided tours.

GET OUTDOORS
Ingleton Waterfalls Trail
ingletonwaterfallstrail.co.uk
The Falls, LA6 3ET | 01524 241930
Open daily from 9am
A delightful four-and-a-half-mile circular trail leads through a landscape of gorge, meadows and woodland, linking waterfalls on the rivers Twiss and Doe. There's a cafe at the start, and a snack centre halfway round, so you'll hardly fade away. Note that the ticket office doesn't accept payment by credit or debit cards.

GO FISHING
Village News
Main Street | 015242 41683
There are about six miles of trout fishing available on local rivers. Buy your permit at the news shop on the high street in Ingleton.

EAT AND DRINK
Country Harvest
country-harvest.co.uk
LA6 3PE | 015242 42223
On the roadside just north of Ingleton, this is a great place to linger on your way home, or to take stock as you enter the Dales proper. The shop offers locally produced food and crafts. You can sample many of the items, including breads baked fresh on the premises, in the excellent coffee shop.

▶ PLACES NEARBY
Explore Britain's largest show caves, with tours to the nearby falls and rivers, or throw a pot at Bentham Pottery.

White Scar Cave
whitescarcave.co.uk
On B6255 north of Ingleton,
LA6 3AW | 015242 41244
Open Feb–Oct daily from 10,
Nov–Jan Sat–Sun from 10
An 80-minute tour passes underground waterfalls and gives you the chance to study the stalactites and stalagmites, with names such as Devil's Tongue and Judge's Head. The last tour starts at 4pm.

Bentham Pottery
benthampottery.com
Oysterber Farm, Low Bentham,
LA2 7ET | 015242 61567
Shop open Mon–Sat 9–5
Want to have a go at throwing or improving your pottery skills? Bentham Pottery's courses cater for all ages and abilities. Or you could cheat, and just buy some of the delicious hand-thrown blue ware from the shop. It's still the Dales, even if it is just over the border into Lancashire...

▶ Jervaulx Abbey MAP REF 336 A5

jervaulxabbey.com
HG4 4PH | 01677 460226 (after 6pm) Open daily dawn until dusk
The high walls of this superb ruined Cistercian monastery, midway between Masham and Layburn, make it a truly evocative place. In summer it is filled with the scent of the glorious wild flowers that grow around the crumbling stonework. Jervaulx is on private land but open access is allowed to visitors, with an honesty box for admission money. There is a very pleasant tea room and gift shop.

Jervaulx was founded in 1156 and eventually owned much of Wensleydale. Sheep, cattle and horses were bred here by the monks, who were the first to make Wensleydale cheese. The last Abbot of Jervaulx, Adam Sedbar, or Sedbergh, was a vociferous opponent of the Dissolution and his protests caused him to be hanged at Tyburn Hill in London.

Despite its ruinous state there's still plenty for you to see here, such as the staircase – known as the Night Stairs – which led from the monks' upstairs dormitory to the church for services held through the night. You can also trace the cloister, the infirmary, the kitchen and the parlour.

EAT AND DRINK
Jervaulx Abbey Tea Rooms
jervaulxabbey.com
Jervaulx, Ripon, HG4 4PH
01677 460391
Just across the road from the abbey ruins, the Abbey Tea Rooms do excellent trade with visitors using the car park. You can sit outside in the garden and enjoy the delicious home-made honeycakes and scones, or take a seat inside for something more substantial.

▶ **Keighley** MAP REF 327 E5

Although only about three miles north of Haworth, Keighley (pronounced 'Keethlee') seems a world away. Brontë pilgrims from America and Asia may flock to nearby Haworth Parsonage, but few have probably even heard of this northern mill town – which, nevertheless, has plenty to offer, not least its status as the terminus for the historic Keighley and Worth Valley Railway. Keen shoppers should note that, as well as the large modern Airedale Shopping Centre, Keighley has several traditional mill shops, selling a variety of quality goods at discount prices.

Your first stop in Keighley should be the excellent Cliffe Castle Museum, a 19th-century mansion northwest of the town centre on the A629. The museum specialises in the geology and natural history of the region and has hands-on exhibits as well as touring exhibitions. The National Trust's East Riddlesden Hall is situated to the northeast of Keighley, on the Bradford road. This 17th-century Yorkshire manor house is set in 12 acres with gardens and a medieval tithe barn housing a fine collection of agricultural implements.

Despite its industrial origins, Keighley still has a surprising amount of wildlife to discover. Bradford City Council and the Canal and Rivers Trust teamed up to devise a three-and-a-half-mile walk which incorporates a stretch of the Leeds–Liverpool Canal towpath at Stockbridge Wharf, and the industrial heartland of the town, where visitors are reminded that they are still in Airedale by the presence of rabbits, foxes and the occasional badger. Details of the walk can be obtained from the Haworth tourist information centre – Keighley doesn't have a centre of its own.

Each July, the village of Oxenhope on the southern edge of Keighley is transformed by the Oxenhope Straw Race, which started back in 1975. Rival teams compete to carry a bale of straw around the village, visiting – and drinking in – as many pubs as feasibly possible on the way. The race, which raises money for local hospitals, took off in a big way and now several hundred people take part – many in fancy dress. Join the several thousand who watch them, and partake of the carnival atmosphere and activities.

◀ Thornton Viaduct, between Bradford, Halifax and Keighley

TAKE IN SOME HISTORY
East Riddlesden Hall
nationaltrust.org.uk
Bradford Road, BD20 5EL
01535 607075 | Open mid-Feb–Oct
Sat–Wed 10.30–4.30, Nov–mid-Dec
Sat–Sun 11–4
The interior of this stern-looking 17th-century manor house is furnished with textiles, Yorkshire oak and pewter, together with fine examples of 17th-century embroidery. The honeysuckle- and rose-covered facade ruin of the Starke Wing provides the backdrop to the garden. Wild flowers, perennials and a fragrant herb border provide a transition of colour throughout the year. Talk to the helpful attendants, who can tell you a wealth of local ghost stories. There's a magnificent old tithe barn in the grounds to explore, too.

VISIT THE MUSEUMS AND GALLERIES
Cliffe Castle Museum and Gallery
bradfordmuseums.org
Spring Gardens Lane, BD20 6LH
01535 618231 | Open Tue–Fri
10–4, Sat–Sun 11–4
Built as a millionaire's mansion, the house displays Victorian interiors, together with collections of local and natural history, ceramics, dolls, geological items and minerals. One popular feature is a model of a giant newt, which used to live in the area. There are also Victorian toys, local historical items and a working beehive, the bees coming in and out through a tube, which leads to a hole in the wall. There's a play area and a magnificent old tithe barn in the grounds, a Riverside Walk and tea rooms.

TAKE A TRAIN RIDE
Keighley and Worth Valley Railway
kwvr.co.uk
Keighley, BD21 4HP
01535 645214 | Open daily in summer, Sat–Sun rest of year
The line was built mainly to serve the valley's mills, and passes through the heart of Brontë country. Beginning at Keighley Station – shared with the mainline – it climbs up to Haworth, and terminates at Oxenhope, which has a storage and restoration building. At Haworth (see page 127) there are locomotive workshops, and at Ingrow West, an award-winning museum. Steam trains operate at weekends and holiday time, but there's also a regular diesel service. Many special events take place throughout the year, including the successful curry and fish-and-chips trains. The much-loved 1970 family movie, *The Railway Children*, featured the KWVR and particularly Oakworth Station.

GO FISHING
K L Tackle
127 North Street, BD21 3LD
01535 667574
Go coarse fishing on the Leeds–Liverpool Canal and the River Aire. Obtain permits from the tackle shop in Keighley.

WATCH RUGBY
Keighley Cougars
keighleycougars.com
Cougar Park, Royd Ings Avenue,
BD21 3RF | 01535 606044
Keighley Rugby League Football
Club was formed in 1876 and
they played their first match on
21 October of that year. You can
now watch the team play
championship level Rugby
League here.

▶ **PLACES NEARBY**
Oakworth is just a 10-minute
drive away from Keighley.

Truewell Hall Riding Centre
truewellequestrian.com
Holme House Lane, Oakworth,
BD22 0QX | 01535 603292
The centre offers a full range of
services including residential
riding holidays and a children's
day camp.

▶ **Kettlewell** MAP REF 327 D1

Kettlewell is a charming old village in Upper Wharfedale, with
solid stone houses dating back to the 17th century. It was once
a more important place than it is today – it had a market way
back in the 13th century, and Fountains and Coverham abbeys
and Bolton Priory all owned big tracts of farmland close by.
Later there were flourishing lead-mining and textile industries
too, which helped create those pleasing old houses.

Today Kettlewell is an excellent base for walking as the
Dales Way passes right through the village, while the road
traffic passes by. A popular route is to take a path heading
south over Knipe Scar and then head along the River Skirfare
and up the lesser-known but delightful Littondale, with
2,000-foot hills on either side of the valley.

To the south, Kilnsey Crag is a limestone bulge that looms
over the main road, the B6160. The cliff stands 170 feet high,
with a 40-foot overhang, which attracts both climbers and
film-makers. Nearby you'll find the Kilnsey Park estate, with
trout-fishing ponds and a farm shop.

When abbeys such as Fountains and Jervaulx were at their
prime, they owned vast amounts of land in the Yorkshire Dales.
They built granges in some of the further places, as bases, and
these were connected to the abbey by drovers' roads, allowing
large flocks of sheep to be moved around the estates. Many
of these roads are still in use as paths and bridleways, an
example being Mastiles Lane, which starts in Malham and goes
all the way across Mastiles and Kilnsey Moor, to emerge at the
River Wharfe near Kilnsey. Kilnsey Old Hall, once a grange for
Fountains Abbey, now provides holiday accommodation.

Visit Kettlewell in mid-August and you might be surprised to
see a lot of strange figures loitering around the village, many in
fancy dress and some definitely up to mischief. Fear not – they

▲ Kettlewell

are merely amiable scarecrows, taking part in the popular Scarecrow Festival.

Take the road north out of Kettlewell towards Gayle and Hawes, and you'll cross Wether Fell and Fleet Moss Pass, reaching a height of 1,857 feet. This is the highest road in the Yorkshire Dales, and one of the highest in England.

GO FISHING

Kilnsey Park and Trout Farm

kilnseyfishing.co.uk

Kilnsey, BD23 5PS | 01756 752150

Hone your fly-fishing skills on the ponds here, to catch rainbow, blue, brown and golden trout. They'll fillet and package your catch, ready to take home, as part of the deal. Enjoy the visitor centre, playground and farm shop, too.

GO RIDING

Kilnsey Trekking and Riding Centre

kilnseyriding.com

Conistone with Kilnsey, BD23 5HS

01756 752861

This family-run riding centre offers trekking, riding lessons and riding holidays. They are suitable for adults and children from the age of four, of all abilities.

▶ Kilburn MAP REF 337 E6

The village of Kilburn lies on the southwestern edge of the
North York Moors National Park (see page 203) and was
mentioned in the Domesday Book, but under the name
'Chileburne'. It has two claims to fame, both of an artistic
nature – the White Horse of Kilburn and woodcarver
Robert Thompson.

The White Horse is a figure cut into the turf that gazes
down from the scarp of Sutton Bank at Roulston Scar, and
is a landmark for miles around. Thomas Taylor, a Kilburn
man who made good in London, was so taken by the famous
White Horse cut into the chalk downs near Uffington in
Oxfordshire that he decided to create his own.

He persuaded John Hodgson, a teacher from Kilburn School,
to involve his pupils in the cutting of the figure. The main
problem was that his chosen hillside, while suitably steep, was
not chalk-based. Hodgson commandeered his pupils to help
create the outline of a gigantic horse, and used gallons of
whitewash to make the design stand out. The White Horse of
Kilburn is almost 325 feet from head to tail, and 227 feet high.
Finished in 1857, it is now the only major landscape figure in
the north of England. Whitewash fades in time, so these days
chalk chippings from the Yorkshire Wolds are used. It is said
about 20 people could stand on the grass island that forms the
eye, though walking on the horse is strongly discouraged.
There is a car park directly below the White Horse for those
who don't want to walk too far. However you get there, please
be careful not to damage the figure by walking on it.

Robert Thompson (1876–1955) was a woodcarver and
cabinet-maker whose fame has travelled far and wide.
Thompson was a self-taught craftsman whose skill with oak
remained largely unappreciated until he was commissioned to
make some furniture for the local church. Encouraged by the
results, Thompson began to specialise in ecclesiastical
furniture. You'll find that many Yorkshire churches have pews,
pulpits and other fixtures made by him, and one of the many
pleasures of visiting them is to search for examples of the
craftsman's trademark: a little carved mouse that stands proud
from its surroundings. There are lots of carved mice to find in
Kilburn's church, where a chapel was dedicated to the
'Mouseman' shortly before his death. Find out more at the
Mouseman Visitor Centre (see opposite).

A stream meanders through Kilburn, supplying part of its
name – unusual, because here a stream is known as a beck
rather than a burn. The 'burn' suffix is a clue that the origins of
the village are Anglo-Saxon not Viking.

VISIT THE WORKSHOP
The Mouseman Visitor Centre
robertthompsons.co.uk
YO61 4AH | 01347 869100
Open Easter–Oct daily 10–5,
Nov Wed–Sun 11–4

Even without the mouse motif, you can recognise Robert Thompson's work by the heavy designs, the dark tones of the oak wood and the rippled effect left by the adze – a heavy hand tool with an arched cutting blade set at a right-angle to the handle. This is furniture made to last not just a lifetime, but many lifetimes.

As the business quickly expanded, Thompson's half-timbered house in Kilburn became a showroom. Behind the building are more recent workshops, in which a new generation of woodworkers follows in his footsteps. You'll see stacks of neatly piled oak planks outside the workshop, being seasoned before they are used. The outbuildings now house an interesting small museum and exhibition centre. If you can't afford one of the substantial pieces of furniture, look for smaller wooden items for sale in the gift shop, all featuring the famous carved mouse. You can also get a good cup of tea in 'T' Café – served on oak tables, of course.

EAT AND DRINK
The Forresters Arms Inn
forrestersarms.com
The Square, YO61 4AH
01347 868386

Next door to the famous Robert Thompson craft workshop, the Forresters Arms has fine examples of his early work, with the distinctive trademark mouse evident in both bars. A sturdy stone-built former coaching inn still catering for travellers, it offers log fires, cask ales and good food.

▶ PLACES NEARBY
Just a little northeast of Kilburn you will find the Black Swan at Oldstead.

The Black Swan at Oldstead ◉◉◉◉
blackswanoldstead.co.uk
Main Street, Oldstead, YO61 4BL
01347 868387

Tucked into the southwestern corner of the North York Moors, Oldstead has been home to the Banks family for centuries. Modest in dimensions, it's a pretty stone-built farmhouse full of charm and classic country style. Antiques and opulent furnishings lift it above the rustic norm.

Tom Banks, in conjunction with a specialist produce gardener, oversees a terraced kitchen garden and orchard, as well as polytunnels out in the fields, to supply his stoves with the backbone of the menu's output. The core of the operation is a nine-course tasting menu, including intermediates, which offers a dazzling excursion through the repertoire, but every last detail on the carte is replete with ingenious care and panache.

Kildale MAP REF 337 F3

This little moorland estate village has a small railway station
on the Esk Valley line between Middlesbrough and Whitby.
Completed in 1865, the Esk Valley line had to make 17 river
crossings between the stations at Kildale and Grosmont, and is
still a valued amenity for locals and visitors.

St Cuthbert's Church is reached via a footbridge over the
railway. Viking relics, including battleaxes and swords, was
found here in 1868 when the church was renovated, showing
that Kildale was once an ancient settlement.

A mound, cut into by the railway line, is now the only clue
that it once had a motte-and-bailey castle. This was one of the
many strongholds of the Percy family, whose name is kept
alive by names such as Percy Cross and Percy Rigg, high on
the moors.

The Cleveland Way drops down briefly from the moors to
pass through Kildale. If you walk the route going north you'll
arrive on the breezy heights of Easby Moor, where a monument
commemorates the life and exploits of Captain James Cook.
From here you can enjoy panoramic views down over Great
Ayton, where the young James Cook spent his formative years
(see page 109).

The road between Kildale and Westerdale offers splendid
moorland scenery, and the watersplash over Baysdale Beck is
a popular spot for a picnic on a summer's day.

Kingston upon Hull

see **Hull**, page 141

Kirkbymoorside MAP REF 338 A5

The market town of Kirkbymoorside lies on the edge of the
moors just outside the National Park, between Helmsley
and Pickering. It's worth leaving the main road to investigate
the old heart of the town. The broad main street is lined
with inns, which are a reminder that Kirkbymoorside was
an important halt in the days of stage coaches. The oldest
inn is the Black Swan, whose elaborately carved entrance
porch bears the date 1632. The market cross, mounted
on a stepped base, can be found in a nearby side street called
The Shambles. The market day hasn't changed from medieval
times – Wednesday.

Kirkbymoorside has a road called Castlegate – and yes it did
have a castle, on a hill behind the parish church. Stones
salvaged from its ruins in the 17th century were used to build

the tollbooth in the market place. Another fortified building was once a hunting lodge built by the Neville family.

If you love old churches, you should rejoin the A170 and travel westwards in the direction of Helmsley for a few hundred yards, before following the sign for St Gregory's Minster. The word 'minster' conjures up some grand edifice, so you may be surprised to find a tiny, dignified church built of grey stone, almost hidden away in beautiful, secluded Kirkdale.

EAT AND DRINK
George & Dragon Hotel
gdhotel-yorkshire.co.uk
17 Market Place, YO62 6AA
01751 433334

This whitewashed coaching inn is welcoming and dog-friendly. Affectionately known as the G&D, it's full of charm – from the log fire in the bar and the collection of sporting paraphernalia, to the fountain in the sheltered courtyard – and there are five well-kept, hand-pulled real ales on offer, including an in-house brew. At lunchtime, tuck into a baguette or panini, or maybe a meal in the Knight's Restaurant with its contemporary decor and leather seats would suit you better. The traditional Sunday carvery is hugely popular.

▶ PLACES NEARBY
As well as St Gregory's Minster to the west you will find a great pub in Sinnington, to the east.

St Gregory's Minster
kirkdalechurches.org.uk
Kirkdale, YO62 7TZ

This ancient and intriguing building was dedicated to St Gregory – the pope who dispatched St Augustine to preach Christianity to the pagan English in AD 597. There has long been a church here – certainly before Anglo-Saxon times, as it had to be rebuilt in c.1060, perhaps following Viking destruction. Recent excavations have revealed a prehistoric standing stone by the west tower, suggesting that Christians reused a pagan site.

We know about the dates of the rebuilding because the details are carved on a three-panelled sundial mounted over the south door. The sun doesn't reach it any more; to protect the sundial, the best Anglo-Saxon example known, a porch was added in the 19th century. The engraved inscription is in Old English. Translated it reads: 'Orm, the son of Gamal, bought St Gregory's Church when it was utterly broken down and fallen, and he rebuilt it from ground level, to Christ and St Gregory, in the days of King Edward and Earl Tostig. Howarth made me and Brand the priest. This is sun's marker at all times'. The Edward is King Edward the Confessor, who ruled between 1042 and 1066; Tostig became Earl of Northumberland in 1055; Howarth made the sundial; Brand was the name of the parish priest. This brief inscription is the longest example of Anglo-Saxon carving to have survived.

Fox & Hounds Country Inn ◉

thefoxandhoundsinn.co.uk
Main Street, Sinnington, YO62 6SQ
01751 431577
This friendly, 18th-century coaching inn on the edge of the North York Moors is run by Andrew and Catherine Stephens. In the wood-panelled bar, under oak beams and (depending on the temperature) warmed by a double-sided log-burner called Big Bertha, a pint of Copper Dragon Best or Black Sheep Special could be waiting. Enjoy food that makes full use of locally farmed produce: light lunches (not Sundays), and early suppers (not Saturdays).

▶ Knaresborough   MAP REF 328 B3

Without doubt Knaresborough is one of the most picturesque market towns in Yorkshire, lying to the east of Harrogate and perched on ridges of rock rising steeply above the River Nidd. A magnificent arched viaduct crosses high above the river, with rowing boats bobbing about beneath. Handsome old houses peek through the trees on one side of the valley, looking across to parkland and woods that conceal Mother Shipton's Cave on the opposite bank.

In the time of the seer Mother Shipton, this land was part of a large royal hunting forest, and Knaresborough must have looked even more beautiful than it does now. Mother Shipton, born Ursula Sontheil in the cave in 1488, gained a famous reputation as a prophet. It is claimed that she foretold the attempted invasion and subsequent defeat of the Spanish Armada in 1588, and predicted the devastating Great Fire of London in 1666. You can visit the cave as part of a self-guided audio tour, along with the Petrifying Well – in which minerals in the water turn any object placed inside it to stone – and a small museum.

The town's official museum is up in the Old Courthouse in the grounds of Knaresborough Castle. Here you'll find local items and a gallery devoted to the Civil War in Knaresborough, but it's enjoyable not least because Knaresborough seems to have had more than its fair share of odd characters over the years, and their doings are well chronicled. For instance, there was Robert Flower, a hermit who lived in a cave on the riverside and was known locally as St Robert because of his alleged powers as a miracle healer. Then there was Eugene Aram, a wicked schoolmaster who murdered a shoemaker in St Robert's Cave and managed to escape justice for 13 years.

And John 'Blind Jack' Metcalfe, who went blind at the age of six but later went on to enjoy various careers including quantity surveyor, road building pioneer, accomplished violinist and part-time smuggler.

Nowadays, Knaresborough Castle is much reduced, but it has also seen its fair share of characters over the years. The murderers of Thomas à Becket sought refuge here, and royal visitors included Edward III, King John and Richard II – who was imprisoned here in 1399. With a small park around the remains, this is a popular spot to sit and enjoy the lovely views over the river.

Not far away is the market place, where you will find the oldest chemist's shop – or apothecary – in Britain, thought to have been established in the 13th century, and trading continuously since 1720. The market is known to have been held in the square each and every Wednesday since 1310.

The Church of St John the Baptist contains some Norman remains, and a Tudor font with a lockable cover to prevent witches stealing the holy water. By the church, a street named Water Bag Bank descends steeply to the river. The unusual name arose because the town's water supply was once brought up here on horseback in leather bags.

The House in the Rock is a folly that was carved out of the rock face by a local weaver, and was still lived in as a private dwelling up until 1996. It can be found up the steps by St Robert's Chapel, also carved out of the rock in 1408. The Chapel is off Abbey Road, beyond Low Bridge.

▼ Knaresborough

VISIT THE MUSEUMS AND GALLERIES

Mother Shipton's Cave

mothershipton.co.uk

Prophecy Lodge, Harrogate Road, HG5 8DD | 01423 864600

Open Apr–Oct daily 10–5.30, Mar Sat–Sun 10–4.30

You'll find plenty of interest at this long-established attraction – it's claimed that tourists have been coming since the 16th century. See the petrifying well, where over a period of just months everyday objects are turned to stone by a process of calcification – you can even buy items like teddies that have been turned to stone in the giftshop. Beyond the cave where Mother Shipton was born, there are more conventional attractions overlooking the river, including a woodland playground and tea room. Dogs are welcome, too.

Knaresborough Castle and Old Courthouse Museum

harrogate.gov.uk

Castle Yard, HG5 8AS | 01423 556188 | Open Apr–Sep daily 11–4, summer holidays 11–5

Towering high above the town, the remains of this 14th-century castle look down over the gorge of the River Nidd. This imposing fortress was once a summer home for the Black Prince. Visit the King's Tower, the secret underground tunnel and the dungeon. Discover Knaresborough's history in the museum and find out about castle life in the hands-on gallery. Play the computer game, 'Time Gate: The Prisoner of Knaresborough Castle'. The dungeon remains just as it was, and there are knowledgeable guides on hand to answer questions and lead regular tours of the sally port (a secret access to the moat). Special events run throughout the year so check the website for further details.

SEE A LOCAL CHURCH

Church of St John the Baptist

knaresboroughanglicans.org.uk

Vicarage Lane, HG5 9AF

Dating back to 1114, there's evidence of the early church to be seen in the string course of brickwork and in the blocked-up windows in the chancel – now flanked on either side by 13th-century chapels. The church is a treasure house, with good Early English features in the chancel, a Jacobean parclose screen, a Perpendicular font with a late 17th-century cover, magnificent 17th-century memorials in the Slingsby family chapel, and some Arts and Crafts stained glass by the William Morris studio.

GO BOATING

Blenkhorns Boat Hire

knaresboroughboats.co.uk

6 Waterside, High Bridge, HG5 9AZ

07973 803186

Hire rowing boats, punts and canoes to see the town from the water.

▶ **PLACES NEARBY**
Just north of Knaresborough lies Ferrensby.

The General Tarleton Inn ◉◉
generaltarleton.co.uk
Boroughbridge Road, Ferrensby,
HG5 0PZ | 01423 340284
This 18th-century coaching inn, renamed in honour of General Banastre Tarleton, who fought in the American War of Independence, lies just north of Knaresborough. The renovated interior retains its old beams and original log fires, while the sofas encourage guests to settle down with a pint of Black Sheep Best Bitter and peruse the seasonal menus which champion local produce: East Coast fish is delivered daily and local vegetables arrive the day they've been picked.

▶ Lastingham   MAP REF 338 A4

At a quick glance, the hamlet of Lastingham has a collection of good-looking houses, a few wellheads and a welcoming inn, but delve deeper and you'll find that it has something less obvious to offer – a unique place in the history of Christianity in the north.

St Cedd left the island of Lindisfarne (Holy Island) in AD 655 and chose this site on which to build a monastery. It was an area which, according to the Venerable Bede, was 'the lurking place of robbers and wild beasts'. St Cedd died of the plague and was buried in his monastery, close to the altar. This early building was later sacked by invading Danes.

In 1078 Abbot Stephen of Whitby moved his own community to Lastingham. He built a crypt dedicated to St Cedd, in which Cedd's remains were re-interred. Apart from cosmetic changes (and the stairs leading down into it from the nave of St Mary's Church) the crypt looks the way it did almost a thousand years ago. It was to have been part of a large abbey, but Stephen's plans were thwarted and the community moved to the larger site of St Mary's Abbey, York.

A closer examination of two of the village's wellheads reveal that one is dedicated to St Cedd, the other to his younger brother, St Chad, who succeeded him as Abbot of Lastingham. The two saints are credited with introducing Christianity to the northern kingdom of Mercia.

SEE A LOCAL CHURCH
St Mary's Church
lastinghamparishchurch.org.uk
Off Anserdale Lane, YO62 6TN
The crypt has a chancel, aisles, an eastern apse, stout Norman pillars, a low vaulted roof and a stone slab for an altar. Here, too, are fragments of ancient crosses. The present church, planned merely as the abbey's chancel, was eventually

consolidated to meet local needs – the congregation was derived from those who lived in many of the surrounding villages.

EAT AND DRINK
Blacksmiths Arms
blacksmithsarmslastingham.co.uk
YO62 6TN | 01751 417247
With a cottage garden and decked outdoor seating area, this 17th-century stone-built pub opposite the church has a wonderful atmosphere. In the small front bar pewter mugs and beer pump clips hang from the low beams, and copper cooking pans decorate the open range. A snug and two dining rooms complete the interior. Home-cooked dishes prepared from local supplies include Yorkshire hotpot and Whitby scampi. Wash down your meal with Theakston's Best Bitter or a guest ale.

Lastingham Grange
lastinghamgrange.com
YO62 6TH | 01751 417345
There are few better places to take tea than in this elegant hotel on the hillside on the edge of Lastingham. The traditional afternoon teas are served in the drawing room, where you can loll on comfy chintz sofas in front of the fire – it's almost like visiting the gracious home of a wealthy great aunt.

▶ Lealholm MAP REF 338 B3

The lovely River Esk runs through the narrow, wooded confines of Crunkly Ghyll, one of the many ancient gorges carved by ice age meltwaters, before flowing through Lealholm's grassy banks. This attractive little village, which sits astride a bend in the river, is a magnet for visitors. Lealholm was a favourite place, too, for Canon Atkinson, Danby's vicar, who wrote lyrically about the village in his 1891 book, *Forty Years in a Moorland Parish*: 'Elsewhere you must go in search of beautiful views; here they offer themselves to be looked at.'

The river is spanned by a well-proportioned bridge of peach-coloured stone; just a few yards away is a line of ancient stepping stones that seem to have an irresistible attraction for small children. Beyond the bridge is the Board Inn, offering refreshment and another vantage point from which to gaze down over the Esk.

Lealholm has no grand buildings of great note; most people come here to enjoy the green, which is common land where you can roam at will and spread a picnic rug. On a sunny summer's day the river bank is a relaxing spot; greedy mallards will eagerly dispose of any leftover sandwiches. Tea rooms and craft shops complete the picture. The National Park Authority has bowed to visitor pressure by providing a car park.

▲ Lealholm

Lealholm can be grouped with other beauty spots, such as Goathland, Hutton-le-Hole and Thornton-le-Dale, as places best avoided on sunny bank holidays, unless you love crowds. Apart from that, it's a delightful place to explore.

EAT AND DRINK

Beck View Tea Room
beckviewtearoom.weebly.com
YO21 2AQ | 01947 897310
There are tables inside this cosy tea room, handily located in the village shop, and outside overlooking the waterfall on the beck. Good-value cream teas and home-made cakes are on offer; the nut slice is particularly scrumptious.

The Board Inn
theboardinn.com
Village Green, Lealholm, YO21 2AJ
01947 897279
There's an inviting welcome in front of the warm fire at The Board Inn. And with more than 60 malt whiskies on offer, there'll be a warm feeling inside too! If you're there for a meal, the beef and lamb come from their own herds.

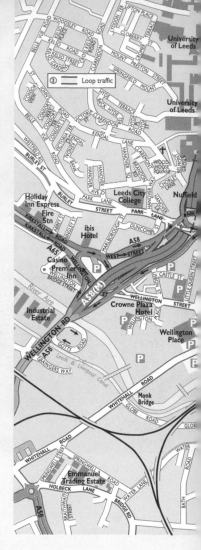

▶ Leeds

MAP REF 328 B6

One of the biggest and fastest-growing cities in England, Leeds displays true northern grit alongside a cultural renaissance. The city is the cultural, financial and commercial heart of West Yorkshire, and is the UK's largest centre for business, legal, and financial services outside London.

When traditional manufacturing industries slumped in the 20th century, the city began a process of reinvention and regeneration, embracing banking and finance, call-centres, digital games development and other service industries. Today, Leeds is a 24/7 business-driven city, with upmarket shopping and thriving sports, culture and nightlife; as well as a large university, and has submitted a bid to be the European capital of culture 2023. The focal point of the city centre is Millennium Square, where you'll find the town hall and several museums and galleries. Trinity Leeds is the vast shopping centre, and among the towering office buildings, Bridgewater Place – nicknamed 'the Dalek' – stands out. At 367 feet, it's Yorkshire's tallest building. Opera North and Northern Ballet Theatre are both resident in the city; there's an international Film Festival each November, and the new mint-green £60 million First Direct Arena opened in 2013 for pop concerts and sporting events. You might even catch a play by local lad Alan Bennett at the Grand Theatre.

Recently, the banks of the River Aire and the Leeds–Liverpool Canal have become a dynamic waterfront area of cafes and shops. You'll also find the Royal Armouries Museum here, which houses the national collection of arms and armour.

This is all quite surprising given the city's roots, which can be traced to the 5th-century forest which gave it its name. It grew up as an agricultural hub, then as a centre for the manufacture of wool and linen. It was ideally placed between the key ports of Hull and Liverpool, and became a hotspot on the canal network – the Aire and Calder Navigation was built in 1699 and the Leeds–Liverpool Canal in 1816. Strong rail links increased Leeds' potential for industrial manufacturing in the mid-19th century, and it became known for the production of clothing as well as printing and engineering. Its civic pride and new-found prosperity are visible in the grand Victorian buildings in the city centre, which include a grand classical town hall and the over-the-top glass-roofed arcades of the Victoria Quarters.

TAKE IN SOME HISTORY
Kirkstall Abbey
leeds.gov.uk

Abbey Road, Kirkstall, LS5 3EH

0113 378 4079| Visitor centre
open Tue–Thu, Sat–Sun 10–4;
abbey access dawn to dusk

The most complete 12th-century Cistercian abbey in the country stands on the banks of the River Aire in Leeds. You can still see many of the original buildings, including the cloister, church and refectory. Regular tours take you around to areas not normally accessible to the public. During the summer the abbey hosts plays, fairs and musical events. There is also a market once a month, selling crafts and local produce. A visitor centre gives an insight into the history of the site and a true sense of how the monks lived in the 15th century.

Temple Newsam Estate
leeds.gov.uk

Temple Newsam Road, off Selby Road, Halton, LS15 0AE

0113 336 7460 | Open all year. House: summer (BST) Tue–Sun 10.30–5, winter (GMT) Tue–Sun 10.30–4; Home Farm: summer Tue–Sun, 10–5, winter Tue–Sun 10–4

Temple Newsam is celebrated as one of Yorkshire's great historic houses and estates, and there's something for all the family at this wonderful site. Set in 1,500 acres of stunning parkland to the east of the city, the mansion contains outstanding collections of fine and decorative art, and there is a rare breeds farm which proves very popular with children. The gardens around it are extensive, and justly famed for their rhododendrons and azaleas. You can stroll down to the lake, to admire the grounds landscaped by Lancelot 'Capability' Brown. Revel in the planting of the walled garden, which holds national collections of delphiniums, phlox, asters and chrysanthemums.

There are two playgrounds, one of which is designed to be accessible to children with special needs and two shops selling gifts, local produce and plants. The cafe serves dishes made with meat reared on the farm, as well as home made cakes.

VISIT THE MUSEUMS AND GALLERIES
Royal Armouries Museum
see highlight panel overleaf

Thackray Medical Museum
thackraymedicalmuseum.co.uk

Beckett Street, LS9 7LN

0113 244 4343 | Open daily 10–5

Your visit transports you into the world of health and medicine – past, present and future. Experience life in the Victorian slums of 1840 and be flabbergasted at the incredible lotions and potions once offered as cures for your ills. See how surgery was performed without the aid of anaesthetics, experience pregnancy by trying on an empathy belly, and step inside the human body in the interactive Life Zone.

Leeds Industrial Museum at Armley Mills

leeds.gov.uk

Canal Road, Armley, LS12 2QF

0113 378 3173 | Open Tue–Sat & BH Mon 10–5, Sun 1–5

Once the world's largest woollen mill, Armley Mills evokes memories of the 18th-century woollen industry, showing the progress of wool from the sheep to knitted clothing. The museum has its own 1930s cinema, illustrating the history of cinema projection, including the first moving pictures taken in Leeds. The museum is set between the Leeds and Liverpool Canal and the River Aire. You'll be able to see demonstrations of static engines and steam locomotives, a printing gallery and take a journey through the working world of textiles and fashion.

Leeds Art Gallery

leeds.gov.uk

The Headrow, LS1 3AA

0113 378 5350 | Open Mon–Tue & Thu–Sat 10–5, Wed 12–5, Sun 1–5

The gallery reopened its doors in October 2017 after an extensive restoration of the original Victorian roof and its Central Court, shedding fresh light on to one of the best collections of 20th-century British art outside London. In addition, there are Victorian and late 19th-century pictures, an outstanding collection of English watercolours, a display of modern sculpture and temporary exhibitions focusing on contemporary art. Look out

5 excitement-filled activities in Yorkshire

▶ **Go 4X4 driving at Yorkshire Outdoors**, Felixkirk, near Thirsk – Some 4 x4s, expert instruction and a 45-acre course – wallow through deep mud and water, climb impossibly steep hills, creep over breathtaking crests.

▶ **Go paragliding at Active Edge**, Pateley Bridge – See Yorkshire from above, while trying your hand at this exhilarating sport. Take control of a paraglider and soar above the rolling Yorkshire Dales.

▶ **Watch a medieval joust at the Royal Armouries Museum**, Leeds – live shows of military and sporting skills-at-arms including archery, falconry, and horse shows all throughout the year in the Tiltyard.

▶ **Experience IMAX at the National Science & Media Museum**, Bradford – Cinema on a giant 48 x 65-foot screen. Be part of the action with larger-than-life pictures and wrap-around sound.

▶ **Go skiing or rock climbing at Xscape Yorkshire**, Castleford, near Pontefract – Experience the outdoors indoors, with everything from the real snow zone for skiing and tobogganing, to rock climbing and skating. Or you could try the less energetic dodgems, cinemas and bowling. For a real adrenaline challenge, go for the Vertical Chill Skyride.

▶ Royal Armouries Museum

MAP REF 328 B6

royalarmouries.org

Armouries Drive, LS10 1LT | 0113 220 1999 | Open daily 10–5

One of Yorkshire's outstanding national museums, the Royal Armouries holds the national collection of arms and armour. Explore the world of the warrior from early medieval knights to the modern-day soldier in five exciting galleries: War, Tournament, Self Defence, Hunting and Oriental. The imposing Hall of Steel features a 100-foot high massed display of over 3,000 objects. Get your hands on history with the interactive displays and handling collections, and test your skills on the crossbow range.

for works by local artists including Henry Moore, Barbara Hepworth and Atkinson Grimshaw, as well as Bridget Riley, Francis Bacon and Paula Rego. The gallery holds an active events programme with regular talks, workshops and demonstrations.

Abbey House Museum

leeds.gov.uk
Abbey Walk, Abbey Road, Kirkstall, LS5 3EH | 0113 378 4079
Open Tue–Fri 10–5, Sat 12–5, Sun 10–5

The displays at Abbey House include an interactive childhood gallery and an exploration of life in Victorian Leeds. Three reconstructed streets allow you to immerse yourself in the sights and sounds of the late 19th century, from the glamorous art furnishers shop to the impoverished widow washerwoman. Well worth a visit.

ENTERTAIN THE FAMILY
Tropical World

leeds.gov.uk
Roundhay Park, LS8 2ER
0113 237 0754 | Open daily 10–4

The atmosphere of the tropics is recreated here as you arrive on the beach and walk through the depths of the swamp into the rainforest. A waterfall cascades into a rock-pool, and other pools contain terrapins and carp. There are reptiles, insects, meerkats and 30 species of butterfly. Feel the dry heat of the desert and look out for fruit bats, pygmy slow lorises and tenrecs in the nocturnal zone. See piranhas and other exotic fish in the depths of the aquarium.

CATCH A PERFORMANCE
Leeds Grand Theatre and Opera House

leedsgrandtheatre.com
46 New Briggate, LS1 6NZ
0844 848 2700

If one top-class theatre wasn't enough in the city, the Grand Theatre presents a fantastic range of performances, including West End and Broadway touring shows, dance and drama. The Theatre is also the home of Opera North and the Northern Ballet, with regular shows from both companies.

O2 Academy Leeds

o2academyleeds.co.uk
55 Cookridge Street, LS2 3AW
0113 389 1555

The site of the former Town and Country Club in the centre of Leeds is now a major performance venue in its own right, with a 2,300-seat auditorium and a second 400-seat club space too. It has a great selection of eclectic bands and club nights – see the website for full details.

West Yorkshire Playhouse

wyp.org.uk
Playhouse Square, Quarry Hill, LS2 7UP | 0113 213 7700

Since 1990, the West Yorkshire Playhouse has hosted a multitude of plays and shows in its two theatres. Productions range from classic drama to European theatre and children's shows.

TAKE IN SOME ART

The Tetley

thetetley.org

Hunslet Road, LS10 1JQ

0113 320 2323

Set in the historic former headquarters of the Tetley Brewery, this is a brand new centre for contemporary art in Leeds. Designed as a platform for creativity, innovation and experimentation, The Tetley is a challenging visit. Take a look at the massive Tetley Collection – a fascinating archive of material from the brewery's industrial past – and there's always an exciting programme of other exhibitions and projects going on.

PLAY A ROUND

As you might expect, Leeds has quite a few top-quality golf courses, starting off with the challenging and impressive municipal course of the Gotts Park Golf Club – with its very steep hills to some greens which require accuracy rather than length from the tees. The 18-hole Wike Ridge at the Leeds Golf Centre is a traditional heathland course designed by Donald Steel. The sand-based greens are constructed to USGA specification, and there are an excellent variety of holes with some very challenging par 5s. The 12-hole, par 3 Oaks is complemented by a floodlit driving range and other practice facilities. The course is the home of the Leeds Golf Academy.

The Sand Moor Golf Club is a beautiful, inland course situated next to Eccup Reservoir on the north side of Leeds. It has been described as the finest example of golfing paradise being created out of a barren moor. With magnificent views of the surrounding countryside, the course has sandy soil and drains exceptionally well. At the Horsforth Golf Club you'll have extensive views across Leeds and on a clear day York Minster can even be seen from the 14th tee. It's a moorland and parkland course combining devilish short holes with some more substantial challenges. The Moor Allerton Golf Club, established in 1923, has 27 holes set in 220 acres of undulating parkland, with testing water hazards and magnificent views extending across the Vale of York. The championship course was designed by Robert Trent Jones, the famous American course architect, and provides a challenge to both high- and low-handicapped golfers.

The South Leeds Golf Club is made of hard-walking parkland, which gets quite windy but has good views. The small undulating greens are a very good test of putting. Cookridge Hall is an American-style course with intimidating water hazards strewn across the course and strategic bunkering, providing a true test for golfers of all abilities, and spectacular views of the Yorkshire Dales.

Gotts Park Golf Club
gottsparkgolfclub.co.uk
Armley Ridge Road, LS12 2QX
0113 231 1896| Open daily

Leeds Golf Centre, Wike Ridge
leedsgolfcentre.com
Wike Ridge Lane, Shadwell, LS17
9JW | 0113 288 6000 | Open daily

Sand Moor Golf Club
sandmoorgolf.co.uk
Alwoodley Lane, LS17 7DJ
0113 268 5180 | Open Sun–Fri

Horsforth Golf Club
horsforthgolfclub.co.uk
Layton Rise, Layton Road, Horsforth,
LS18 5EX | 0113 258 6819
Open Sun–Fri

Moor Allerton Golf Club
magc.co.uk
Coal Road, Wike, LS17 9NH
0113 266 1154 | Open daily

South Leeds Golf Club
southleedsgolfclub.co.uk
Gipsy Lane, Beeston, LS11 5TU
0113 277 1676 | Open daily

Cookridge Hall Golf Club
cookridgehall.co.uk
Cookridge Lane, LS16 7NL
0113 230 0641 | Open daily

EAT AND DRINK
The Cross Keys
the-crosskeys.com
107 Water Lane, LS11 5WD
0113 243 3711

Built in 1802, The Cross Keys was a watering hole for local foundry workers and is where James Watt, famed inventor of the steam engine, reputedly hired a room to spy on his competitor, Matthew Murray. As the story goes, to learn Murray's trade secrets Watt bought drinks for foundry workers relaxing here after work. Incredibly, this historic landmark was closed in the 1980s and was a tyre storage depot for a local garage until it was restored in 2005. This city centre pub has a country inn atmosphere. Now, hand-pulled pints from local microbreweries complement traditional British dishes recreated from long-lost recipes.

Jamie's Italian, Leeds
jamieoliver.com/italian/leeds
35 Park Row, LS1 5JL
0113 322 5400
A thorough makeover has transformed a once-grand banking temple into a warehouse eatery in the modern idiom, its original features still visible amid the girdering, tiling and brickwork. Sit up on high stools at a counter, or around cafeteria-style booth tables, for the enjoyable Jamie-goes-to-Italy experience. Should the British affection for simple Italian food ever pall, the empire may come juddering to a halt, but thankfully no such disaffection is in evidence here.

Malmaison Leeds ◉

malmaison.com/locations/leeds
1 Swinegate, LS1 4AG
0113 398 1000

The Malmaison group's Leeds branch has been carved out of an impressive building that used to be the headquarters of Leeds City Tramway. In common with other hotels in the group, it is decorated and furnished to a high standard, creating the atmosphere of a contemporary boutique hotel. The brasserie is no exception, with soft lighting, plush leather booths and open fireplaces under its elegant ceiling. The cooking is built on a framework of quality ingredients, and talented professionals are clearly at work here.

North Bar

northbar.com
24 New Briggate, LS1 6NU
0113 242 4540

This pioneering beer bar opened in 1997 in the heart of Leeds and is heaven for ale aficionados as it offers up to 130 bottled beers from around the globe at any one time, plus 16 draught beers and a selection of around 50 whiskies. Yet, pride of place on the vast bar are hand-pumped beers from local microbreweries, notably Roosters ales. It's a trendy European-style bar, full of characters and great conversation, as well as a venue for music and local art exhibitions. Don't miss the regular beer festivals – check online for details.

Salvo's Restaurant & Salumeria ◉

salvos.co.uk
115 Otley Road, Headingley, LS6 3PX | 0113 275 5017

Since it first opened in 1976, Salvo's has served the local Headingley community and built a deserved reputation. It's lively, family-friendly and family-run, and will sort you out for some rustic and hearty regional Italian cooking. The Salumeria, which is a café-deli during the day and opens in the evening for musical soirees and the like, lies a few doors down from the restaurant. If you've come for a pizza because nothing else will do, the classics are all present and correct and you won't leave disappointed. But there is so much more to explore on the menu here.

Thorpe Park Hotel & Spa ◉

restaurant-and-bar.co.uk/leeds
Century Way, Thorpe Park, LS15 8ZB | 0113 264 1000

Close to the M1 and with quick access into Leeds or the countryside, the Thorpe Park Hotel is a handy base for exploring the area while offering plenty of enticements to stick around. There's a spa, conference and leisure facilities, and the Restaurant & Bar, a great drinking and dining option. The open plan and split-level dining room has a contemporary finish with a pale wooden floor, artwork on the walls and black leather-style chairs.

Town Hall Tavern ◉
townhalltavernleeds.co.uk
17 Westgate, LS1 2RA
0113 244 0765
Located between the law
courts and the Park Square
Business Centre, this bustling
city-centre pub looks like any
old boozer from the outside,
but the interior is stylish and
comfortable. The cooking,
too, is a cut above your
standard pub norm, with an
all-day menu offering a wide
choice of appealing options

▶ **PLACES NEARBY**
Lotherton Hall is a beautiful
Edwardian country house to the
east of Leeds.

Lotherton Hall
leeds.gov.uk
Aberford, LS25 3EB | 0113 281 3259
Hall open summer Tue–Sat 10–5,
Sun 1–5, winter Tue–Sat 10–4, Sun
12–4; estate 8am–8pm; bird garden
summer 10–5, winter 10–4
Lotherton Hall is home to a
treasure trove of arts and
crafts, with paintings, silver,
ceramics and costume – and
forms part of Leeds Museums
and Galleries. The house itself
is Edwardian, although there is
some evidence of a Georgian
house on the site. The Chapel,
dedicated to St James, dates
from the 12th century. It's
all set within an estate with
formal gardens and a red deer
park, including an adventure
playground, walking trails
and a large bird garden that is
home to around 500 rare and
endangered birds.

5 companies founded in Yorkshire

▶ **Asda**: Founded in Leeds in
1949 as Associated Dairies &
Farm Stores Limited, and
known as Asda since 1965,
the company expanded out
of the north in the late 1980s,
and has since become a
familiar sight all over the UK.

▶ **Marks & Spencer**: Formed
by Michael Marks and Tom
Spencer in Leeds, 1894,
Marks & Spencer called
their new stores 'Penny
Bazaars'. By 1900 Marks &
Spencer had 36 Bazaars and
12 high street stores. The
rest is retail history.

▶ **Optare**: Founded in 1985 and
based in Leeds, Optare is a
bus manufacturer which
opened on the site of the old
Charles H Roe bodybuilders.
Optare buses are used
throughout the world.

▶ **Sumo Digital**: Most gamers
will have played a Sumo
game in the last decade.
Since forming in Sheffield,
the company has produced
titles such as *Sonic & Sega
All-Stars Racing*, *F1 2011*,
Virtua Tennis and *Doctor Who:
The Adventure Games*.

▶ **Tetley's Brewery**: Founded
in 1822 by Joshua Tetley, the
brewery went big time in
1961, through mergers that
formed Allied Breweries,
then the world's largest
brewing concern. Tetley is
now owned by Carlsberg,
and the Leeds brewery was
demolished in 2012. The
former headquarters now
houses The Tetley (see
page 176).

▶ Levisham & Lockton   MAP REF 338 C4

Levisham and Lockton are a pair of delectable villages lying off the A169, about five miles north of Pickering. Lockton has a church, a youth hostel, a duck pond and limestone cottages set back from wide grass verges.

Neighbouring Levisham is just a mile away, but it's a really long mile if you happen to be walking – the villages are divided by a deep gorge. At the bottom, close to Levisham Beck, is a converted watermill and the ruins of St Mary's Church. Though it was built in this isolated spot to be equidistant from both villages, the church can hardly be said to be convenient for either.

When you get there, houses and the Horseshoe Inn surround an expansive village green. Pass the pub to join a single track road, with long views along well-wooded Newton Dale. Keep ahead down the road to arrive at Levisham Station, one of the stops for steam trains on the preserved railway line between Grosmont and Pickering (see page 110 and page 217), where the public road ends.

EAT AND DRINK
The Horseshoe Inn
horseshoelevisham.co.uk
Main Street, Levisham, YO18 7NL
01751 460240

On the edge of the North York Moors National Park, here is a village pub where you can stay overnight while touring the area. Charles and Toby Wood have created an inviting atmosphere that's especially apparent in the beamed and wooden-floored bar, where a gilt-edged mirror hangs above the open fire, and the real ales are from Black Sheep and Cropton. Local suppliers play a big part behind the scenes so that the kitchen can prepare hearty plates of Whitby scampi and chips, steak-and-ale pie, and sausage and mash.

▼ The North Yorkshire Moors at Levisham

▶ Leyburn   MAP REF 335 F4

Leyburn is one of several Dales towns that stakes a claim to being the unofficial capital of Wensleydale. Come on a Friday for the flourishing market in the square. A modern addition is a purpose-built auction centre on Harmby Road – the largest outside London – which holds general and specialist sales two or three times a month.

In the business park close by is a ceramics workshop where you will find the Teapottery, an unusual and eccentric place which makes and displays nothing but teapots in wacky designs. You'll find many other craft shops and galleries in Leyburn, which are scattered in between the mainly 19th-century solid town houses.

On the western edge of the town, beginning in Shawl Terrace not far from the tourist information centre, is the walk known as the Leyburn Shawl. This easy stroll to an open grassy area is a winner with everybody, as it leads very quickly to some glorious views of Wensleydale. The name 'shawl' is linked to a legend that Mary, Queen of Scots, dropped hers here as she was escaping from incarceration in nearby Bolton Castle.

VISIT THE WORKSHOP
Teapottery
teapottery.co.uk
Leyburn Business Park, Leyburn
DL8 5QA | 01937 588235
Open Apr–Oct daily 9.30–4,
Nov–Mar Mon–Sat 10–4
You can watch the craftspeople at work in the visitor centre, making teapots in every shape and size, from a golden syrup tin to an AGA.

GO FISHING
Both coarse and fly fishing are possible along the River Ure and its tributary, the River Cover, which has a good stock of trout and grayling. You can buy your permits in The Cover Bridge Inn, at Fast Witton (see right) – and possibly have a meal there afterwards.

EAT AND DRINK
The Blue Lion
thebluelion.co.uk
East Witton, DL8 4SN
01969 624273
This well maintained 18th-century coaching inn has built a reputation as one of North Yorkshire's finest. The interior is best described as rural chic, oozing stacks of atmosphere and charm. The classic bar with its open fire and flagstone floor is a beer drinker's haven.

The Cover Bridge Inn
thecoverbridgeinn.co.uk
East Witton, DL8 4SQ
01969 623250
The oldest part of this magnificent little pub was probably built around 1670, to cater for the increasing trade on the drovers' route from

Coverdale. Wholesome fodder, including home-made pies, and their famous ham and eggs.

Sandpiper Inn
sandpiperinn.co.uk
Market Place, DL8 5AT
01969 622206
The ivy-clad Sandpiper may only have been a pub for 30 years or so, but it's Leyburn's oldest building, dating to the 17th century. The bar and snug offer real ales from a small army of Yorkshire breweries, while the restaurant, distinguished by an impressively huge stone lintel above an open fireplace, offers modern British food.

▶ Malham   MAP REF 326 C2

Malham is one of the biggest tourist attractions in the Yorkshire Dales while Malham Cove is one of Britain's most impressive and recognised natural features, and so the area has become almost too popular. At busy times the National Park Centre car park overflows and the roadside verges disappear under the wheels of parked vehicles. The village cafes, pubs, outdoor shops and guest houses are kept very busy accommodating the crowds.

In their haste to see Malham Cove, many people miss seeing the two old bridges in the village. The New Bridge, as it is known, is also called the Monks' Bridge and was built in the 17th century. It can be seen near the post office. Malham's older bridge dates from the 16th century and is of clapper design, with large slabs of limestone placed on stone supports in the stream. This is the Wash-Dub or Moon Bridge, named after Prior Moon, the last Prior of Bolton Abbey, who had a grange in Malham. Both cross Malham Beck, which is the start of the River Aire.

The Pennine Way (see page 216) runs through the village, and there are lots of well-trodden footpaths around. The half-mile walk to Malham Cove is signed from the village centre. The limestone rock face seems to tumble down the 250-foot cliffs, and extends for about 1,000 feet. Try to picture the water that once flowed over the cliff face, helping create today what has been described as a dry waterfall. This natural amphitheatre was formed by movements of the earth's crust, and is simply the most visible part of the Craven Fault. It is a steep climb up man-made steps to the top, but your reward is an exhilarating view over the moors, north to Malham Tarn, and over the limestone pavements that stretch away from beneath your feet. It's in the grykes and clints of these limestone pavements that some of the area's wide variety of unusual plants can be found.

Malham Tarn, to the north of the village, is in the care of the National Trust and the Field Studies Council. The Tarn is 1,229 feet above sea level, the highest natural lake in England, and both the tarn and the area around it have been declared a Site of Special Scientific Interest. A track leads down past Tarn House, where regular courses are run on the natural history of the area. It is a particularly important area for plant life and as a breeding ground for many birds: a hide enables you to view parts of the lake that can't be accessed on foot. Tarn House, a former shooting lodge, was the home of the wealthy Victorian businessman Walter Morrison, whose visitors at various times included Charles Darwin, John Ruskin and Charles Kingsley. It was while staying here that Kingsley was inspired to write his children's classic, *The Water Babies* (1863).

Malham's other impressive natural attractions include Gordale Scar and Janet's Foss – one a limestone gorge, the other a magical waterfall. The village of Kirkby Malham, a little way to the south, is also worth exploring. The church has many notable features, but one of the most significant is one of the three bells. It was cast in 1601 and weighs 1.25 tonnes, making it the second largest bell in Britain.

GET OUTDOORS
Yorkshire Dales National Park Centre
yorkshiredales.org.uk
BD23 4DA | 01729 833200
Open daily Apr–Oct 10–5; check ahead at other times; closed Jan
Discover local literature and displays on natural history, the local community and the work of conservation bodies. There's a useful 24-hour information screen.

EAT AND DRINK
The Lister Arms
listerarms.co.uk
BD23 4DB | 01729 830330
This handsome old 17th-century stone coaching inn sits right in the heart of Malham, opposite the village green, which makes it an ideal place to stop for morning coffee, or perhaps a pint of Thwaites Wainwright bitter, named after the great walker Alfred Wainwright. History is visible wherever you look: outside, there's a traditional mounting block where riders would effortlessly climb onto their horses, and a beautiful tiled entrance; inside, the renovated ground floor is divided into little nooks, with original beams, flagged floors and wood-burning stoves. The kitchen team serve up food that is seasonal, local and always freshly prepared. Children, well-behaved dogs, muddy boots and cycles are also happily welcomed here.

▶ View over Malham (overleaf)

▶ **PLACES NEARBY**
Visit Town End Farm and its
farm shop, south of Malham.

Town End Farm
townendfarmshop.co.uk
Scosthrop, Airton, Skipton,
BD23 4BE | 01729 830902

Town End Farm has a tea room
and a farm shop filled with
goodies. When you've tasted
their light snacks you can stock
up on some of the best locally
produced food in the area,
including 'Limestone Country'
grass-fed beef.

▶ **Malton** MAP REF 330 A1

Malton is a pleasing old town on the River Derwent. Based on
the site of a Roman settlement – now largely buried under
Orchard Fields – Malton grew up as a medieval market town,
and has managed to maintain a range of small, traditional
independent shops alongside the familiar high street names.
Good food is a priority here, from rare breed pork to locally
grown asparagus, and the town is fostering a growing
reputation as the foodie capital of Yorkshire. There's a thriving
market scene, with a monthly food market attracting big names
– and an annual food festival in May.

The White Rose Way – the long-distance walking route
between Leeds and Scarborough – passes through the town.

TAKE IN SOME HISTORY
Castle Howard
see highlight panel opposite

VISIT THE MUSEUM
**Eden Camp Modern History
Theme Museum**
see highlight panel overleaf

SEE A LOCAL CHURCH
St Mary's Priory Church
stmarysmalton.org.uk
Malton | 01653 692370
On the edge of the town stands
the sturdy grey St Mary's
Church, the remnant of a
Gilbertine priory founded in
1150 and lost at the Dissolution.
In the churchyard one of the
magnificent original Norman-
arched doorways has been
reconstructed, its stonework

recovered from its recycled use
as a cattle trough. The
medieval and Victorian carved
misericords inside the church
are well worth a look.

EAT AND DRINK
The New Malton
thenewmalton.co.uk
2–4 Market Place, YO17 7LX
01653 693998
Overlooking the market place
in Malton, this prominent
18th-century building has had
an interesting history and is
now a family-friendly pub. Beer
drinkers are spoilt for choice,
with the range of local ales
changing weekly. An extensive
menu features a mix of pub
classics, along with more
ambitious dishes.

▶ Castle Howard MAP REF 329 F2

castlehoward.co.uk

YO60 7DA | 01653 648333 | House open end Mar–early Nov
& end Nov–mid-Dec, daily 10–5; gardens open all year

The full magnificence of this grand 18th-century stately home is best appreciated from the south, where it is viewed in dramatic outline against the horizon. It may well seem familiar to you – two versions of Evelyn Waugh's tale of love and loss, *Brideshead Revisited*, have been filmed here. There are formal gardens and grounds of around 1,000 acres to explore.

Inside, the sheer scale of the Grand Staircase and the vast, echoing rooms are imposing, and there is no denying the splendour of the bedrooms and dressing rooms that follow, even if the opulent taste is over the top. Queen Victoria slept in the 18th-century bed with its unusual circular top, which dominates the Dressing Room. On the occasion of her visit in 1850, gas was first installed in the castle, and her entrance was heralded with a display of flames spelling out 'God Save the Queen' on the hall balcony.

The Great Hall is a triumph of architect John Vanbrugh's art on an altogether different scale. Its vastness is accentuated by the heavy pillars that draw the eye upwards to the wrought-iron balcony of the gallery and the dizzying height of the painted dome. By comparison, the rest of the house seems positively domestic, but a series of glittering state rooms provide the setting for a collection of fabulous paintings.

▶ Eden Camp Modern History Theme Museum MAP REF 330 A1

edencamp.co.uk
Eden Camp, YO17 6RT | 01653 697777
Open early Jan–late Dec daily 10–5

This national award-winning museum presents the most comprehensive display of British civilian life during World War II, in the unique setting of an original prisoner of war camp built in 1942 to house Italian and German POWs. Life-size tableaux and dioramas incorporate sound, light and even smell effects to create the atmosphere of the 1940s. Other sections of the museum cover military and political events of the war, and British military history from World War I to modern warfare in Iraq and Afghanistan. The museum also houses an extensive collection of military vehicles, artillery and associated equipment. Look out for the popular re-enactment weekends through the year.

The Talbot Hotel ◉◉
www.talbotmalton.co.uk
Yorkersgate, YO17 7AJ
01653 639096

The Talbot stands on a B-road running to the north of the River Derwent. It's a rugged but pastoral setting for a country-house hotel, in a house owned by the same family since the second George. A dining room, in pale green and gold, showcases contemporary cooking of distinctive flair.

▶ PLACES NEARBY

Flamingo Land Resort
see highlight panel overleaf

Scampston Hall
www.scampston.co.uk
Scampston Hall, YO17 8NG
01944 759000 | Garden open mid-Apr to Oct, Tue–Sun 10–5; house open late May to mid-Aug, Tue–Fri, Sun; tours 1–3

Scampston Hall is a privately owned country house just east of Malton, with extensive landscaped grounds and a remarkable modern, formal garden. The house itself was extensively remodelled in 1801 by the architect Thomas Leverton with fine Regency interiors, and has some good works of art. The current owners, Charles and Miranda Legard, came to the property in 1987; in 1998 they called in Dutch designer Piet Oudolf to remodel the kitchen garden and create an excitingly modern design within its walls. The result is a breathtaking display which is well worth a visit.

5 family days out

▶ **Flamingo Land Resort**
This family theme park has more than 100 rides and activities. There are five family shows, plus the UK's largest privately owned zoo. The latest white-knuckle ride is Hero, which delivers the sensation of free flight with swooping turns and breathtaking drops.
page 190

▶ **The Forbidden Corner**
Tupgill Park is a four-acre garden, full of tunnels, follies and oddities –a huge pyramid of glass; strange statues of mythical figures; paths and passages that lead nowhere.
page 197

▶ **Lightwater Valley Theme Park**
Lightwater is home to Europe's longest roller-coaster ride. Also here are the thrilling Raptor Attack and Eagle's Claw. There's a falconry centre, a farm, and crazy golf.
page 236

▶ **Tropical Butterfly House Wildlife and Falconry Centre**
There's not just butterflies here – handle snakes and birds of prey, and feed the marmoset, monkeys, lorikeets and many more.
page 246

▶ **Yorkshire Sculpture Park**
In the grounds of a 500-acre country estate, this is one of the world's leading open-air galleries. See sculptures by Yorkshire-born Henry Moore and Barbara Hepworth, among others.
page 283

▶ **Flamingo Land Resort** MAP REF 338 B6

flamingoland.co.uk
Kirby Misperton, YO17 6UX | 0871 9118000 | Open Apr–Oct daily from
9.30; Nov–Mar selected days

If you're seeking thrills and spills, then this theme park is the
place for you – and with around 1.8 million visitors a year, it's one
of Yorkshire's most popular attractions. It's set in 375 acres of
North Yorkshire countryside, and with over 100 rides and activities,
there's something for everyone at Flamingo Land. Enjoy a dozen
stomach-churning white-knuckle rides, take a monorail ride and
stroll through the extensive zoo, where you'll find tigers, giraffes,
hippos and rhinos. The theme park also boasts five great family
shows and Mumbo Jumbo – with the steepest drop on any roller
coaster in the world. The scale is vast – there are at least 18
different places to eat for a start – so plan ahead if you can, and
consider advance purchase of the Q-buster tokens, via the website.

**The Garden Restaurant
at Scampston**
scampston.co.uk
Walled Garden, Scampston Hall,
YO17 8NG | 01944 759000
A range of teas, coffee and
lunches are served in this light
and airy modern establishment,
using produce from the gardens
and ingredients from other
local sources. You can buy
home-made pickles, jams,
cookery books, crockery
and paintings, and cookery
courses and demonstrations
are a feature in a specially
designed kitchen. You don't
have to pay the Hall's entrance
fee to visit the restaurant.

Wolds Way Lavender
woldswaylavender.co.uk
Sandy Lane, Wintringham,
YO17 8HW | 01944 758641
Open Jun–Aug daily 10–5,
Apr–May & Sep–Oct Sun–Thu 10–4
The medicinal benefits of
lavender are extolled at this
12-acre site. Six acres are
currently planted with lavender,
and there's a wood-burning still
for the extraction of lavender
oil. Be calmed by the Sensory
Areas, enjoy a cuppa in the tea
room, and purchase many
lavender items in the shop.
Harvest and distillation takes
place in the last week of July
and throughout August.

▶ Marsden MAP REF 322 B2

Marsden is a large former industrial village, surrounded by
high moorland, on the edge of the Pennines and on one of the
main routes over the tops and Saddleworth Moor to Greater
Manchester. Lots of transport routes meet here – the River
Colne and the Wessenden Brook, the Huddersfield Narrow
Canal and the Huddersfield–Manchester Railway all pass
through Marsden.

Its location on an important through-route was recognised
from earliest times, and there are two historic packhorse
bridges to be seen – Mellor Bridge and Close Gate Bridge.
'Blind Jack' Metcalfe of Knaresborough (see page 164)
engineered the first coach road through the village in 1765.
Cotton, silk and wool were all spun and woven in Marsden at
one time or another – many of the mills which stretched down
the Colne Valley have been demolished for housing, but some
are preserved as part of the Marsden Conservation Area. The
last mill, Bank Bottom, closed in 2003. The clock tower of the
Mechanics Institute is a local landmark on the main shopping
thoroughfare, Peel Street.

To the west of the town, Standedge Tunnel is Britain's
longest and highest canal tunnel, opened in 1811 and
stretching for three-and-a-quarter dark miles – pity the poor
bargemen who had to work the narrowboats through by lying
on their backs and pushing against the walls with their feet.

Wild and remote Marsden Moor, which surrounds the village to the west and south, is largely in the care of the National Trust. The estate – along with several reservoirs also to be found on the moors – forms an area of outstanding scenery ideal for walking, with around 100 miles of footpaths and trails. Buckstones car park, on the A640, is a good place to start.

TAKE A BOAT TRIP
Standedge Tunnel and Visitor Centre
canalrivertrust.org.uk
Waters Road, Marsden, HD7 6NQ
01484 844298
Fancy a canal ride with a difference? Then this is for you, as you can take a trip through the longest canal tunnel in Britain on family-friendly guided boat trips. Afterwards, you can stop for a bite to eat at the Watersedge cafe where the children can let off steam in the playground and explore the wildlife centre.

EAT AND DRINK
A Month of Sundaes
amonthofsundaes.com
Marsden, HD7 6BR
01484 845868
This is a place where all the family can enjoy a traditional ice cream sundae, or two. There are 18 flavours to choose from, all changing on a regular basis,

so there's always something different to try. It's not just the sundaes, though – they have a great range of ice cream cakes too, and don't forget to try one of their gourmet beef burgers. Artwork and photographs are displayed on the walls of The Gallery, upstairs.

The Olive Branch
olivebranch.uk.com
Manchester Road, HD7 6LU
01484 844487
Enter this traditional 19th-century inn on a former packhorse route above the River Colne and the Huddersfield Canal and you'll find yourself in a rambling series of rooms, fire-warmed in winter. There's some good brasserie-style food, and you can enjoy a pint of Greenfield Dobcross Bitter from Saddleworth on the sun deck and admire the views of Marsden Moor.

▶ Masham MAP REF 336 A6
Masham's (pronounced Massam) most obvious and welcoming feature is its vast central Market Place, one of the largest in the country and providing ample convenient car parking in the middle of the town – handy if you want to discover the craft galleries or stock up on some local produce. Its scale is an indication that Masham was once much more important than it appears today – a pleasant but less bustling town than many.

Masham's location was its making, between Wensleydale's sheep-filled hills and the flatter arable lands of the Vale of York. It was also within easy reach of both Fountains Abbey to the south and Jervaulx Abbey to the north. The Market Place filled up at the weekly markets and during its annual Sheep Fair, both of which date back to 1250.

In medieval times the town belonged to York Minster, and held the status of a peculiar, or outling parish – a name exploited with great success by the Theakston Brewery, famous for its 'Old Peculier' ale. Today, the brewery has a visitor centre and you can see some of the country's few remaining coopers at work, constructing their barrels. The rival Black Sheep Brewery was started by a renegade member of the Theakston family (the black sheep – geddit?), and is also worth further exploration.

For one weekend at the end of each September, Masham hosts the annual jamboree of the Sheep Fair, with rare and prize sheep on display, sheepdog demonstrations, woolly crafts and lots of other fun attractions. The origins of this fair go back to medieval times, when as many as 70,000 sheep changed hands. The event was revived in 1986 when local woman, Susan Cunliffe-Lister, decided that Sheep Aid could be added to events like Live Aid and Fashion Aid as a means of raising money to help alleviate the African famines.

To the west of Masham is one of the least-known Dales, the lonely Colsterdale, with a road that leads to some peace and fine views. It is a fitting place for a memorial to the Yorkshire regiment known as the Leeds Pals, who were massacred in July 1916 during the Battle of the Somme.

TOUR THE BREWERIES
Theakston Brewery and Visitor Centre
theakstons.co.uk
The Brewery, HG4 4YD
01765 680000 | Open daily all year from 10.30; closing times vary according to time of year
The Theakston Brewery was first established in 1827 by Robert Theakston. At the Brewery Visitor Centre – originally the stables which housed the dray horses – you can discover how the famous ales are brewed. The centre is called The Black Bull in Paradise after the first inn and the land (Paradise Field) that Theakston bought. Experience the taste and aromas of English hops and malted barley before sampling the beers in the brewery tap. There is plenty to do and see, including the working cooperage where the cooper hand-crafts the oak barrels – one of the last two remaining craft brewery coopers in the country. Guided tours run four times a day – book well ahead.

10 quirky things to do

- **Go Husky Trekking**
  Pesky Husky – peskyhusky.co.uk
  page 223
- **Go Mountain Boarding**
  Another World Adventure Centre – anotherworld adventurecentre.co.uk
  page 116
- **Explore the Lakes in a Coracle**
  Swinton Park Hotel – swintonpark.com
  page 194
- **Get Digging**
  DIG – digyork.com
  page 310
- **Get Scared**
  Whitby Walks – whitbywalks.com
  page 298
- **Drive a Steam Train**
  North Yorkshire Moors Railway – nymr.co.uk
  page 206
- **Travel through a Canal Tunnel**
  Standedge Tunnel and Visitor Centre – canalrivertrust.org.uk
  page 192
- **Relive the Cold War**
  York Cold War Bunker – english-heritage.org.uk
  page 307
- **Get On a Bike**
  3 Peaks Cycles – 3peakscycles.com
  page 257
- **Go Whale Watching**
  Whitby Whale Watching – whitbywhalewatching.net
  page 298

Black Sheep Brewery Visitor Centre
blacksheepbrewery.com
Wellgarth, HG4 4EN
01765 680100 | Mon–Wed 10–5, Thu–Sat 10am–11pm, Sun 10–5
Set up by Paul Theakston in the former Wellgarth Maltings in 1992, the complex includes an excellent visitor centre and a popular bar-cum-bistro. Tour the brewhouse and fermenting room to learn how beer is made, then take in the wonderful views over the River Ure and surrounding countryside as you sup tip-top pints of Riggwelter and Golden Sheep. Finally, tuck into a good plate of food. There are plenty of black sheep-themed goodies in the gift shop, too. Tours are popular, so book ahead.

GET ON THE WATER

Swinton Park Hotel
swintonpark.com
Masham, HG4 4JH | 01765 680900
Fancy learning about the 10,000-year history and construction of coracles while exploring the lakes at Swinton Park? Coracle-maker Dave Purvis is on hand to explain all – and there's even the option of a two-day coracle building course too, but make sure you book this in advance.

EAT AND DRINK

Bordar House
13 The Market Place, HG4 4DZ
01765 689118
Sit in Masham's huge market square and enjoy a delicious afternoon tea with Yorkshire

teacakes or home-made fruitcake and Wensleydale cheese. This is a proper old-fashioned tea shop where light lunches of omelette and chips, or toasted sandwiches are the order of the day. A blackboard has daily specials.

Samuel's at Swinton Park ●●●

swintonpark.com
HG4 4JH | 01765 680900
Swinton Park provides the opportunity to get a taste of grand Downton Abbey-style aristocratic life in a truly splendid house, originally built in the 1690s but added to over the years, and owned by the same family since the 1880s. The 200-acre estate provides produce for the restaurant – Samuel's is the jewel in this sparkly crown, and it's headed-up by Simon Crannage, a man with prodigious talent and a passion for contemporary culinary goings on. The dining room is an unruffled space with an ornate ceiling and views over the lake and gardens. There's a cookery school in the former Georgian stable block.

Vennell's ●●

vennellsrestaurant.co.uk
7 Silver Street, HG4 4DX
01765 689000
Vennell's is one of the town's irresistible lures – it's the sort of neighbourhood eatery that, by punching above its weight, has become a destination for out-of-towners. Four dinners and one lunch a week keep things on a tight rein, and enable a style of cooking that's all about minute attention to detail.

The White Bear

thewhitebearhotel.co.uk
Wellgarth, HG4 4EN
01765 689319
Theakston Brewery's flagship inn stands just a short stroll from the legendary brewhouse and the market square. There's a snug taproom for quaffing pints of Old Peculier by the glowing fire, oak-floored lounges with deep sofas and chairs for perusing the daily papers, and an elegant dining room. Menus promise good Yorkshire fare and there's regular live music.

▶ **PLACES NEARBY**

Visit Marmion Tower, with its royal connection, go fishing on Leighton Reservoir or riding in Swinton.

Marmion Tower

english-heritage.org.uk
West Tanfield | 0370 333 1181
Open daily 10–4
Southwest of Masham, seek out this solid-looking 15th-century gatehouse near the church in West Tanfield, which once led to the stately riverside home of the Marmion family. William Parr, brother of Catherine, Henry VIII's last wife, later owned the place. You can walk through the vaulted gate passage, and look up to see an elegant little oriel window on the outside wall. The spiral

stairs lead up inside the square tower to what were once the living chambers.

Leighton Reservoir

leightonflyfishing.co.uk
01765 689024 / 01765 689224
Day tickets for fishing are for sale in the car park – you'll need the correct money, as payment uses an envelope system. Rainbow trout are in the quarry.

Masham Riding & Trekking Centre

mashamridingcentre.com
Home Farm, Swinton, HG4 4JH
01765 689636
This small rural riding centre provides trekking and basic riding lessons in an outdoor arena. There are 18 horses and ponies to choose from and the riding centre caters for all levels of riding skill and all ages of rider.

▶ Middleham   MAP REF 335 F4

Middleham's claim to be the smallest town in Yorkshire is not the least of its noteworthy features; it also has two cobbled market squares and a collection of around 15 horseracing stables that have seen it referred to as the 'Newmarket of the North'. It has certainly produced its share of race winners since the first racehorses were trained here in the 1730s, and of course the racecourses of Thirsk, Ripon, Wetherby and York are all nearby. Stay here overnight and you'll probably wake up to the sound of hooves on cobbles as the stable lads and lasses ride the horses up to the gallops on the moors above the town for an early-morning workout.

The most important landmark in the town is its magnificent Norman castle – which is in a pretty good state of preservation, thanks to the care of English Heritage. Bits of it date back to 1170. Middleham Castle was put on the map by Richard III, who first came here in 1461 when he was Duke of Gloucester. His tutor in riding and other skills was Richard Neville, the Earl of Warwick – better known to history as Warwick the Kingmaker – and Richard married Neville's daughter, Anne, in 1472. They stayed at Middleham after marriage – their son, Edward, was born in the castle – and lived here until Richard became king in 1483, when he was required to leave for London. Edward died at the age of just 11 in 1484, swiftly followed by his mother. Richard himself was killed in 1485 at the Battle of Bosworth Field, and Middleham fell back into obscurity.

As Duke of Gloucester, Richard would have attended Middleham's church, St Alkelda's, much of which dates back to the 13th and 14th centuries. The dedication is to a Saxon princess, murdered by Danes around AD 800 – she also gives

▲ Middleham Castle

her name to a nearby holy well, or spring. Inside the church you can see a replica of the Middleham Jewel, a 15th-century gold reliquary pendant discovered near the castle by an enthusiast with a metal detector.

From the lower marketplace are good views down the dale – and with plenty of accommodation, pubs, tea shops, gift shops and eating places, Middleham shows that it's indeed a small town with much to offer.

TAKE IN SOME HISTORY
Middleham Castle
english-heritage.org.uk
Castle Hill, DL8 4QG
01969 623899 | Open Apr–Oct daily 10–6, Nov–Mar Sat–Sun 10–4
Explore the maze of rooms and passageways at this impressive castle, once the boyhood home of the ill-fated Richard III. Head to the oak viewing gallery for magnificent views over Wensleydale.

ENTERTAIN THE FAMILY
The Forbidden Corner
theforbiddencorner.co.uk
Tupgill Park Estate, Middleham,
DL8 4TJ | 01969 640638
Open Mar–Oct Mon–Sat 12–6, Sun 10–6, Nov–Dec Sun 12–6; advance booking essential
This is an unusual place, and its reputation grows year by year. Tupgill Park is a four-acre fantasy garden, full of tunnels, follies and surprises. It started almost by accident in 1989 as a private affair, went public five years later and now it's even spawned its own interactive tales for kids. There are strange statues of mythical figures, a huge pyramid of translucent glass, paths and passages that lead nowhere – all very odd.

EAT AND DRINK
The White Swan
whiteswanhotel.co.uk
Market Place, DL8 4PE
01969 622093
Paul Klein's Tudor coaching inn stands in the cobbled market square in the shadow of the castle and – like the village – is steeped in the history of horses and the turf, with several top horseracing stables located in the area. Here, you'll find oak beams, flagstones and roaring log fires in the atmospheric bar, where you can quaff tip-top Black Sheep, Theakstons Best or Wensleydale ales and enjoy modern British and Italian pub food. The menu makes the most of quality Yorkshire produce, and children's portions are available.

▶ Middlesbrough   MAP REF 337 D2

Middlesbrough lies on the extreme northeastern edge of Yorkshire, a sprawling industrial conurbation on the south bank of the River Tees that seems to run effortlessly into Stockton-on-Tees and Billingham. Its landmark feature – and the town's proud symbol – is the magnificent Tees Transporter Bridge, built in 1911, which connects to Port Clarence, across the river.

Middlesbrough grew up on unpromising marshland in the middle of the 19th century, in response to the need to store and ship coal from Witton Park Colliery. When ironstone was found in the Eston Hills, a foundry and rolling mill were built here, and the industrial growth of 'Ironopolis' started in earnest. Later chemical industries are associated with the giant ICI, which pulled out in 2006 to the detriment of the local economy, but the town is still the third largest port in the UK, handling millions of tons of raw materials each year.

Captain James Cook was born in Marton, a farming hamlet long ago swallowed up by the city, but the modern museum opened on the site, in Stewart Park, is well worth seeking out.

TAKE IN SOME HISTORY
Ormesby Hall
nationaltrust.org.uk
Ladgate Lane, Ormesby, TS3 0SR
01642 324188 | Open mid-Mar–Oct, Sat–Sun 1.30–5
Southeast of the town centre lies Ormesby Hall, a handsome Georgian mansion with stables attributed to John Carr of York. Inside the Pennyman family home, you'll see superb examples of plasterwork, furniture and 18th-century pictures. There's also a large model railway, perfect for railway buffs.

VISIT THE MUSEUMS
Captain Cook
Birthplace Museum
captcook-ne.co.uk

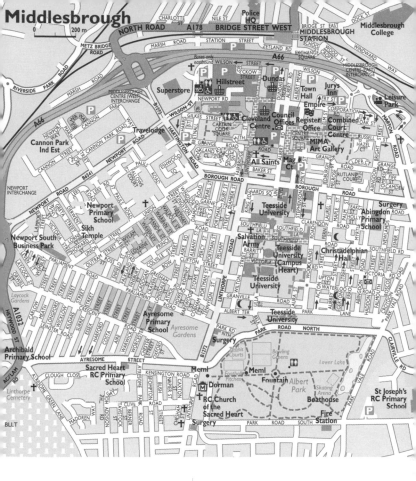

Middlesbrough

Stewart Park, Marton TS7 8AT
01642 311211 | Open Jun–Oct
Tue–Sun 10.30–3.30
Opened to mark the 250th anniversary of the birth of the voyager in 1728, this is a super little museum illustrating the early life of James Cook and his discoveries. Signage around the town is poor, but persist in your search – you'll be rewarded with a wonderful collection of artefacts from Australia, New Zealand and the Pacific, as well as items linked directly to Cook and his voyages of exploration around the globe.

Dorman Museum

dormanmuseum.co.uk
Linthorpe Road, TS5 6LA
01642 813781 | Open Tue–Sun 10.30–3.30
This is Middlesbrough's main museum, with eight galleries and two further exhibition spaces, including plenty of hands-on activities and children's trails. A highlight is the exhibition of pieces from the Linthorpe Pottery, a Victorian success in the town which lasted just 10 years – chief designer was the stylish Christopher Dresser (1834–1904). The pottery is avidly collected today.

10 Yorkshire folk who made good

▶ **James Cook** (1728–1779) – Marton, Middlesbrough – captain who explored and charted the Pacific.

▶ **William Wilberforce** (1759–1833) – Hull – politician and philanthropist, spearheaded the successful campaign to abolish slavery across the British Empire.

▶ **Charlotte Brontë** (1816–55) – Thornton, Bradford – novelist and poet; author of *Jane Eyre*.

▶ **Harry Brearley** (1871–1948) – Sheffield – philanthropist and metallurgist who invented stainless steel.

▶ **Henry Moore** (1898–1986) – Castleford – artist known for semi-abstract sculptures of reclining people.

▶ **Amy Johnson** (1903–41) – Hull – aviatrix, first woman to fly solo to Australia, died after crash into the Thames.

▶ **Harold Wilson** (1916–95) – Huddersfield – Labour Prime Minister twice, winner of four general elections.

▶ **Ted Hughes** (1930–98) – Mytholmroyd – Poet Laureate, Mr Sylvia Plath, and award-winning writer for children (*The Iron Man*).

▶ **Fred Trueman** (1931–2006) – Stainton – cricketing legend, one of the greatest ever fast bowlers, played for England 67 times.

▶ **John Barry** (1933–2011) – York – film score composer; lots of James Bond, *Out of Africa* and *Zulu*.

GET INDUSTRIAL
Tees Transporter Bridge and Visitor Centre
middlesbrough.gov.uk
Ferry Road, TS2 1PL | 01642 247563
This unique structure dominates the Middlesbrough skyline, transporting cars and passengers across the River Tees in just a couple of minutes. The visitor centre tells the history of this fascinating piece of engineering.

TAKE IN SOME ART
Middlesbrough Institute of Modern Art
visitmima.com
Centre Square, TS1 2AZ | 01642 931232 | Open Tue, Wed, Fri and Sat 10–4.30; Thu 10-7; Sun 12–4
Family-friendly art gallery, with a range of special events and exhibitions organised throughout the year. The building is pretty special as well, with its roof terrace providing excellent views of the surrounding area.

Chadwicks Inn Maltby ◉◉
chadwicksinnmaltby.co.uk
High Lane, Maltby, TS8 0BG
01642 590300
Chadwicks is a traditional country pub with an award-winning restaurant. Close to the nearby Thornaby airfields, original memorabilia from World War II is on display. Have a drink in the bar, with its wood-burner and squashy sofas, and dine either in the red-walled snug or under beams in the relaxed and comfortable restaurant.

▶ Newby Hall & Gardens   MAP REF 328 B2

newbyhallandgardens.com

HG4 5AJ | 0845 4504068 | Open Apr–Sep Tue–Sun, Jul–Aug daily;
gardens 11–5.30; house guided tours only

Newby Hall is the epitome of an elegant Georgian stately home,
hidden away in the countryside southeast of Ripon off the
B6265, near Skelton-on-Ure. Still owned by the Compton
family, it's famous for its Robert Adam interiors, and for the
superb herbaceous borders in its extensive gardens.

Its stylish rooms and period furnishings made Newby a
gift for filmmakers seeking the perfect backdrop to Jane
Austen's *Mansfield Park* in 2007. The billiard room is
particularly fine, and contains a splendid portrait of Frederick
Grantham Vyner, an ancestor who was murdered by Greek
bandits. There is a statue gallery, Chippendale furniture to
admire, an overwhelming tapestry room hung all around with
18th-century French tapestries – and, by way of contrast, an
extraordinary collection of more than 100 potties in the
chamber-pot room.

The award-winning gardens are extensive and will appeal as
much to horticultural experts for their plantings as to those
who can simply admire the beauty of their design. The credit
for their creation goes to the present owner's grandfather,
Major Edward Compton, who transformed the grounds from a
nine-hole golf course into gardens that offer something
different in every season of the year.

One leaflet suggests the best walks to appreciate the many
seasonal highlights, and another details the National Collection
of Cornus, or dogwood, which is held here. The Woodland
Discovery Walk leads through an orchard down to the River
Ure, crossing a restored rustic bridge before returning through
Bragget Wood. The walk has been created with the help of
Yorkshire Wildlife Trust, so there's a wealth of good information
in the booklet.

Children will enjoy the miniature railway which runs
alongside the banks of the River Ure, and nearby is an
adventure garden with a timber fort, climbing frames,
pedaloes, swing boats and an interactive water play area.

As you approach the restaurant at Newby Hall, an
old wooden door to the left of the entrance gates bears
the inscription: 'Through these gates Jack Sheppard,
highwayman, escaped from Newgate Prison, 30th August
1724'. The doors were brought to Newby in the 19th century
when the Hall passed by marriage to the Vyner family from
Lincolnshire. Several Vyner ancestors had been Lord Mayor
of London.

▶ **Nidderdale** MAP REF 327 E1

Beautiful Nidderdale might have felt snubbed when it was left out of the Yorkshire Dales National Park – it's since gained some protection from over-development by claiming the status of an Area of Outstanding Natural Beauty. It forms the upper valley of the River Nidd, flowing down from the fells of Great Whernside, and its capital is the bustling market town of Pateley Bridge (see page 213), with the Nidderdale Museum devoted to the area.

The Nidderdale Way is an attractive circular route from the town, covering 53 miles over moorland and meadows around the dale. Nidderdale also features large in the Six Dales Trail (38 miles). There are plenty of shorter walks in the area too – for a good selection to download, see the Nidderdale AONB visitor centre website, visitnidderdaleaonb.com.

Great reservoirs dominate the upper reaches of the valley, constructed to supply Bradford – Gouthwaite Reservoir, northwest of Pateley Bridge, doubles as a bird reserve. Ramsgill is the village at its foot – scenes for the film *Fairy Tale: A True Story* (1997) were shot here. It told the true story of two Yorkshire girls who hoaxed many – including author Arthur Conan Doyle – into believing they had photographed fairies in Cottingley, Bradford.

TREK WITH LLAMAS
Nidderdale Llamas
nidderdalellamas.org
Kiln Farm, Wilsill, Pateley Bridge,
HG3 5EE | 01423 711052
How about discovering Nidderdale's landscape in a different way – with a llama. You don't actually ride a llama, but they make great walking companions, and they even carry your gear for you. A real alternative to walking the dog.

▼ How Stean Gorge in Nidderdale

▸ North York Moors National Park

MAP REF 338 B3

The North York Moors became a National Park in 1952, and covers an area of 554 sq miles, with 26 miles of coastline and scores of appealing little stone villages. It contains one of the largest expanses of heather moorland in the UK – in fact about 40 per cent of the National Park is made up of heather moorland. To see the moors at their colourful best– a sea of pinky-purple – make your visit in the late summer months when the heather is in bloom.

This is agricultural country, with sheep on the tops and cattle on the lower ground. The hardy, black-faced Swaledale sheep are at home on the open moors, and are brought down into the valleys only at lambing times. Take care as you drive along the moorland ridge and roads, as the sheep have only the most rudimentary road sense and are liable to dash into your path without warning. Grouse, raised for shooting, also occupy the moors in significant number.

▾ Captain Cook's Monument, Cleveland Way

The eastern edge of the National Park is defined by the physical boundary of the cliffs which overlook the North Sea. The northern boundary follows the steep scarp slopes of the Cleveland Hills, edging the Tees lowlands and the Hambleton Hills above the Vale of Mowbray to the west. The southern edge follows the indented line of the Tabular Hills and the Vale of Pickering.

The park is a walker's paradise, with around 1,400 miles of public rights of way, including the 110-mile Cleveland Way National Trail, which forms a horseshoe around the area. If you are a fan of great scenic drives, then the North York Moors has some fantastic ones for you – including

▲ Lake Gormire

Chimney Bank in Rosedale, which vies with Cumbria's Hardknott Pass for the steepest road in England, with a gradient of 1 in 3.

The east–west branch line rail link from Whitby to Middlesbrough in the north provides connections to the North Yorkshire Moors steam railway, which operates from Pickering to Whitby via Grosmont (see page 206).

For more information, visit the National Park centres at Sutton Bank and Danby, and check out the website northyorkmoors.org.uk.

▶ North Yorkshire Moors Railway
MAP REF 338 B4

nymr.co.uk

12 Park Street, Pickering, YO18 7AJ | 01751 472508 | Open Apr–Oct daily, Nov–Mar certain days only

The restored North Yorkshire Moors Railway is a remarkable success story. No visit to the area would be complete without a trip along this most scenic and nostalgic of lines. Today the railway is recreational, but it was commerce and industry that provided the original spur for the line to be built. Two centuries ago Whitby was one of the most important ports in the country. By the early 1800s, however, the town's traditional industries – whaling, shipbuilding and alum mining – were in decline and Whitby's traders decided that the town needed to improve the communications over land. In 1831, engineer George Stephenson surveyed the terrain between Whitby and Pickering, recommending a railway line on which the carriages would be horse-drawn. A veritable army of navvies was hired to drive the line over the moors. Armed only with pick and shovel they tackled the rough terrain. The line from Whitby to Pickering opened with the usual fanfare in 1836, when a trainload of dignitaries was pulled along the track at a sedate 10 mph.

The line revitalised the area – a variety of industries, such as ironstone mining, sprang up once a regular train service had been established. A few years later it was converted to carry steam

engines; the first one chugged noisily into Whitby in 1847. The rather troublesome Beck Hole Incline was bypassed by blasting a new route between Beck Hole and Goathland. By the time a new century dawned, the moors and coast were well served with rail links; the trains not only transported goods, they also began to bring visitors from the crowded cities to enjoy the moorland landscape.

In 1965, nearly 130 years of rail services came to a halt. The Esk Valley line was reprieved from the Beeching cuts, but the section of railway line between Pickering and Grosmont was unceremoniously closed. Eight years of careful restoration and hard work later, the line was reopened by the North Yorkshire Moors Railway Preservation Society. More than just another line run by enthusiasts, the North Yorkshire Moors Railway operates a full timetable from April to October.

The 18-mile rail journey takes you into the very heart of the moors – and more than 300,000 passengers travel on it every year, making the railway the biggest single attraction within the National Park. Board the train at Pickering Station (see page 217), which dates from 1845. The line climbs into the spectacular steep-sided, wooded gorge of Newton Dale, before arriving at Levisham Station. Trains also call at Newtondale Halt, the starting point for a number of waymarked walks. The next stop is popular Goathland (see page 105). The northern terminus was traditionally Grosmont (see page 110), but now a selection of services carry on to the main Northern Rail line to Whitby (see page 292).

▶ Northallerton MAP REF 336 C5

Northallerton is a large and prosperous market town in the Vale of Mowbray, between the Pennines and the North York Moors. The town is known for its traditional market, which takes over both sides of the broad High Street on Wednesdays and Saturdays. Don't worry if you see cows in the High Street as there is still a cattle market held in the town as well. Northallerton is the administrative capital of North Yorkshire, and offers a wide choice of independent shops in addition to the omnipresent national chains.

Located on the main Roman highway to the North, the town at one time had a castle, and was fought over by English and Scots seeking advantage. Cattle, sheep and horses would have been driven down the broad main street for the fairs, held four times a year. Today Northallerton makes a great base for exploring the countryside around – with both the Dales and the Moors on your doorstep.

For a more relaxing way to discover the countryside, the Wensleydale Railway runs between Leeming Bar and Redmire in the Yorkshire Dales, offering a scenic and pleasant journey through Herriot Country. Getting to the Wensleydale Railway couldn't be easier – there's a half-hourly bus service from Northallerton to Leeming Bar, which takes just 14 minutes. Other attractions within easy reach include Kiplin Hall (see page 230), The Big Sheep and Little Cow Farm (see page 61) and Mount Grace Priory (see page 210).

PLAY A ROUND
Romanby Golf and Country Club
romanby.com
Yafforth Road, DL7 0PE
01609 778855
Open daily
Set in 200 acres of natural undulating terrain with the River Wiske meandering through, this course offers a testing round of golf for all abilities. In addition to the river, two attractive lakes come into play on the 2nd, 5th and 11th holes. It also has a covered 12-bay floodlit driving range, and a par-3 academy course comprising 6 holes.

EAT AND DRINK
Bettys Café Tea Rooms
bettys.co.uk
188 High Street, DL7 8LF
01609 775154
This branch of Bettys is situated in a listed Georgian building with a domed glass roof, huge window mirrors and a Chusan palm. During the warmer months you can enjoy afternoon tea 'alfresco' in the walled courtyard. Two set teas are offered: a Yorkshire Cream Tea and the Bettys Traditional Afternoon Tea with a choice of sandwiches, a sultana scone with butter, jam and cream, and a selection of miniature cakes.

▶ Nunnington Hall   MAP REF 338 A6

nationaltrust.org.uk
Nunnington, YO62 5UY | 01439 748283 | Open mid-Feb–Oct
Tue–Sun 11–5, Nov–mid-Dec Sat–Sun 11–4

Set in beautiful gardens across the River Rye from tiny
Nunnington village is honey-coloured Nunnington Hall. It's a
tranquil setting that offers no clue to the house's turbulent past
– this isn't one of those stately homes that cruised serenely
through the centuries, while leaving barely a ripple.

Nunnington Hall's early history is sketchy; it is thought to
have been built on the site of a nunnery – hence its name. It
was started by William Parr, brother of Henry VIII's sixth wife
Catherine – he lost the estate after the scandal of trying to set
Lady Jane Grey on the throne. It passed through many hands,
including the Abbot of St Mary's at York.

Most of the building – a concoction of Tudor and Stuart
styles – dates from the 17th century. Among other attractions
you can see the extraordinary hunting trophies in the entrance
hall and the entrancing Carlisle collection of miniature rooms
displayed in the attics. There are also regular art and
photography exhibitions.

It's worth crossing the three-arched bridge and exploring
the village on foot – Nunnington's handsome grey stone houses
are hidden from sight to those who drive straight through. The
church dates largely from the 13th century. Here, in an alcove,
you'll find the effigy of a knight in chain mail. This recumbent
figure commemorates Sir Walter de Teyes, Lord of the Manor of
Nunnington and Stonegrave until his death in 1325.

▼ Nunnington Hall

EAT AND DRINK
Nunnington Hall
nationaltrust.org.uk
Nunnington, YO62 5UY
01439 748283
The food here is top-notch. Cream teas, cakes (try the special Nunnington Fruit Loaf) and light lunches will tempt you. If you're there later in the season, you'll find old apple varieties from the orchard used in pies, crumbles and soups.

The Star Inn ◎◎
thestaratharome.co.uk
Harome, YO62 5JE | 01439 770397
The thatched country pub in a moorland village just outside Helmsley is a perfect crooked house. There's a rustic bar, an old dining room with chunky tables, a real fire and knick-knacks galore, and a newer bar with a bright, contemporary feel. The Star has it all, including friendly staff.

▶ Osmotherley MAP REF 337 D4

This handsome village on the western fringe of the North York Moors, is the starting point of a 42-mile route march across the moors to Ravenscar (see page 222), known as the Lyke Wake Walk. Every weekend walkers climb from their cars, don boots and waterproofs, and head for the high ground. If you're feeling less energetic, you can stroll around the village and explore its tiny handful of shops. Those who manage to work up a healthy appetite will find excellent food on offer in the pubs that surround the old market place.

The Lyke Wake Walk takes its inspiration from the old corpse roads that crossed the moors, along which the deceased were carried to – often distant – burial grounds. Lyke refers to a corpse, as in a church lychgate; wake is the party after a funeral. This fine high-level walk between Osmotherley and Ravenscar was begun in 1955 as a challenge walk, the challenge being to complete the 42 miles within 24 hours.

Northwest of Osmotherley is Mount Grace Priory, though you need to make a rather inconvenient loop on the A19 dual carriageway to reach it. No matter – this is the best preserved of the nine Carthusian priories that were built in England.

TAKE IN SOME HISTORY
Mount Grace Priory
nationaltrust.org.uk
Staddlebridge, DL6 3JG
01609 883494 | Open Apr–Oct
Thu–Mon 10–6, Nov–Mar
Sat–Sun 10–4

The ruins of a 14th-century priory, where monks lived in silence and were isolated as hermits within their own cells. It's set in breathtakingly beautiful woodland surroundings, including a herb garden. Mount Grace was founded in 1398 by Thomas de Holland. The monks were given land, which they rented out to tenant farmers. At the height of their wealth, the income generated by the monks here was even greater than that of their Cistercian neighbours at Rievaulx Abbey (see page 231). Yet the very success of the Carthusian communities contributed to their downfall. Henry VIII ordered them to be disbanded, and in 1539 Mount Grace Priory shut down.

EAT AND DRINK
The Golden Lion
goldenlionosmotherley.co.uk
6 West End, DL6 3AA
01609 883526
There's a warm and welcoming feel to the The Golden Lion, which has been standing for over 250 years. The open fires, bench seating, fresh flowers and whitewashed walls bring a great feel to dining here. The extensive menu ranges through basic pub grub to more refined dishes. Some 60 single malt whiskies are on offer, together with three real ales.

▶ **Otley** MAP REF 327 F4

When the TV soap *Emmerdale* wanted a town that could give them a bustling livestock market for filming, they chose Otley in Lower Wharfedale. You'll still find cattle markets on Mondays and Fridays, with general street markets on Tuesdays, Fridays and Saturdays. Otley also has one of the oldest agricultural shows in the country, dating back to 1796. At first just a cattle show, today it is a highlight of the Otley calendar and includes rare breeds and the splendid shire horses – catch it in May.

Otley is a busy working town, but with attractive 17th- and 18th-century buildings and streets with ancient names, such as Kirkgate, Bondgate and Boroughgate. As well as the cotton and woollen mills that you might expect to find along the River Wharfe, the town developed particular skills at the end of the 19th century in paper-making and printing.

Thomas Chippendale (1718–79), one of the world's most celebrated furniture makers and designers, was born here. His family were joiners and he served his apprenticeship here, probably at a shop in Boroughgate. You'll find a statue of him by the former grammar school.

In the churchyard of All Saints, look out for a memorial fashioned as a miniature castellated tunnel-mouth. It's a representation of the nearby Bramhope railway tunnel, and dedicated to the 24 men who died in its construction between 1845 and 1849. A curious long, low Toblerone-shaped construction in the same churchyard, nicknamed the Donkey Stone, apparently marks the grave of Methodist preacher John

▲ Lower Wharfedale

Wesley's faithful horse, Robert, who died in 1782. Wesley was a frequent visitor to the town, where he would stay with his good friends the Ritchie family, on Boroughgate.

The hill behind the town is Otley Chevin, and stone quarried from here went to build the Houses of Parliament in London. Its forest park offers good facilities for walkers and cyclists, with great views over the surrounding countryside.

GET OUTDOORS
Otley Chevin Forest Park
chevinforest.co.uk
The Whitehouse Café and Visitor Centre, LS21 3JL | 01943 465023
This escarpment above the town is preserved as a nature reserve, with varied woodland, heathland and meadow habitats. Great Dib Wood is noted for the geological feature, the Otley Shell Bed – fossilised marine creatures are sandwiched between the mudstone and the limestone. Park at East Chevin Quarry or Surprise View (J M W Turner loved this view), and explore the network of paths and bridleways. There are plenty of self-guided walks through the forest, but if you're feeling a bit braver how about a spot of orienteering, or the new craze of geocaching?

WATCH RUGBY
Otley Rugby Union Football Club
pitchero.com/clubs/otley
Cross Green, LS21 1HE
01943 461180
Watch a local game at this famous club, founded in 1865. The First XV team play in National League Two, while the second team, Saracens, play in the Yorkshire Premier League. Occasional international matches are played here, too.

EAT AND DRINK
Black Bull
Market Place, Otley, LS21 3AQ
01943 462288
Cromwell's troops are believed to have stopped here for refreshments on their way to battle at Marston Moor in 1644. Modern visitors can enjoy the excellent food and award-winning beers.

**Chevin Country Park
Hotel & Spa**
crerarhotels.com
Yorkgate, LS21 3NU | 01943 467818
Part of a Scottish chain, this
hotel is tucked away in 40 acres
of private woodland, complete
with three lakes, extensive
gardens and abundant wildlife
– which makes the short drive
from Leeds/Bradford Airport
seem a world away. And it's not
your usual hotel either – the
restaurant is actually housed
in a huge log cabin, and the
bedrooms are mostly scattered
around the grounds in chalets.
The modern menus – including
à la carte and a steak and grill
menu – are full of crowd-
pleasers, and local produce
features strongly. The spa is a
perfect place to relax after a
hectic day out in Yorkshire.

▶ Pateley Bridge MAP REF 327 F2

The main attraction at Pateley Bridge (often shortened to
Pateley) is the Nidderdale Museum, housed in the town's
former workhouse, but this bustling little market town is also
a good base for visiting places of interest nearby. Many of the
buildings date from the 18th and 19th centuries, when the town
flourished with thriving local industries and a vital railway link.
A relic of that bustling age is The Oldest Sweet Shop in the
World – in business since 1827, and its claim officially
confirmed by the *Guinness Book of World Records* in 2014 – a
heavenly emporium full of handmade and retro confectionery.

North of Pateley Bridge, near Lofthouse, is How Stean Gorge
– Yorkshire's 'Little Switzerland'. The ravine of up to 80 feet
deep was hacked out of the limestone in the Ice Age.

To the west of Pateley Bridge, on the B6265, are the Stump
Cross Caverns. Only discovered in the mid-19th century, these
showcaves have given up fossil bones as much as 200,000
years old, from creatures such as bison, reindeer and
wolverines that once wandered the region.

VISIT THE MUSEUMS
AND GALLERIES
Nidderdale Museum
nidderdalemuseum.com
The Old Workhouse, King Street,
HG3 5LE | 01423 711225
Open Easter–Oct daily 1.30–4.30,
Nov–Easter Sat– Sun 1.30–4.30
Everything you could want
to know about life in
Nidderdale is here, from the
spread of religion and the
development of transport to
collections of cameras and
razors that have been owned
by local people. Some of the
most enjoyable exhibits are the
reconstructed cobbler's shop,
general store, milliner's shop,
joiner's shop and solicitor's
office. All of them contain
fascinating memorabilia, and
the whole museum is much
loved and well looked after.

GO PARAGLIDING
Active Edge
activeedge.co.uk

The Mill, Glasshouses, HG3 5QH

0845 1298286 or 07793 678133

Ever wanted to see the beautiful Yorkshire countryside from above? You'll get a bird's-eye view while trying your hand at an exhilarating new sport. Find out what it's like to take control of a paraglider and soar above the rolling Yorkshire Dales on a paragliding fun day.

GO SHOPPING
The Oldest Sweet Shop in the World
oldestsweetshop.co.uk

39 High Street, HG3 5JZ

01423 712371

Throw caution and dental cares to the wind and indulge in a bag of whatever you fancy, from humbugs, pear drops or parma violets to space dust, raspberry bonbons and pomfret cakes.

EAT AND DRINK
The Old Granary Tea Shop
oldgranary.net

17 High Street, HG3 5AP

01423 711852

In the centre of the town, you'll find that the Granary is perfect for a quick bite or a light lunch. As well as teas and coffees, the tasty homemade apple crumble is popular.

High Street Fisheries
16 High Street, HG3 5AW

01423 711831

It might be the only fish and chip shop in Pateley Bridge, but that certainly doesn't mean they rest on their laurels here. Their traditional British fish and chips are arguably some of the best in the Harrogate district – and they'll be welcome after a walk in the countryside.

▶ PLACES NEARBY
This part of the world is defined by its landscape, and nearby there are many gorges and caverns to explore. Fishing at Scar House Reservoir is popular, and south of Pateley Bridge is the Bewerley Riding Centre. Be sure to see Andrew Sabin's impressive sculpture at Greenhow Hill.

How Stean Gorge
howstean.co.uk

Near Lofthouse, HG3 5SY

01423 755666 | Open daily 10–5

Pay your entrance fee, don a hard hat and follow the rocky pathways that lead by the fast-flowing river through ferns and by lush, dank undergrowth; there are bridges on different levels and fenced galleries on rocky ledges. There are also caves here, the best known being Tom Taylor's Cave, with a 530-foot walk underground – you might want to take a torch. Wellies are recommended. The tea room serves up 'traditional Yorkshire grub' – roast beef and Yorkshire pudding is a speciality, but the raspberry pavlovas have also acquired a following. Delicious cakes and aromatic freshly ground coffee may also tempt you to linger here.

▲ How Stean Gorge

Stump Cross Caverns

stumpcrosscaverns.co.uk
Greenhow Hill, HG3 5JL
01756 752780 | Open mid-Feb–Nov
daily 10–5.30, Dec–mid-Feb Sat–Sun
10–5.30

Discovered by the Newbould
brothers in 1860, Stump Cross
Caverns have been an attraction
for visitors since 1863, when
one shilling was charged for
entrance. Among the few
limestone show caves in
Britain, these require no special
clothing, experience or
equipment. Stalagmites,
stalactites and calcite
precipitation make for an eerie
day out, west of Pateley Bridge.

Scar House Reservoir

nidderdaleaonb.org.uk
01423 712950

Fishing for wild brown trout
here is controlled by the
Nidderdale Angling Club. Day
tickets are available from
Pateley Bridge and Lofthouse
post offices.

Bewerley Riding Centre

bewerleyridingcentre.co.uk
Bewerley Old Hall Cottage,
HG3 5JA | 01423 712249
The centre offers tailor-made
riding holidays for adults and
children of all abilities.

The *Coldstones Cut*

thecoldstonescut.org
Greenhow Hill, HG3 5JL
Just to the west of Pateley
Bridge is Yorkshire's largest
free attraction. Created by the
artist Andrew Sabin, *Coldstones
Cut* is a massive sculpture
which overlooks the huge
working Coldstones Quarry. Be
prepared for a trek, as the
footpath to the top climbs 130
feet over 1,640 feet from the car
park at the Toft Gate Lime Kiln.

Crown Hotel

Middlesmoor, HG3 5ST
01423 755204
Nearly 1,000 feet up, towards
the head of Nidderdale,
Middlesmoor commands a fine
view over Gouthwaite Reservoir.
This family-run free house
dates back to the 17th century
and is perfect for anyone
following the popular
Nidderdale Way. Enjoy a pint of
local beer and food by the
roaring fire, or outside in the
sunny pub garden. A large
selection of malt whiskies is
also on offer.

▶ The Pennine Way MAP REF 326 C3, 334 C4

nationaltrail.co.uk

Britain's first long-distance footpath is the ultimate challenge for many keen walkers, and is now designated a National Trail. Its 256 miles from Derbyshire to Scotland includes a 60-mile stretch in the Yorkshire Dales, entering near Keighley and leaving past the lonely Tan Hill Inn (see page 277), where Yorkshire gives way to Durham. It's named for the Pennine mountain range, which runs down northern England like a knobbly backbone.

One of the walk's main instigators was Tom Stephenson, secretary of the Ramblers' Association at the time, and 2,000 ramblers attended the route's official opening on 24 April 1965 on Malham Moor. Though the route near Pen-y-Ghent gives a rugged climb over moors scarred by caves and potholes, there are easier and more low-lying stretches, such as along Airedale, south of Malham, which are all well signposted.

▼ Haworth Moor close to Top Withins on the Pennine Way

▶ Pen-y-Ghent MAP REF 334 C6

The lowest but not the least of Yorkshire's Three Peaks,
Pen-y-Ghent in profile seems to be thrusting a jaw out defiantly
– as if challenging anyone to climb to the top of its 2,277 feet.
Many people assume it is the third highest peak in the
Yorkshire Dales – as it is the third highest of the Three Peaks
– but that's not the case. That honour goes to Buckden Pike,
some 10 miles across Wharfedale, which is 25 feet higher than
Pen-y-Ghent. Unusually for a Yorkshire hill, Pen-y-Ghent
carries a Celtic name, meaning 'hill of the border', and it once
marked the edge of a British tribe's kingdom. If you fancy
climbing to the top, the most common route is a three-mile
hike from Horton-in-Ribblesdale (see page 135), following the
signs for the Pennine Way, which passes right over the summit
of the hill (see page 216).

At the end of the track out of Horton, just beyond the point
where the route turns sharp right towards the hill, there are
two potholes. The larger is the huge gaping hole known as Hull
Pot, into which Hull Pot Beck disappears. You should treat both
these potholes with extreme caution.

The climb to the summit of Pen-y-Ghent is steep in places,
with a little bit of scrambling, but it's well worth the climb. At
the top you are rewarded with views across to the other peaks,
north across the fells of Langstrothdale Chase, and south over
Ribblesdale and Lancashire's Forest of Bowland.

▶ Pickering MAP REF 338 B5

Historic Pickering lies just to the south of the National Park,
dominated by the spectacular walls of its ruined medieval
motte and bailey castle. It's a bustling place, terminus of the
popular North Yorkshire Moors Railway (see page 206), and
home to the Beck Isle Museum, which is stuffed full of local
curiosities – this is a good place to explore if you're waiting for
the train. Pickering Beck, which flows down from the moors
and straight past the museum house, has an unfortunate
tendency to flood – in 2013 the go-ahead for a flood defence
scheme for the town was finally given, and with luck the
museum and the rest of the lower town will keep its feet dry
in the future.

Overlooking the marketplace is the large parish church
dedicated to saints Peter and Paul. Hemmed in by houses and
shops, the building is approached by narrow gates (streets) and
ginnels (alleys). Inside you can see some remarkably vivid
15th-century frescoes illustrating scenes from the lives of
saints and martyrs. St George slays a dragon, Thomas à Becket

expires in the cathedral; St Edmund raises his eyes towards heaven as arrows fired by Vikings pierce his flesh.

After the Norman Conquest, William I created outposts in the north to establish order and quell uprisings – Pickering was one of these strategic sites. The first castle was built to a basic motte-and-bailey design; by the 12th century, the wooden keep and outer palisade had been rebuilt in stone. It was besieged by Robert the Bruce on one of his incursions south of the border. When the Scots inflicted a heavy defeat on the army led by Edward II in 1322, the King found shelter here. The castle saw no further military action, and was used by a succession of monarchs as a hunting lodge. Some parts of the old forest are still royal properties, but Pickering Castle is now in the hands of English Heritage.

TAKE IN SOME HISTORY
Pickering Castle
english-heritage.org.uk
Castlegate, YO18 7AX
01751 474989 | Open Apr–Jun, Sep
Thu–Mon 10–5, Jul–Aug daily 10–6
A splendid 12th-century castle, originally built by William the Conqueror. Visit the exhibition on the castle's history and take in the views from the keep.

VISIT THE MUSEUM
Beck Isle Museum
beckislemuseum.org.uk
Bridge Street, YO18 8DU
01751 473653 | Open mid-Feb to
Nov daily 10–5 (Feb–Mar & Oct–
Nov 10–4)

Housed in a fine Regency-era town house close to Pickering Beck, the museum offers fascinating glimpses into the more recent past. Successive rooms are devoted to different aspects of bygone life in town and country; you can visit the cobbler's, gents' outfitters, kitchen, barber's shop and even the bar of a public house.

GO WALKING
Newtondale Horse Trail
ldwa.org.uk
Follow this 37-mile circuit, waymarked on bridleways and roads, through the dramatic gorge of Newtondale between Pickering and Grosmont. It's a route for serious walkers and

▼ Pickering station

you should plan your route carefully. The landscape is varied and remote, encompassing farmland, forest and open high moor.

EAT AND DRINK
The White Swan Inn ◉◉
white-swan.co.uk
Market Place, YO18 7AA
01751 472288
The White Swan is a venerable stone-built inn dating from the Tudor period, and was once a stopping-off point for the York-to-Whitby stagecoach. Today it's run with a clear eye to its role in the community, being a welcoming hostelry for locals, and a prime destination for regionally sourced eating. The kitchen philosophy is all about feeding patrons on good Yorkshire produce that isn't overly mucked about with ('we don't do froths and smudges', says chef). Rare-breed meats from the celebrated Ginger Pig butcher in nearby Levisham, local cheeses, fish from Whitby and veg from the allotment all feature proudly. There are vegetarian options, and children are also welcome.

▶ Pocklington MAP REF 330 A4

Pocklington is more than just a commuter town for York, Hull and Leeds – although its Wolds location gives it that convenient advantage. Pock – as the locals call it – is a classic market town, its skyline dominated by the 15th-century tower of All Saints Church, known as the Cathedral of the Wolds. Things might have been different in this now modest town – at the time of the Domesday survey, it was second only to York in size. The canal spur that facilitated its status as a wool trading centre, by linking it to the River Derwent, was abandoned in the mid-20th century, but is gradually being coaxed back to life by local enthusiasts. Meanwhile the sleepy backwater makes a pleasant place to stroll and enjoy the wildlife.

GO ROUND THE GARDENS
Burnby Hall Garden and Stewart Museum
burnbyhallgardens.com
33 The Balk, YO42 2QF
01759 307125 | Open daily, mid–Mar-Oct 10–5.30, Nov–mid-Mar 10–4
The two lakes in this garden hold the National Collection of more than 100 varieties of hardy water lilies. The lakes stand within nine acres of beautiful gardens: heather beds, a rock garden, an aviary garden with spring and summer bedding, a woodland walk, a stumpery and a Victorian garden. The museum contains sporting trophies and ethnic material gathered on Major Percy Stewart's world-wide travels between 1906 and 1926. Listen out for band concerts every other Sunday and various events throughout the summer.

▶ Pontefract MAP REF 324 A1

Almost overshadowed by neighbouring Wakefield, this historic town nevertheless has two very particular claims to fame – its famous racecourse, and a liquorice sweet manufactured in the town and even named after it.

There's a pub in the market place uniquely named The Liquorice Bush, in celebration of the liquorice that used to be grown in the fields around here. It's a plant that requires well-drained sandy soil, and its fibrous roots are boiled up to produce a sweet extract or flavouring widely used in the tobacco industry. Chemist George Dunhill of Pontefract was the first to use it to flavour sweetened confectionery in 1760, producing tarry, chewy coin-like discs called Pontefract or Pomfret cakes. Haribo took over the original Dunhills factory in 1972 and are still making the sweet today, although the liquorice is no longer grown locally. Its contribution to the town is celebrated each July in the Liquorice Festival – allsorts are welcome.

The history of racing in the town goes back further, to the days when there was a castle here – before Cromwell's men got their hands on it in the Civil War and reduced it to rings of rubble. Flat meadows on the edge of town made the perfect spot for the sport, until interest died out in Georgian times. The fashion revived in the 19th century, however, and the three-mile circuit is now one of the best known in Yorkshire.

TAKE IN SOME HISTORY
Pontefract Castle
pontefractcastle.co.uk
Castle Chain, WF8 1QH
01977 723440 | Grounds open
Mon–Fri 8.30–4.30, Sat–Sun
9.30–4.30; Visitor Centre open
daily 11–3

Pontefract Castle, or Pomfret Castle as it was also known, was once one of the greatest fortresses in England. You can explore the underground magazine which was cut out of the solid rock – and see where Civil War prisoners carved their names into the cell walls. King Richard II is said to have been murdered in the castle in 1399.

GO TO THE RACES
Pontefract Racecourse
pontefract-races.co.uk
Park Road, Pontefract, WF8 4QD
01977 781307

Racing is recorded in Pontefract as early as 1648, just before the castle was taken by the forces of Oliver Cromwell. Pontefract's course holds a full programme of racing and special events.

▶ PLACES NEARBY

A mix of entertainment and wildlife is near Pontefract. Just off the M62 is Xscape Yorkshire, to the northwest is Diggerland and the RSPB Fairburn Ings reserve is to the north.

▲ Pontefract Castle

Xscape Yorkshire

xscapeyorkshire.co.uk

Xscape Yorkshire, Colorado Way, Castleford, WF10 4TA

01977 664794

This huge leisure complex northwest of Pontefract offers a vast array of family activities, including a large artificial indoor snow slope, a real wave simulating surf venue, a kids' soft play centre, a 14-screen cinema, a climbing wall, an aerial assault course, cosmic golf and laser games, 20 bowling lanes, Yorkshire's first trampoline park, an indoor skate-park, urban and outdoor retailers and a wide variety of bars and restaurants. Phew...

Diggerland

diggerland.com

Willowbridge Lane, Whitwood, WF10 5NW | 0871 227 7007

Contact Diggerland for details of opening times

Experience the thrills of driving real big and mean earth-moving equipment at this family adventure park. There are many challenges to complete, including the Dumper Truck Challenge, or perhaps dig for buried treasure (supervised by an instructor). Rides include JCB Robots, Diggerland Dodgems, Go-karts, Land Rover Safari, Spin Dizzy and the Diggerland Tractors. Snack wagons, picnic areas and an indoor play area complete the day. Diggerland is northwest of the town, west of Castleford.

RSPB Nature Reserve Fairburn Ings

rspb.org.uk

The Visitor Centre, Newton Lane, Ledston, WF10 2BH | 01977 628191

Open Mar–Oct daily 9–5, Nov–Feb 9–4

One-third of the 700-acre RSPB reserve is open water,

and more than 270 species of birds have been recorded. A visitor centre provides information, and there's an elevated boardwalk suitable for visitors with disabilities. You'll see lots of wildlife here whatever the season.

Wentbridge House Hotel ⚫⚫
wentbridgehouse.co.uk
The Great North Road, Wentbridge, WF8 3JJ | 01977 620444
Set in 20 acres of landscaped grounds in a West Yorkshire conservation village, Wentbridge is a stone-built grand manor house built at the turn of the 18th century. It had long associations with the Leatham family, luminaries of Barclays Bank, but became a country hotel in 1960. A degree of glossy formality prevails within, not least in the Fleur de Lys dining room, where candy-coloured upholstery creates a light, bright effect, and the cooking reaches out in all directions for its references.

▶ Ravenscar   MAP REF 339 D3

Great things were planned for the tiny village of Ravenscar. At the end of the 19th century, a developer called John Septimus Bland decided to build a holiday resort that he thought would rival Whitby and Scarborough. A station was built and Bland laid out the town's network of roads and began to build shops and houses. But Bland's company went bankrupt, and work stopped. Despite the panoramic sea views, this exposed site was clearly unsuitable for such a development. It is geologically unstable, and visitors would have been faced with an awkward descent to the stony beach far below.

You can see Ravenscar's street layout today, though grass is growing where the buildings ought to have been. When the Raven Hall Hotel was built in 1774, it was simply Raven Hall. Converted to a hotel in 1895, it was to have been the centrepiece of the resort; now it stands alone, its mock battlements a landmark for miles around.

The Romans built a signal station here; its foundations and an inscribed stone (on display in Whitby Museum and Pannett Art Gallery, see page 296) were found when Raven Hall's own foundations were being laid. The signal station relayed warnings of Anglo-Saxon invaders to military bases.

This part of the coastline was exploited in the 17th century for alum, used in dyeing to fix colours permanently. Remains of the quarries and buildings can be found to the north of the town.

The geology of this coastline is worth a closer look. You can clearly see the fault line that runs along the coast between

Boulby and Scarborough at Ravenscar. At low tide the rocky shoreline is revealed as a series of concentric curves, formed from layers of hard and soft rock, eroded by the waves over millions of years.

This is excellent walking country, on either the beach or cliff top. The Cleveland Way and the trackbed of the old Whitby–Scarborough railway, open to walkers and cyclists, are nearby. Ravenscar is also the finish of the 42-mile hike across the moors from Osmotherley, known as the Lyke Wake Walk (see page 210).

GET INDUSTRIAL
Ravenscar Coastal Centre
nationaltrust.org.uk
Ravenscar | 01723 870423
Open Apr–Nov 10–4.30
Find out more about the area and its history. There's also an exhibition at the Old Coastguard Station.

GO HUSKY TREKKING
Pesky Husky
peskyhusky.co.uk
Meeting House Farm,
Staintondale, YO13 0EL
01723 870521
As days out go, it doesn't get much better than this for dog-lovers. Siberian huskies love to run as a team, and with Pesky Husky Trekking you become a 'musher' – an integral part of the team. You can also try out two-wheeled Pawtrekker scooters – powered by two of the strongest huskies. You can meet the dogs and join them for walkies year-round, but they're used to working in cool conditions so trekking operates from October to the end of March only.

PLAY A ROUND
Raven Hall Country House Hotel
ravenhall.co.uk
YO13 0ET | 01723 870353
Open daily
Opened by the Earl of Cranbrook in 1898, this nine-hole clifftop course is sloping and with good-quality small greens. Because of its clifftop position it is subject to strong winds which make it lively to play, especially the sixth hole.

EAT AND DRINK
Ravenscar Tea Rooms
ravenscartearooms.com
1 Station Square, Ravenscar,
YO13 0LU | 01723 870444
With 12 sorts of tea and six coffees, this corner cafe offers a wide choice. Based in one of the few buildings – part of the station – that were erected in what was planned to be a coastal resort to rival Scarborough, the cafe also offers home-baked cakes, hot food and spectacular cliff-top and sea views.

▶ Reeth MAP REF 335 E3

Tucked quietly away in the junction where Arkengarthdale meets Swaledale, Reeth has an air of being larger and more important than the other Swaledale villages. The huge open green surrounded by 18th-century houses certainly helps with that view, and a well-known landmark is the miniature suspension bridge across the River Swale. Today, Reeth is an attractive centre for tourism, with general shops, craft shops, pubs, guest houses and one of the Dales' most popular museums. The Friday market is a rather small affair compared to others in the Dales, but there's an annual agricultural show around the beginning of September each year.

The Swaledale Folk Museum, which also acts as an information centre for visitors, is hidden away behind the post office on the far eastern side of the Green. Inside there are particularly good displays on the local industries over the years: farming and lead-mining, as well as knitting and dry-stone walling. The farming is still here, but the lead mining is long gone.

About three miles west of Reeth, on the minor road that goes north from Feetham, is Surrender Bridge. Over the bridge on the right is a track that takes you to the remains of the Surrender Lead Smelting Mill, now a scheduled Ancient Monument. There were extensive lead workings in this area, and the industry dates from Roman times, reaching its peak in the 18th century.

VISIT THE MUSEUM

Swaledale Folk Museum
swaledalemuseum.org
The Green, DL11 6TX
01748 884118 | Open Apr–Sep
An excellent museum run by volunteers that illustrates the history of the area.

GO FISHING

You can fish the River Swale from Keld to Grinton Bridge. Day tickets are available from the Bridge Inn, Grinton and from the post office in Reeth. Water levels can be unreliable in summer, so seek some local advice first.

▶ PLACES NEARBY

Near to Reeth you can hire a bike, see a working farm and eat at a couple of good pubs.

Dales Bike Centre
dalesbikecentre.co.uk
Parks Barn, Fremington, DL11 6AW
01748 884908
Hire a bike and go exploring on one of their top-quality Trek hire bikes. The price includes a helmet, route map, pump and a handy spares pack.

Hazel Brow Farm
hazelbrow.co.uk
Low Row, DL11 6NE
01748 886224

West of Reeth you'll find this 200-acre organic working farm where you can interact with the livestock, discover nature trails and watch the sheep-shearing demonstrations and other events. April and May are the best months to see lambs. With tray bakes, fresh scones, carrot cake and perhaps a 'Hazelbrowman's lunch', the organic cafe at Hazel Brow strives very hard to ensure as much of its produce as possible is certified organic. You'll find an imaginative specials board keeps the savoury options fresh, and you can buy produce in the farm's shop.

The Bridge Inn

bridgeinn-grinton.co.uk
Grinton, DL11 6HH
01748 884224

This 13th-century riverside pub has a beamed old bar, serving baguettes and rye squares, and a more tranquil restaurant. The menu is inspired by seasonal local game, meats and fish. Expect traditional English dishes with a modern twist.

Charles Bathurst Inn ◉

cbinn.co.uk
Arkengarthdale, DL11 6EN
01748 884567

This 18th-century inn takes its name from the son of Oliver Cromwell's physician who built it for his workers in what was once a busy lead-mining area. In winter, it caters for serious ramblers tackling The Pennine Way and the Coast to Coast route, and it offers a welcome

escape from the rigours of the moors. Many a tale has been swapped over pints of Black Sheep or Theakston ale. The 'Terrace Room' features handcrafted tables and chairs from Robert Thompson's craftsmen in nearby Kilburn. English classics meet modern European dishes on a menu written up on the mirror above the stone fireplace, and the provenance is impeccable.

5 special rail routes in Yorkshire

▶ Ribblehead Viaduct MAP REF 334 B5

The Ribblehead Viaduct is England's most iconic railway land bridge, striding out dramatically across Batty Moss and photogenic in all weathers. There are 24 arches to count, and it stretches up to 104 feet above the valley floor, with foundations reaching a further 25 feet into the peat bog below. Designed by engineer John Sydney Crossley and stretching for a quarter of a mile, it took four years and scores of lives to build, finally opening in 1874. Now it's part of the most scenic stretch of the Settle–Carlisle cross-country railway route. Ribblehead railway station lies half a mile to the south, with the Blea Moor Tunnel – the longest on the route – to the north.

The need for the viaduct in the first place came from the Midland Railway's desire to run trains all the way to Carlisle – and beyond. The problem was the Midland's line ended at Ingleton, and their passengers and goods had to be taken northwards by rival London and North Western Railway (LNWR). Relations between the Midland and the LNWR were never great – the latter would handle the through-carriages of its rival with deliberate obstructiveness by attaching the coaches to slow freight trains instead of fast passenger ones. The Midland decided this would not do, and so gained approval from Parliament for a new line to Scotland in June 1866.

Despite second thoughts about the cost of the line, work on the route commenced in November 1869.

The whole Settle–Carlisle railway came under the threat of closure during the 1980s, largely blamed on the costs needed to repair the Ribblehead Viaduct. After much protest, the figures quoted for the work were found to be wildly high and the closure proposals were dropped. Today, the viaduct, along with the rest of the line, has been repaired and there are no longer any plans to close it – which is just as well, as it now carries record numbers of passenger and freight services.

Explore around the footings of the viaduct and you may come across some trenches, which are all that remain of Batty Green. This was the name that was given to the village of wooden huts that housed up to 2,000 navvies in the 1870s, when they were building the railway. There are some excellent interpretative panels by the site and a further display in the station outlining the extent of the village – which is astonishing when you see what the site looks like today. Batty Green and other shanty-towns were Britain's own Wild West in Victorian times, with saloons, religious missions, good-time girls and fearsome reputations.

▼ Ribblehead Viaduct

▶ Richmond   MAP REF 336 A4

You should approach Richmond from Swaledale to gain a sense of the importance of this town to the dale. With the road winding through lovely wooded valleys, the sight at the end is the magnificent Richmond Castle, standing on its hill high above the river. It dates from the Norman period, and inside you'll see Scolland's Hall, which dates from the 11th century – it's claimed to be the oldest hall in England. The panoramic views down the river and over the surrounding area are splendid.

Take a walk behind the castle and you'll find Richmond's huge cobbled Market Place, with its Market Cross (a tall cigar-shaped structure) and the unusual sight of Holy Trinity Church – unusual because there are shops and a museum built into the base of the building. Since its construction around 1150, it has been almost destroyed several times.

The curfew bell sounds from the church's clock tower at 8am and 8pm every day. It's also known as the 'Prentice Bell' because, as well as sounding the curfew, it marked the start and end of the apprentices' working day. At one time the town crier, who lived beneath the bell, was responsible for ringing it each day.

The museum in the church is that of the Green Howards, one of Yorkshire's proudest regiments. Military concerns are important here – Catterick army camp is close by. If you're a history or military buff, you'll love the smart modern displays to be found here, but it's actually only one of three museums in Richmond.

The Richmondshire Museum itself is a typical collection of historical items, from prehistoric times to the age of television and James Herriot. Here's a great story: when the BBC finished filming the first series of *All Creatures Great and Small*, they sold the set of James Herriot's surgery to the museum – not realising what a huge success the show would become. When the second series was commissioned, the Beeb asked if they could buy it back, but the museum refused, knowing by then that the exhibit was of great interest to visitors. So the BBC was forced to build a replacement. No doubt James Herriot himself would have enjoyed these canny Yorkshire business dealings.

After the castle, Richmond's best historic site is the Georgian Theatre Royal. The theatre, built late in the 18th century, is the only one in the world that still survives in its original state. As well as attending a show in the evenings, you should take one of the guided tours to have a glimpse behind the stage, into the dressing rooms and inside the original box office. It's the volunteer guides who make the place come alive.

A mile southeast of the town centre, via a walk along the banks of the Swale, is Easby Abbey. This English Heritage-owned ruin isn't as grand as the more celebrated Fountains Abbey further south, but it's a good destination for a lovely walk.

TAKE IN SOME HISTORY

Richmond Castle
english-heritage.org.uk
Riverside Road, DL10 4QW
01748 822493 | Open Mar–Sep daily 10–6, Oct–Nov 10–5, Dec–Feb Sat–Sun 10–4
Commanding a powerful position on the banks of the River Swale, this mighty fortress was never put to the test, for Richmond has never seen military action. Its location is textbook, with steep cliffs protecting one side, and thick walls defending the others.

The Normans started constructing a castle here in the 1080s, and it is thought that Scolland's Hall – a fine, two-storeyed hall with typical round-headed windows – is one of the earliest stone-built halls in England. The towers at Richmond have romantic names: Robin Hood Tower, now in ruins, is said to have been the prison of William the Lion, King of Scotland; the Gold Hole Tower may have a poetic name, but it was actually the latrine tower, complete with pits at its base. The largest building of the complex is the keep, which was a gatehouse in the 11th century, but in the mid-12th century was extended upwards to a height of 100 feet.

Georgian Theatre Royal
georgiantheatreroyal.co.uk
Victoria Road, DL10 4DW
01748 823710
Dating back to 1788, when it was built by actor-manager Samuel Butler, the theatre closed down in 1848 and remained shut until it was restored and re-opened in 1963. The theatre, Britain's most complete Georgian playhouse, is still used for live productions – music, comedy, drama – and it has a museum with old playbills, photographs and the oldest complete set of painted scenery in England.

Easby Abbey
english-heritage.org.uk
DL10 7JU | 0370 333 1181
Open Apr–Sep daily 10–6, Oct daily 10–5, Nov–Mar 10–4
Set beside the River Swale, this Premonstratensian Abbey was founded in 1155 and dedicated to St Agatha. You can see extensive remains of the monks' domestic buildings, including the gatehouse and the refectory. The rich decoration on the upper floors indicates it may have been used to accommodate guests. The parish church next door has some interesting medieval wall paintings.

VISIT THE MUSEUMS
Richmondshire Museum
richmondshiremuseum.org.uk
Ryders Wynd, DL10 4JA
01748 825611 | Open Easter–mid-
Oct Mon–Sat 10.30–4.30
A museum of local history,
from Roman times to the
modern age.

Green Howards Regimental Museum
greenhowards.org.uk
Trinity Church Square, DL10 4QN
01748 826561 | Open Mon–Sat
10–4.30
This museum traces the
military history of the
Green Howards from the
late 17th century onwards.
The exhibits include uniforms,
weapons and medals –
beautifully displayed in the
newly reworked space.

EAT AND DRINK
The Frenchgate Restaurant and Hotel
thefrenchgate.co.uk
59–61 Frenchgate, DL10 7AE
01748 822087
Compounded of two original
town houses in photogenic
Richmond, The Frenchgate is a
modern boutique hotel with
bags of character. Works by
local artists are hung about the
place, as well as some not so
local. Can that really be an
original Pissarro in the dining
room? Yep. Uncovered wood
surfaces lend the place an
agreeably informal feel, and
the whole thing is kept on a
manageable scale, with just a
few tables and a shortish menu.

▶ PLACES NEARBY
For 400 years of history, take
a trip down the road to Kiplin
Hall, in the village of the
same name.

Kiplin Hall
kiplinhall.co.uk
Near Scorton, DL10 6AT
01748 818178 | Open Apr–Oct
Sat–Wed 2–5; grounds 10–5
Kiplin Hall is a red-brick
Jacobean mansion dating back
to 1620, with extensive gardens.
It stands by the River Swale in
the Vale of Mowbray and was
built by George Calvert, who
rose from comparatively
humble beginnings to the
highest political eminence.
After graduating from Trinity
College, Oxford, he became
an MP in 1619. James I made
him Secretary of State and
he later became first Lord
Baltimore and founder of
Maryland in what is now part
of the United States.

This intriguing house
is now furnished as a
comfortable Victorian home,
with 17 rooms open to the
public. It's crowded with an
eclectic mix of previous
owners' furniture, paintings,
portraits and personalia,
including many Arts and Crafts
items. Among numerous
original paintings are works by
Beuckelaer, Carlevarijs,
Kauffman and Watts.
Ornamental gardens, a
productive walled garden,
woodland and lakeside walks
and a popular tea room add to
the enjoyment of any visit.

▶ Rievaulx Abbey MAP REF 337 E6

english-heritage.org.uk

Rievaulx, YO62 5LB | 01439 798228 | Open Apr–Sep daily 10–6,
Oct Thu–Mon 10–5, Nov–Mar Sat–Sun 10–4

A short drive (or pleasant, well signposted stroll) from Helmsley
(see page 131) is one of Yorkshire's finest treasures. Today the
setting of Rievaulx Abbey is sheltered and inviting, but when Walter
l'Espec dispatched a group of French monks to find a suitable site
on which to build a new community it was reported to be fit only for

'wild beasts and robbers'. At that time there were no roads in the area; instead of neat copses and lush meadows there were only impenetrable thickets. To the devoutly ascetic Cistercian monks, this part of the Rye Valley represented the sort of challenge on which they thrived.

In 1131, the monks began to build the mother church of the Cistercian order in England – and it's still one of the finest abbeys in the country. The nave is Norman, but the rest of the buildings reflect the Early English style.

Enough remains of all the buildings on site to give you a very clear impression of what monastic life was like all those centuries ago. The monks may have started out with a strictly ascetic attitude towards wealth and lifestyle – indeed the establishment of the Cistercian order was partly due to what they considered to be the wicked corruption of the Benedictine orders. But the 140 monks and nearly 600 lay brothers of Rievaulx Abbey succeeded in creating wealth and influence.

The monks farmed sheep, cultivated vegetables, ground corn and smelted iron – a process that required the felling of perhaps 40 trees to make a hundred-weight of metal. They even built canals to enable the iron to be transported. Stone for the buildings was brought here from local quarries by the same method. By 1538, when the Dissolution destroyed their way of life for ever, the monks had become very wealthy indeed.

The delightful little village of Rievaulx, with its thatched cottages of honey-coloured stone, grew up only after the Reformation. It's inevitable that many of the houses were built from stone salvaged from the ruins of the abbey.

GO FOR A STROLL
Rievaulx Terrace
and Temples
nationaltrust.org.uk
Rievaulx, YO62 5LJ
01439 748283
Open mid-Feb–Oct daily 11–5
As if the abbey were not delightful enough on its own, cut into the hillside above the ruined buildings is Rievaulx Terrace – a level, curved grassy promenade. The terrace at Rievaulx was designed in 1758 by Thomas Duncombe – who had inherited it and whose family built nearby Duncombe Park. It is now owned by the National Trust after they purchased the site in 1972. It offers strollers tantalising glimpses of the abbey between the trees below, with fantastic views of the Rye Valley and Hambleton Hills. There are two Grecian-style temple follies to walk between, one apparently built for the use of hunting parties, the other for quiet contemplation. There are some lovely walks to be had through the beech woods and the garden has a display of spring flowers.

▶ Ripley MAP REF 328 A3

Ripley is an estate village built around Ripley Castle, which has been home to the Ingilby family since the 1320s. The village was largely built in the 1820s by Sir William Amcotts Ingilby, an affable eccentric who modelled it on an estate village he had seen in Alsace-Lorraine. The delightful result is the only place in Yorkshire which has a *hotel de ville* rather than a town hall. The cobbled Market Square with its stocks, the listed cottages and the aged church all make this an unusual and pleasurable place to visit.

TAKE IN SOME HISTORY
Ripley Castle
ripleycastle.co.uk
HG3 3AY | 01423 770152
Castle open for guided tours only, see website for details; garden open daily 9–4.30

The medieval fortifications of Ripley Castle were built to provide protection from marauding Scots, but later baronets added a tower and a mansion house. Designed by John Carr of York in the 18th century, this is the most elegant part of the castle, with furniture by Chippendale – his father was a joiner on the Ripley estate – and Hepplewhite. Continental influences from the family's grand tours are reflected in the Venetian chandeliers and the Italian plasterwork ceilings and statuary. Most fascinating of all are the tower rooms: the library, with its huge table, 5,000 books and the 1386 foundation charter of Mount Grace Priory; above it, the Tower Room, with a fabulous plasterwork ceiling, where James I slept in 1603; and, on the third storey, the gem of the castle, the perfectly preserved Knight's Chamber of 1555.

You'll also find a priest hole hidden behind the panelling, and the door to a spiral staircase that has a prominent false handle to delay attackers.

The colourful and eccentric Ingilbys have lived at Ripley Castle since the 1320s, when Thomas Ingilby married Edeline Thweng, heiress to the estate. Thomas saved the life of Edward III when he was attacked by a wounded boar while hunting, and was rewarded with a knighthood, but the Ingilby's Catholicism later cost them dear. Sir William joined the conspirators in the 'Pilgrimage of Grace' and was saved from execution by Henry VIII only because he had advised against taking action. His son, Francis, trained as a Jesuit priest in the seminary at Rheims, returning to England in 1584; captured two years later, he was convicted of treason and hung, drawn and quartered at York. Beatified in 1987, he is the only Ingilby likely to become a saint. His brother William narrowly avoided execution for treason when he was unjustly implicated in the Gunpowder Plot. Loyalty to the Crown proved equally hazardous: Sir William was fined over £700 for 'delinquency' in supporting Charles I during the Civil War, and his son briefly fled into exile with James II. More prosaically, in 1794, the then baronet and his wife abandoned their six small children when escaping to Europe to avoid their creditors. It was 10 years before he could pay off their debts and return home.

EAT AND DRINK

Ripley Castle Tea Rooms
HG3 3AY | 01423 770152
After looking around the castle and gardens, a visit to the tea rooms is a must. Fashioned from the old kiln and potter's shop in the stable yard, the tea rooms cater for thousands of visitors every year, and yet everything is freshly made on the premises. You can sip one of seven blends of tea with your traditional cream tea or a light lunch.

▶ **PLACES NEARBY**
Just east of Ripley is Nidd Hall, built in the 1820s for a Bradford wool magnate.

Nidd Hall Hotel ⊛⊛
warnerleisurehotels.co.uk
Nidd, HG3 3BN | 01423 771598
Nidd Hall, set in 45 acres of superb garden, is an early example of 19th-century pastiche, a glorious hodge-podge of architectural and stylistic references that take in everything from stained window panels, marble and oak floors to Tuscan columns. The colossal double-height fireplace and distant copper ceiling in the dining room give notice that the place was once grand enough to host the first meeting between Edward VIII and Mrs Simpson – possibly. Ancestral paintings and antlered heads surround you in the Terrace restaurant, which offers a graceful version of modern British cooking.

▶ **Ripon** MAP REF 328 B2

If you like your churches with history, then check out Ripon Cathedral. In AD 672 St Wilfrid built a church on this spot. You can still see the crypt of that church – it's the oldest complete Saxon crypt in any English cathedral. That alone would make the cathedral worth a visit, but it has lots of good things in its own right. The impressive west front dates from 1220, the east front from 1290, and inside there are 500-year-old woodcarvings, a 16th-century nave and some exceptional stained glass to enjoy. All-in-all, it's a building not to be missed.

Ripon may be a pocket-sized city, largely by-passed by the heavy industry which dominated so much of Yorkshire, but there are plenty of things to see and do here. In St Mary's Gate, the Ripon Prison and Police Museum tells the vivid story of

Yorkshire law and disorder through the ages. It's one of a series of sites making up the Yorkshire Law and Order Trail, which will also take you to the Old Workhouse Museum and the Courthouse Museum.

Every night at 9pm the Ripon Hornblower blows his horn in the market place and then once more outside the home of the mayor. The ceremony marks the setting of the watch, informing the citizens that their safekeeping overnight was the charge of the wakeman – an important consideration when marauding Vikings or Scots were around. The office of wakeman disappeared in 1604, but the tradition lives on. Also at 9pm, the curfew bell at Ripon Cathedral is sounded – unless a concert is taking place. This custom comes from the Normans, when it was an instruction that all fires should be covered for the night – an essential safety precaution in the days of timber houses. The word curfew comes from the French *couvre-feu* – 'cover the fire'.

The 50-mile circuit, the Ripon Rowel Walk, starts from the cathedral. It is named after the rowels – the small spiked wheels fitted to the back of a horse-rider's spurs – that were the city's speciality in the 16th and 17th centuries. So famous were the rowels that a royal charter recognised their superiority, and they gave rise to a common folk saying, 'As true steel as Ripon rowels'. A spur appears on Ripon's coat of arms – along with a horn – and can be seen on the

▼ Ripon Cathedral

top of the obelisk in the Market Square, designed by Nicholas Hawkssmoor.

All around Ripon attractions vie for attention, and Fountains Abbey is probably the most significant (see page 102). The Lightwater Valley Theme Park, with its enormous rollercoasters and other rides, is high on the list for families. There are, naturally, lots of eating places and gift shops, and the Lightwater Village, a shopping centre with factory, fashion and food shops.

Just two miles east of Lightwater Valley is Norton Conyers, a lovely country house which dates back to the mid-14th century, and is linked to novelist Charlotte Brontë.

VISIT THE MUSEUM
Ripon Prison and Police Museum
riponmuseums.co.uk
01765 690799 | Open mid-Feb–Nov daily 1–4 (10–4 in school holidays)
Housed in the cell block of what was first the Ripon Liberty Prison and later its Police Station, the Prison and Police Museum has some chilling – but never gruesome – displays. You can also see the former Courthouse and the Victorian workhouse around the town.

GO TO THE RACES
Ripon Racecourse
ripon-races.co.uk
Boroughbridge Road, HG4 1UG
01765 530530
Ripon has hosted some of the most exciting, prestigious and enjoyable racing in the country for more than 300 years. The season starts in April, and the racecourse stages 16 race meetings and several special events throughout each year.

EAT AND DRINK
The Royal Oak
royaloakripon.co.uk
36 Kirkgate, HG4 1PB
01765 602284
This former coaching inn stands in the centre of Ripon. Built in the 18th-century, it is an ideal base for exploring nearby York and Harrogate. Well-kept local cask ales from Timothy Taylor and Saltaire breweries can be enjoyed in the bar, as well as wines from a carefully chosen list. Sandwiches and 'pub classics' appear on the menu alongside local steaks and interesting signature dishes.

▶ PLACES NEARBY
With the thrills and spills of Lightwater Valley and the history of Aldborough Roman Site all nearby, Ripon is a great based for exploring. You can also visit Norton Conyers and a couple of great pubs.

Lightwater Valley Theme Park
lightwatervalley.co.uk
North Stainley, HG4 3HT | 0871 720 0011 | Open selected dates from Apr–Nov; phone for details

Set in 175 acres of North Yorkshire parkland just outside Ripon, Lightwater Valley Theme Park, with its falconry centre, has got a friendly and welcoming atmosphere. The theme park line-up includes Europe's longest roller coaster – The Ultimate – as well as the stomach-churning mighty Eagle's Claw and the Wild River Rapids. Step aboard the terrifying Whirlwind or risk a one-on-one encounter in Raptor Attack's abandoned mineshaft. The Falconry shows you how these amazing birds are trained and handled – watch dramatic flying shows at 2pm and 4pm every day. You can save a significant amount of money by booking tickets ahead online.

Norton Conyers

Wath, HG4 5EQ | 01765 640333
Garden open selected days, please phone for opening times.
This lovely country house with its high Dutch-style gables, dates back to the mid-14th century. Charles I and James II both visited in their time, but more significant was a visit by the novelist Charlotte Brontë in 1839. It is assumed that she heard the tale of a madwoman locked in the attic here in the previous century, and that this gave her the idea for the unfortunate Mrs Rochester in *Jane Eyre*, published in 1847. Today the gardens are also well worth exploring, with their elegant little orangery making a focal point for wedding parties.

Aldborough Roman Site

english-heritage.org.uk
Boroughbridge, YO51 9ES
01423 322768 | Open Apr–Sep
Sat–Sun 11–5
See two spectacular mosaic pavements and discover the remains of the Roman town, the capital of the Romanised Brigantes – once the largest tribe in Britain. Boroughbridge is southeast of Ripon, on the far side of the A1.

The Buck Inn

Thornton Watlass, HG4 4AH
01677 422461
Very much the heart of the local community, this traditional pub is welcoming and relaxed. Cricketing memorabilia adorns the Long Room, which overlooks the village green and cricket pitch (the pub is part of the boundary). There are several separate dining areas, and the menu ranges from sandwiches to freshly prepared pub fare. There's live jazz music most Sunday lunchtimes.

The George at Wath ◉◉

thegeorgeatwath.co.uk
Main Street, Wath, HG4 5EN
01765 641324
The George at Wath, a brick-built double-fronted free house dating from the 18th century, is just three miles from the centre of Ripon. Enjoy the log fires and cosy atmosphere. The contemporary dining room proffers seasonal and locally sourced ingredients for its mix of classic and bistro-style dishes.

▶ Robin Hood's Bay MAP REF 339 D3

Robin Hood's Bay vies with Staithes for the title of the prettiest fishing village on Yorkshire's coastline. Both communities have to juggle the conflicting demands of tourism with the needs of local people. When you come here you'll have to leave your car at the top of the hill, where there are two large car parks – the steep, narrow road down to the beach is a cul-de-sac and visitors' cars are barred.

The houses – which cling precariously to the side of the cliff – are reached by narrow alleyways and steps from the single access road. The result is a cheerful jumble of whitewashed cottages and red-tiled roofs leading down the main street and almost into the sea. An old story tells of a ship which at high tide came so close to shore that its bowsprit knocked out the window of a pub!

There is no harbour. Where once there were more than a hundred fishing boats, there are now just a handful, and they are launched down a slipway from the beach. There's a good stretch of sandy beach and a rocky foreshore, noted for its fossils; children love to investigate the little rock pools left in these scars by the receding tide. Take care – it is easy to get cut off by the tide when it starts coming in again.

Robin Hood's Bay has had its share of storms, their effects exacerbated by the softness of the shale that forms the cliffs of the bay. A sea wall helps to blunt the worst of the buffeting, though every winter still brings memorable storms.

The only community of any size between Whitby and Scarborough, the relative isolation of Robin Hood's Bay helped to make it a haunt of smugglers. It used to be said that a boat-load of contraband could be beached, and the load transferred to the top of the village through a maze of secret passages between the tightly packed houses, all without seeing the light of day.

You can walk at low tide along the beach to Ravenscar (see page 222) – keeping an eye out for the incoming tide – or along a section of the Cleveland Way. On your way, about a mile from Robin Hood's Bay, is Boggle Hole, a little wooded cove. An old water mill, once powered by Mill Beck, is now a youth hostel conveniently situated for Cleveland Wayfarers.

But the Cleveland Way isn't the only long-distance walk in the area. Spend any time in the village, and you'll certainly spot a few battle-hardened folk who have conquered the Coast to Coast walk – Alfred Wainwright's classic cross-country hike of some 190 miles.

◀ Robin Hood's Bay from Ravenscar

5 top beaches

With over 45 miles of coast, Yorkshire has an impressive selection of great beaches – here are our top five.

▶ **Cayton Bay** – South of Scarborough, this is often quiet even during the school holidays – possibly thanks to the steep trek to get to it. It's worth the climb though, as the beach is excellent, and WWII fortifications are popular with the kids. Be sure to bring everything you need for the day, to avoid too much trekking.

▶ **Filey Beach** – Often overlooked, Filey has a long sandy beach set in a wide bay. Head slightly north, and Filey Brigg has lots of wildlife living in rock pools.

▶ **Hornsea Beach** – A classic seaside resort, with a long promenade to stroll along, and easy access to the town. The recently landscaped gardens make Hornsea's seafront a top spot. Beach-wise it's sand and shingle, with plenty of parking too.

▶ **Robin Hood's Bay** – Although it's a dock for small boats, the bay does have some sandy areas and rock pools at low tide. It also has good local pubs and restaurants around it.

▶ **Scarborough North Bay** – Scarborough's often forgotten North Bay is the wilder of the two beaches, lacking the views towards the seaside coast, but gaining a free and rugged feel. Surfers love it, as do dog owners.

VISIT THE MUSEUM
Robin Hood's Bay and Fylingdales Museum
museum.rhbay.co.uk
New Road, YO22 4ST
Open Jun–Sep Sun–Fri afternoons, plus selected afternoons during school holidays and rest of year

Located in an old cottage that once served as the district coroner's office, this is a gem of a museum, stuffed full of treasures and tales about the village and the life of the hardy men and women who lived along this coastline. The stories of shipwrecks and rescues that affected this tight little community are particularly poignant.

HIT THE BEACH

Although it's a dock for small boats, the bay does have some sandy areas and many rock pools at low tide. It also has some good local pubs and restaurants around it. For long-distance walkers, it's well-known as the end of the Coast to Coast route.

SADDLE UP
Farsyde Riding Centre
farsydefarmcottages.co.uk
Farsyde Farm Cottages, YO22 4UG
01947 880249

Farsyde offers access for riders of all abilities to the spectacular countryside around Robin Hood's Bay – with the sea itself rarely far from view. Cross-country routes are geared to small groups of capable riders – more experienced riders may go on to the beach, and even novices can enjoy the quiet lanes. Not suitable for younger children.

EAT AND DRINK

Laurel Inn

New Road, YO22 4SE

01947 880400

Given its location it's hardly surprising that this was once the haunt of smugglers who used a network of underground tunnels and secret passages to bring the booty ashore. Nowadays it's the haunt of holidaymakers and walkers, and the setting for this small, traditional pub which retains lots of character features, including beams and an open fire. The bar is decorated with old photographs, Victorian prints and an international collection of lager bottles. This popular free house serves Adnams and Theakston Old Peculier and Best Bitter.

The Old Bakery Tea Rooms

Chapel Street, YO22 4SQ

01947 880709

A lovely, traditional tea room, situated in the heart of the village, that serves hot food all day. The bread and cakes are produced in the attached bakery. Scones with home made preserves are a favourite, along with the chocolate and coffee cakes. There's an enclosed balcony overlooking the stream – it's a good place to rest and watch the world go by.

▶ Roseberry Topping MAP REF 337 E3

Roseberry Topping, which lies just to the north of Great Ayton, is Yorkshire's very own 'Matterhorn'. Its height – just 1,056 feet – doesn't really qualify it as a major peak, yet it is a prominent landmark for miles around, standing aloof from the surrounding Cleveland Hills.

To see Roseberry Topping as nature intended – as an almost symmetrical cone – you will have to look at old pictures. As soon as its mineral wealth was realised, it was exploited for its alum, iron ore, jet and roadstone. So heavily was it mined and quarried that a great chunk of the hill fell away in a landslip, making the residents of the nearby village of Newton under Roseberry fear for their lives.

And it's this landslip which created the distinctive profile you can see today. If you climb to the top, to the northwest you can see the industrial heartland of Middlesbrough (see page 198), its urban sprawl creeping inexorably outwards; to the south are views across the moors.

Roseberry Topping's prominence has made it an important landmark for more than a millennium. There is some evidence that it was even an object of veneration. Roseberry is a corruption of the old Viking name, 'Othenesberg' – Odin's Hill – indicating it was probably sacred to the Danish god of creation. Topping, also of Scandinavian origin, means a peak. Several 17th-century references have it as 'Osbury Toppyne', at a time when it was one of the many beacon hills on which fires were built – to be set alight if the Spanish Armada were sighted at sea.

▶ Rosedale MAP REF 338 A3

Ah, the peace of Rosedale... a lovely tranquil valley today, making you feel a world away from the noise and grime of Yorkshire's industrial heartlands. But appearances can be deceptive. Just a hundred years ago the scene was very different: Rosedale was a veritable moorland 'Klondike'.

Ironstone had been mined here, on and off, since the Iron Age, and during the 13th century mining even added to the wealth of the monks of Byland Abbey. In the middle of the 19th century the extent of Rosedale's subterranean wealth was fully realised, with the discovery of massive quantities of top-grade iron ore. This was the Industrial Revolution, and the demand for iron came from the blast furnaces on the rivers Tees and Tyne, for building ships, railways and general engineering. But it's one thing to dig it out of the ground, another to get it to where it's needed – especially from isolated Rosedale.

So in 1861 the North Eastern Railway built a line from Battersby Junction on the Stockton–Whitby line, over the bleak moorland to Rosedale West. In 1865 a branch was built around the head of Rosedale to the east mines, joining the original line at Blakey Junction, just below the Lion Inn on Blakey Ridge. To reach Teesside the wagons, now laden with ore, were winched down the steep descent of the Ingleby Incline. The engines that plied the high-level line between the Rosedale mines and the incline never came down from their moorland heights, except when they had to be repaired.

This Rosedale railway was closed in 1929, by which time the valley's mining boom was over. Though the demand for iron was as buoyant as ever, ore could be mined more cheaply elsewhere – now you can walk along the route. The valley is quietly returning to a natural state, but the massive calcining kilns (where ironstone was roasted to reduce its weight) are being preserved, so that Rosedale's mining past will not be forgotten.

The old Rosedale railway is ideal for cycling for much of its length, as it is relatively level and surfaced with ash ballast.

▲ Rosedale from Bank

The best section is from Rosedale Bank Top to Blakey Junction, near the Lion Inn (four miles) and then across the moors to Ingleby Bank Top, another seven miles. You could even cycle down the Incline – but remember: what goes down must come up again.

You'll search in vain for the abbey that gave the village of Rosedale Abbey its name. The truth is that you can see the remains of the abbey – or rather it was a priory – wherever you look, as the population explosion of the mid-19th century meant that the priory was plundered for its building stone to build homes for the ironstone miners.

GET ACTIVE
Wild Country Walkabouts
wildcountrywalkabouts.co.uk
YO18 9AE | 01751 417950
With a fantastic range of activities on offer, from courses in bushcraft and archery to wildlife awareness, there's something different and interesting to take on with the team at Wild Country Walkabouts. It's essential to dress with regard to the weather and terrain.

EAT AND DRINK
Abbey Tea Room and Store
abbeytearoom.co.uk
Rosedale Abbey, YO18 8SA
01751 417475
As well as plain, fruit and cheese scones, you can find cherry scones, scones made with treacle, scones made with blueberries and ginger... and you can spread them with blueberry-and-lavender jam. If you're more peckish, try the Yorkshire ham afternoon tea.

▶ Rotherham MAP REF 324 A5

Rotherham grew up as a town based on coal mining and steel production – two industries which declined sharply at the end of the 20th century. Always overshadowed by its much bigger and noisier neighbour, Sheffield, it's been undergoing a quiet regeneration in recent years.

The Romans were the first to spot the potential of this spot on the River Don, building a fort at what is now Templeborough. A settlement grew, to the extent that in the 1480s Thomas Rotherham, Archbishop of York, earmarked his home town for a centre of learning to rival those of Cambridge and Oxford. His founding of the College of Jesus was a great success – at least, until it was quashed in 1547. Bits of its original brick walls have been incorporated into buildings along College Street, but Rotherham's scholarly hopes were dashed.

Instead, iron and steel came to the fore, with foundries fuelled by coal. Cast iron was king, used for everything from the city's own-brand plough to the plating that encased Brunel's SS *Great Eastern*. Other industries thrived here, including glassmaking.

Today, the coal mines have just about gone, and the steel industry employs a fraction of what it once did. The opening of the Meadowhall shopping centre, only two miles away, stalled much of the town-centre trade, and the city might have become a ghost town. However, thanks in part to private and foreign investment, things are looking up, and Rotherham has a feel of a town being reborn, with a mix of apartments, retail and restaurant space along the waterfront, a new leisure complex, and new council buildings too.

VISIT THE MUSEUM
Clifton Park and Museum
cliftonparkrotherham.co.uk
Clifton Lane, S65 2AA
01709 254588 | Mon–Fri 10–5,
Sat 9.30–5, Sun 1.30–4.30.
Closed Sun Oct–Mar
This imposing Georgian mansion was originally the home of the Walker family, who were early industrialists involved in the manufacture of iron and steel. It's now a lively modern museum about life and history in the Rotherham area – and admission is free.

The former grounds are a public park, with a land-train

▼ Clifton Park and Museum

to take you around and a great water splash area for hot days – random jets of water squirt high into the air, and you can observe the ensuing fun from the comfort of the cafe.

leisure centre, within walking or cycling distance of the town centre. It offers a range of activities from swimming to squash and racket ball, or scale the dizzying heights of the climbing wall.

ENTERTAIN THE FAMILY
Magna Science Adventure Centre
visitmagna.co.uk
Sheffield Road, S60 1DX
01709 720002 | Open summer daily 10–5, rest of year Tue–Sun but may vary so check ahead
Magna has brought the cavernous former Templeborough steelworks back to life. There are four pavilions where you can explore the elements – earth, air, fire and water. It's the ultimate interactive experience – you can have fun firing a giant water cannon, launch rockets, board an airship and spin in a gyroscopic chair, see lightning bolts, explode rock faces and work real JCBs. The outdoor playgrounds of Sci-Tek and Aqua-Tek are a must for children.

Top tip – if you're going to get properly stuck in, then expect to get wet and bring some dry clothing.

GET ACTIVE
Rotherham Leisure Complex
placesforpeopleleisure.org
Effingham Street, S65 1BL
01709 722555 | Open Mon–Fri 7am–10pm, Sat–Sun 7.30am–8pm
Get active at this big modern

PLAY A ROUND
Rotherham has three great courses, starting with the correctly named Rotherham Golf Club, which is a parkland course with easy walking along the tree-lined fairways. Sitwell Park Golf Club is an undulating course designed in 1913 by Dr Alister MacKenzie, retaining many of his greens and complete with its own 'Amen Corner', aptly named 'The Jungle'. It's a good test of golf for all levels of player. Grange Park Golf Club is a parkland/meadowland course, with panoramic views. The golf is testing, particularly at the 1st, 4th and 18th holes (par 4), and 8th, 12th and 15th (par 5).

Rotherham Golf Club
rotherhamgolfclub.com
Thrybergh Park, Doncaster Road, Thrybergh, S65 4NU
01709 850500 | Open Thu–Tue

Sitwell Park Golf Club
sitwellgolf.co.uk
Shrogswood Road, S60 4BY
01709 541046 | Open Sun–Fri

Grange Park Golf Club
grangeparkgolfclub.org
Upper Wortley Road, S61 2SJ
01709 559497

▶ **PLACES NEARBY**

On the outskirts of Maltby, east of Rotherham, are the ruins of Roche Abbey. Further south is the Tropical Butterfly House in North Anston, while stately home Wentworth Woodhouse is in Wentworth.

Roche Abbey

english-heritage.org.uk
Maltby, S66 8NW | 01709 812739
Open Apr–Sep Thu–Sun 11–4

Roche Abbey was founded on a curve of Maltby Dyke in 1147 for monks of the Cistercian order. The buildings were largely dismantled at the Dissolution, but among the ruins two impressively high limestone sections of the Gothic transept survive. In the 18th century 'Capability' Brown was given free rein in the valley, and the landscaping is picturesque.

Wentworth Woodhouse

wentworthwoodhouse.co.uk
Wentworth, Rotherham, S62 7TQ
01226 351161 | Check website for tour details

Built between 1725 and 1750 for the Marquesses of Rockingham, the house has a frontage believed to be the longest in Europe, over 200 rooms and is twice the size of Buckingham Palace. The Wentworth Woodhouse Preservation Trust bought the estate for £7 million in March 2017, and is planning to spend £42 million on restoration of the house, associated buildings and gardens.

Tropical Butterfly House Wildlife and Falconry Centre

butterflyhouse.co.uk
Woodsetts Road, North Anston
S25 4EQ | 01909 569416
Open daily 10–4, school holidays 10–4.30

You'll find much more than butterflies here. Get close to lots of free-roaming animals, handle exotic snakes and magnificent birds of prey, and feed the marmoset monkeys, lorikeets and many more amazing creatures.

▶ Runswick Bay MAP REF 338 B2

A long arc of sand extends south to form one of the loveliest bays on the Yorkshire coast. Sheltered by protective cliffs, many a ship's captain has been relieved to find safe harbour here. The cliffs that protect the bay take a battering each winter – whole chunks can disappear in a storm.

Since medieval records began this eastern coastline has continued to change dramatically, with villages creeping ever closer to the shore. You only have to look at old maps to realise the 'lost' villages of Yorkshire's coast can be counted in scores.

The village of Runswick fell into the sea in 1682. Fortunately no lives were lost as all the villagers were evacuated in time. Today Runswick comprises a rather pleasing collection of small red-roofed cottages, clinging limpet-like to the cliff, and the sheltering bay, good soil and southerly aspect make the village a pretty suntrap, attracting artists. The attractive thatched and whitewashed house on the headland was formerly the coastguard's cottage.

HIT THE BEACH

Runswick Bay's lovely sandy beach is a family-friendly place for rock pooling, fossil hunting and coastal walks. You can bring a surf board to catch a few waves or perhaps take a boat ride out to sea instead.

EAT AND DRINK

The Cliffemount Hotel
cliffemounthotel.co.uk
Runswick Bay, TS13 5HU
01947 840103

Perched high on the dramatic cliffs overlooking the petite fishing village of Runswick Bay – a windy perch – is The Cliffemount Hotel. Indeed, the bluster off the sea is about as turbulent as things get in this sublimely peaceful spot, and the plainly decorated dining room enjoys the best of the views. The cooking keeps things reasonably simple but very effective, using the freshest locally sourced ingredients.

▶ Saltaire   MAP REF 327 F5

Titus Salt (1803–76) was a paternal Leeds-born wool merchant who decided that the best way was his way. Accordingly, he constructed a 'model' village on the edge of Bradford for his textile factory workers, removing them from slum dwellings and combining care for their welfare with a shrewd business sense of people management.

With its buildings of pale gold stone reflecting the Italianate style so popular here in the mid-19th century, Saltaire has a charm and completeness about it, and is now preserved as a World Heritage Site – though it's still very much lived in. As you explore, you can identify the neatly laid out terraced houses built for the workers, and the larger houses for middle and senior management. The cottage hospital and church are easy to spot – there was also a school, and a riverside park for recreation. Streets are named after Salt's wife Caroline and 11 children.

The vast mill building on the bank of the River Aire was the focus of the village, of course – at the height of production 3,000 people worked here. There were 1,200 looms clattering away, weaving as much as 30,000 yards of cloth every working day, using wool and alpaca fibres. It's now a smart art gallery with a dedicated collection by the popular Bradford-born artist David Hockney (b.1937).

▶ Sandsend   MAP REF 338 C2

The approach to lovely Sandsend along the A174 is steeply
downhill from Lythe – views open up of a long sandy beach and,
in the distance, Whitby Abbey dominates the horizon. Here is
a place name that, for once, doesn't require interpretation.
Sandsend marks the northern end of a sandy beach, one of the
best on Yorkshire's coast, stretching down as far as Whitby
harbour (see page 292).

The village has been busy with industry for centuries,
starting with the Romans who had a cement works here. More
recently the bare outcrop of Sandsend Ness was mined for
alum and it is still bare today, because of the heaps of mining
waste. Remarkably, these mines were worked steadily for

250 years. When Yorkshire's coastal area had its railway, Sandsend was overlooked by a long viaduct, raised high above the red-tiled rooftops on tall pillars. Sadly, both the railway and the viaduct disappeared in the 1960s.

Today, Sandsend is a peaceful spot, sheltered from the rough battering of north winds and fearsome seas by Sandsend Ness. Mickleby Beck and East Row Beck reach the sea at Sandsend a mere 97 feet apart; rather than staring out to sea, most of the cottages are neatly clustered either side of their banks. Several paths accompany these two valleys into Mulgrave Woods, which you'll find is a traditional broadleaved woodland.

On the narrow ridge between these valleys is the splendid Georgian pile of Mulgrave Castle. Guests in the past included William Wordsworth and Charles Dickens – both wrote glowingly about the fine views to be enjoyed from here. In the grounds are the evocative, ivy-clad ruins of a much earlier castle, dating from the 13th century.

It was while strolling along the this fine sandy beach that Lewis Carroll first had the idea for his surreal poem about the Walrus and the Carpenter. If you fancy it, you can follow in his footsteps – at low tide it's a stroll of about two-and-a-half miles. Will you, won't you, will you, won't you: you decide.

◄ East Row, Sandsend

EAT AND DRINK
Estbek House ◉◉
estbekhouse.co.uk
East Row, YO21 3SU | 01947 893424
Overlooking the North Sea, Estbek House is perfectly positioned to source its materials from the chilly waters out front and the rolling moors behind, and that's exactly what the kitchen team does. It all takes place in a handsome Regency house (Grade II listed) that operates as a soothingly modern restaurant with rooms of considerable charm. Wild fish is the main passion here, hauled from local waters and prepared simply in the open-plan kitchen.

▶ Scarborough MAP REF 339 E5

Scarborough can rightly claim to be one of the oldest seaside resorts in the country. Trace its prosperity back to the occasion in the year 1620, when a visitor, Mrs Elizabeth Farrow, was drinking a glass of spring water. Finding the water acidic in taste, she came to the natural conclusion that something that tasted so unpleasant must surely have medicinal qualities too. Subsequent claims that Scarborough's spring water would cure many ills – even hypochondria – ensured folk flocked to the town to take the miraculous waters.

Scarborough's spring water certainly contains a cocktail of minerals, and it was definitely good for one thing – giving the town's economy a much-needed boost. The taking of the waters was soon put on a more commercial footing. Scarborough became known as a spa town – a place where the well-heeled might come to recuperate at leisure.

Then a local doctor started to extol the health-giving properties of sea-bathing. One way or another Scarborough's waters were responsible for its success.

Scarborough's first spa house was built over the original spa well in 1700. However, it was to suffer the fate of many other local buildings, by falling into the sea. Ever more elaborate spa houses were built, each one getting the royal stamp of approval for the water's efficacy. By the time Queen Victoria ascended the throne, Scarborough was arguably the North's finest resort, and many of the town's most distinguished buildings date from her reign. The magnificent Grand Hotel, overlooking the South Bay, seems to sum up the prosperity of Scarborough during the busiest time in its long history.

The town is not just about holidays, as you'll soon discover – there's a working port and harbour where fresh fish are still landed and sold at the market.

While many British resorts have lost out to the ease of foreign travel, Scarborough has enough attractions to keep the most fastidious visitors coming back for more. Cricket-lovers eagerly anticipate the Scarborough Festival, traditionally held towards the end of the season. Playwright Sir Alan Ayckbourn keeps faith with local theatregoers by premiering most of his plays here in the acclaimed Stephen Joseph Theatre before they are transferred to London's West End.

Scarborough has two top beaches. The North Bay is quieter, and a favourite with dog-owners – but watch out for canine restrictions in summer. Families can enjoy the

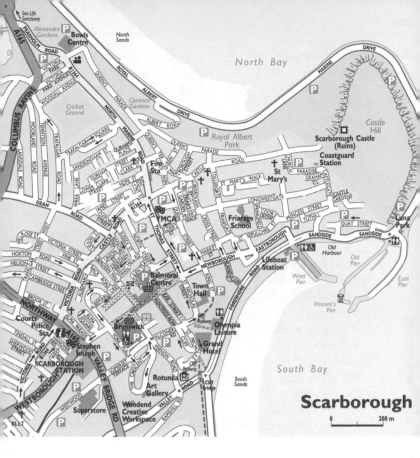

miniature North Bay Railway, which runs between Peasholm Park and the Sea Life Sanctuary at Scalby Mills. There you can see a colourful Caribbean-style coral reef, with hundreds of fish, turtles and sharks. The North Bay also has Peasholm Park, with its boating lake, and donkey rides on the beach in summer. Or take a walk along to the South Bay via the Victorian promenade.

Scarborough Castle has dominated the town with an air of fortress-like impregnability for the best part of a thousand years. Standing proudly on its headland, between the North and South Bays, it enjoys an uninterrupted view over the town and out to sea. Remains of even earlier defences have been unearthed, including an Iron Age settlement and a Roman signal station.

St Mary's Church suffered artillery damage – which you can still see – when caught in the cross-fire of a fight at the castle in the mid-17th century. Poet and novelist Anne Brontë is buried in the churchyard here – she loved the seaside, and was visiting Scarborough in 1849 for her health when she succumbed to tuberculosis and died.

TAKE IN SOME HISTORY
Scarborough Castle
english-heritage.org.uk
Castle Road, YO11 1HY
01723 372451 | Open Apr–Sep
daily 10–6. Oct–Nov 10–5, Dec–Mar
Sat–Sun 10–4

Unlike most medieval castles, Scarborough saw action in World War I, when shells from German battleships struck it. Historical records indicate that this was not the first time that the castle had come under attack, and several English kings received bills for repairs, from Henry II to James I.

The rocky headland on which the castle was built had been an important site for hundreds of years before the Normans came, the cliffs providing a natural defence, which was further strengthened by curtain walls. The keep, now in ruins, was built by Henry II on the site of an earlier tower. It was originally 100 feet high, and had walls up to 12 feet thick.

The Norman version you see today dates back to the year 1136, when William de Gros decided to rebuild in stone an earlier wooden fort. Henry II, concerned that many of his noblemen were growing too powerful, set about destroying their castles. He spared Scarborough, however. Impressed by its air of impregnability, he requisitioned the castle and kept it for himself.

Besieged on a number of occasions, Scarborough Castle was never taken by force, but attackers did manage to starve the defenders into surrendering. On one occasion, in 1645, Hugh Chomley's Royalist troops were besieged by John Meldrum's Scottish army and the Great Keep was badly damaged by the Scottish artillery. Unable to hold out any longer, they were allowed to surrender with honour intact; those men who could still stand were allowed to march out of the castle. The castle was heavily besieged again in 1648 when the Parliamentary garrison, discontented because they had not been paid, went over to the King's side; they too were starved into submission. Should all this make you feel peckish yourself, there's fortunately now a tea room located in the Master Gunner's House.

MEET THE SEALIFE
Sea Life Sanctuary
visitsealife.com
Scalby Mills, North Bay,
YO12 6RP | 01723 373414
Open all year daily 10–4

Made up of three large white pyramids, this impressive marine sanctuary overlooks the white sandy beaches of the North Bay and Peasholm Park. You can see lots of creatures, including otters and penguins, touch crustacea in the rockpool and feed the sharks and rays. There is also a pair of resident common seals – it's probably the best chance you'll have to get up close to these charming North Sea natives.

VISIT THE MUSEUMS AND GALLERIES

Scarborough Art Gallery

scarboroughmuseumstrust.com
The Crescent, YO11 2PW
01723 374753 | Open Tue–Sun 10–5

An Italianate villa is the setting for the town's art collection, including lots of views of Scarborough itself through the ages – it's a good way to see a visual history of this coastline. In the basement, creative modern artists work and exhibit in the Crescent Arts Workshop.

Woodend Creative Workspace

woodendcreative.co.uk
The Crescent, YO11 2PW
01723 384500

A modern art gallery where everything's for sale! See some of Yorkshire's finest modern arts and crafts – it's free to look.

The Rotunda Museum

scarboroughmuseumstrust.com
Vernon Road, YO11 2NH
01723 353665 | Open Tue–Sun 10–5

This distinctive pepper-pot building, dating from 1829, is where you can learn more about the geology of Scarborough and the Yorkshire coast, with fossils including a Bronze Age skeleton known as Gisthorpe Man, and dinosaur bones.

TAKE A TRAIN RIDE

North Bay Railway

nbr.org.uk
Burniston Road, Scarborough, YO12 6PF | 01723 368791
Open late Mar–Nov daily 10–5.30

Catch the miniature steam-hauled train between Peasholm Park and Scalby Mills – pushchairs and wheelchairs are accommodated, and it's handy for the Sea Life Sanctuary, too. Opened in 1931, the line runs for around three quarters of a mile, offering good views of Scarborough's North Bay. If you want to try your hand at being a train driver, driver experience courses take place ouside operating hours.

HIT THE BEACH

Cayton Bay

Just south of Scarborough is the best beach in Yorkshire: Cayton Bay. It's often quiet even during the school holidays – possibly thanks to the steep trek down (and up) to get to it through the cliffs. You should persevere though, as the beach is excellent, and much loved by surfers, windsurfers and kite-flyers. The World War II fortifications prove a great den for the kids. Just be prepared to bring everything you need for the day, to avoid trekking up and down more than strictly necessary.

North Bay

Scarborough's often forgotten North Bay is the wilder of Scarborough's two beaches, lacking the views towards the traditional seaside coast, but gaining a free, easy and rugged feel. Surfers love this beach, as do dog-owners, whose four-legged friends can play in the sea towards the north end.

CATCH A PERFORMANCE
Stephen Joseph Theatre
sjt.uk.com
Westborough, YO11 1JW
01723 370541

Daring theatrical pioneer Stephen Joseph founded Britain's first theatre-in-the-round here in 1955, and it moved to its present home – the old Odeon Cinema – in 1996, when still under the artistic directorship of playwright and farce-master Alan Ayckbourn. Today it's one of Britain's finest small theatres, and known for showcasing innovative new plays. With a 404-seat auditorium in the round and a further 165-seat cinema, it offers a fantastic programme of shows throughout the year.

GO FISHING
MV Queensferry
queensferrycruises.com
West Pier Slipway, Scarborough
Harbour, YO11 1PD
01723 379126

Scarborough has several providers who operate fishing trips out at sea. MV *Queensferry* sails daily, weather and numbers permitting. The Skipper, Neil Horsley, is an MCA-qualified local man with extensive inshore and offshore angling experience.

For details of other providers, contact Scarborough Tourist Information Centre – 01723 383636.

WATCH CRICKET
Scarborough Cricket Club
scarboroughcricketclub.co.uk
North Marine Road, YO12 7TJ
01723 365625

Founded in 1849, the club has its ground today at North Marine Road – and is second only in capacity to the Test Match venues. The club runs no fewer than seven teams, so there's often a game to watch in summer. The ground also hosts Yorkshire County Cricket Club for a number of four-day and one-day matches, and the famous Scarborough Cricket Festival is scheduled in August.

PLAY A ROUND
Two notable courses have Scarborough as their base. The Scarborough North Cliff Golf Club is situated on a clifftop overlooking North Bay and the Castle. It's a seaside course winding inland through parkland with stunning views of the North Yorkshire moors. The nearby Scarborough South Cliff Golf Club is a parkland and seaside course which falls into two parts, divided from one another by the main road from Scarborough to Filey.

Scarborough North Cliff Golf Club
northcliffgolfclub.co.uk
North Cliff Avenue, YO12 6PP
01723 355397 | Open daily

Scarborough South Cliff Golf Club
southcliffgolfclub.com
Deepdale Avenue, YO11 2UE
01723 360522 | Open daily

EAT AND DRINK

Lanterna Ristorante ◉

lanterna-ristorante.co.uk
33 Queen Street, YO11 1HQ
01723 363616

It has been honoured by Italian
newspaper *La Stampa* as 'the
English temple of Italian
cuisine', which seems an
extraordinary accolade for an
unassuming, albeit heartily
convivial, place in Scarborough,
but then Lanterna has been
here for nigh on 40 years.
There are warm contrasting
colour-schemes of reds and
oranges, and sunny yellow and
sky-blue, in the two dining
rooms, and the menu continues
to fly the flag for simple,
well-handled Italian cooking
of the classic school.

Palm Court Hotel ◉

palmcourtscarborough.co.uk
St Nicholas Cliff, YO11 2ES
01723 368161

This grand old Victorian hotel
has moved with the times, with
a modern makeover sitting
comfortably beside its elegant
period features. Run by the
same family for 30 years, it's a
popular spot for the British
institution that is afternoon tea,
which should keep you ticking
over until dinner in the elegant,
neutral-toned restaurant,
where tables swathed in linen
sit beneath chandeliers. The
kitchen doesn't try to reinvent
the wheel here, relying on
top-class local produce allied
with tried-and-true culinary
principles for its effect.

▶ Selby MAP REF 329 E6

Believed to have originated from a settlement called Seletum,
Selby grew from around its impressive abbey, dating back to
medieval times. By the 18th century the town had become a
major port and upwards of 360,000 tonnes of shipping used the
River Ouse between Selby and the North Sea each year. Today,
Selby owes its modern fortunes to power generation, but it still
retains much of its heritage with its regular Monday market.

SEE A LOCAL CHURCH

Selby Abbey

selbyabbey.org.uk
The Crescent, YO8 4PU
01757 703123

In 1069, monk Benedict from
Auxerre in France was granted
permission from William the
Conqueror to establish an
abbey at Selby. His successor,
Hugh, planned and constructed
the great church and the
associated buildings, and all
was fine for many years until
the time of the Dissolution
under Henry VIII, when the
abbey fell. Against the odds,
the abbey church was left alone
until 1906 when a massive fire
ripped through the building.
Fortunately the church was
restored at a cost of £40,000.
With no other church matching
it for size, age or beauty, Selby
Abbey certainly is Yorkshire's
hidden gem.

▶ Semerwater MAP REF 335 D4

Semerwater was formed at the end of the last ice age. Glacial meltwater attempted to drain away down the valley which the glacier had gouged out of the limestone, but was prevented from doing so by a wall of boulder clay, dumped by the glacier itself, across the valley's end. So the water built up, forming a lake which once stretched three miles up Raydale.

Natural silting has gradually filled the upper part of the lake bed, leaving Semerwater – at half a mile long, Yorkshire's second largest natural lake. Semerwater is now a very popular place, busy with anglers, boaters, watersports enthusiasts, nature lovers, swimmers, walkers and those who simply want to stop and admire the open views.

You can walk all the way round the lake, which is ringed by three pretty little villages – Countersett, Marsett and Stalling Busk. The circular walk covers about five miles. A fourth settlement is said to be lying on the bed of the lake – legend has it that a beautiful city once stood here. An angel, disguised as a beggar, went round appealing for food and drink, but was turned away at every home. The angel left the city and finally found food and shelter in the home of a poor man and his wife. On departing the next morning, the angel turned to the city and proclaimed:

Semerwater rise – Semerwater sink,
And cover all save this little house
that gave me meat and drink.

The waters did indeed rise to create the lake, and beneath its surface you may just hear the occasional sound of bells ringing from the long-drowned city. The poor man's cottage survived, and is said to be at Low Blean, on the eastern edge of Semerwater.

▶ Settle MAP REF 326 B2

You should try to visit Settle on a Tuesday – market day – when stalls are crammed into Market Square and visitors jostle with locals from the surrounding farms and villages. The Ribblesdale town is quite a lot smaller than nearby Skipton, but it is still a great place for shopping, with some old-fashioned family-run stores adding to the appeal of its 18th- and 19th-century buildings.

The composer Edward Elgar had a very good friend in Settle, a Dr Buck. Elgar stayed with him often, in his house

▲ Settle

overlooking the Market Square, where today a plaque commemorates the connection. Also overlooking the square is a two-storey row of shops known as the Shambles. In the 17th century this was an open market hall, which later became a butcher's shop. Arches and cottages were added in the 18th century, and then the second storey was built above the cottages in 1898.

In front of the Shambles is a fountain pillar erected in 1863 to replace the former market cross – and in front of this is a cafe with one of the oddest names you'll ever come across: Ye Olde Naked Man Café.

The town's most unusual building is the impressive Richard's Folly, on School Hill, close to the Market Square. The house was built in 1675 for a local tanner, Richard Preston. He called it Tanner Hall, but it earned its 'folly' nickname because it stood empty long after Richard's death. It has since been restored and a part of it houses a museum.

The railway reached this cotton-spinning town in 1875, and today it's well known as the southern terminus for the 72-mile scenic rail route through the Dales and up to Carlisle.

Settle's most famous son is probably the Reverend Benjamin Waugh (1839–1908), a Victorian social reformer who founded the National Society for the Prevention of Cruelty to Children (NSPCC). He was born in a saddler's shop in what is now Lloyds Bank, off the Market Square.

Northwest of Settle you'll find Giggleswick. The village is renowned for its public school founded in 1553, and it's a much quieter place than Settle to wander around.

EXPLORE BY BIKE
3 Peaks Cycles
3peakscycles.com
Market Place, Settle, BD24 99EJ
01729 824232
Take time out to enjoy the countryside in one of the best cycling areas of the Dales. The team here offers self-guided tours to suit everyone – or you can simply hire a bike, saddle up and spend the day exploring the countryside at your own pace.

EAT AND DRINK

The Lion at Settle
thelionsettle.co.uk
Duke Street, BD24 9DU
01729 822203
Owned by Thwaites and set in the market place, The Lion has interiors that ooze atmosphere and history – original inglenook fireplaces, wooden floors and a grand staircase lined with pictures that trace the town's history. Expect decent cask ales and a classic pub menu.

Ye Olde Naked Man Café
yeoldenakedmancafe.com
Market Place, BD24 9ED
01729 823230
This busy tea shop and bakery takes its name from a strange relief carved above the doorway, dated 1663. Inside, you can fill up on tempting cakes or pastries or try a savoury pie. You can buy the cafe's produce and their delicious breads in the shop.

▶ **PLACES NEARBY**
Just outside Settle, is the Settle Falconry at Feizor.

Settle Falconry
settlefalconry.co.uk
Feizor, Settle | 07879 645522
It's not a falconry centre open to the general public; this is a small experience for four people at a time enabling you to get hands-on with a beautiful trained bird of prey.

▶ Sheffield MAP REF 323 F5

Now the fourth largest city in England, Sheffield rose to prominence during the 19th century to become the steel capital of the world. The legend 'Made in Sheffield', engraved on tools and cutlery, has long been a byword for quality. Yet that industrial Sheffield lies on the edge of the Peak District National Park, next to some of the finest scenery in the North.

Sheffield today still has its industry, but has worked hard to be a modern, vibrant place. Its two universities guarantee a lively nightlife and the city is being revitalised as a centre for leisure activities, conferences and sporting excellence. The Sheffield Arena is South Yorkshire's major entertainment venue, hosting most Yorkshire gigs of the biggest names, and the theatres in the centre offer a wealth of art and culture.

The city might have lost its famous Don Valley Stadium, but its replacement Woodbourn Road has been refurbished to a high standard to maintain Sheffield's ambition to be the sporting capital of the North. The healthy long-term competition between local rivals the 'Blades' and 'Owls' is still a feature of the footballing scene, in the city regarded as the birthplace of the modern game.

Sheffield

If football isn't your thing, Sheffield is also home of the World Snooker Championship at the famous Crucible Theatre, and the Ponds Forge International Sports Centre, which boasts Olympic-standard swimming facilities.

Sheffield's steelmaking hasn't been thrown away though – the city is still a hive of industry, and in fact more steel and cutlery is made here today than ever before. At the lively Kelham Island Museum, on Alma Street, you can trace the history of Sheffield's industrial development over the last 400 years, with displays of working machinery and some of the products that have made Sheffield famous, particularly iron, steel and silverware.

Sheffield's Supertram is an enviable public transport system that is quiet, quick and comfortable. It's so good, Leeds have wanted one for years. The trams offer the most convenient way to get to both the Woodbourn Road Stadium and the Meadowhall shopping centre – the largest shopping centre in Yorkshire, built on the site of what was the city's largest steelworks.

10 actors from Yorkshire

- ▶ **Sean Bean** – Sheffield
- ▶ **Brian Blessed** – Mexborough
- ▶ **Judi Dench** – York
- ▶ **Ben Kingsley** – Scarborough
- ▶ **Anna Maxwell Martin** – Beverley
- ▶ **Felicity Montagu** – Leeds
- ▶ **Diana Rigg** – Doncaster
- ▶ **Patrick Stewart** – Mirfield
- ▶ **Tom Wilkinson** – Leeds
- ▶ **Penelope Wilton** – Scarborough

VISIT THE MUSEUMS AND GALLERIES

Kelham Island Museum

simt.co.uk

Alma Street, S3 8RY

0114 2722106 | Open Mon–Thu 10–4, Sun 11–4.45

Set on a man-made island that is over 900 years old, Kelham Island Museum is the showcase of Sheffield's industrial history from early industrialisation to modern times. Don't miss the penknife with no fewer than 365 retractable blades. The massive and mighty River Don steam engine – the largest in the world – once powered a steel-rolling mill and it can still be seen 'in steam'. Skilled cutlers, using traditional methods, can be seen at work in the 'Little Mesters' workshops – this is a 'living' museum. Learn what it was like to live and work in Sheffield's past, and see how steel-making forged both the city of today and the world.

Millennium Gallery

museums-sheffield.org.uk

Arundel Gate, S1 2PP

0114 2782600 | Open Mon–Sat 10–5, Sun 11–4

With four different galleries under one roof, the Millennium Gallery has something for everyone. Enjoy new exhibitions drawn from Sheffield's collections and those of Britain's national galleries and museums, including the Victoria and Albert Museum and the Tate Gallery. See the best of contemporary craft and design in a range of exhibitions by established and up-and-coming makers. Be dazzled by Sheffield's magnificent and internationally important collection of decorative and domestic metalwork and silverware. Discover the Ruskin Collection, with its wonderful array of treasures by Victorian artist and writer John Ruskin. The best of all, it's free – though you may be charged for some special exhibitions.

Weston Park

museums-sheffield.org.uk

Western Bank, S10 2TP

0114 2782600 | Open Mon–Sat 10–5, Sun 11–4

This award-winning museum tells the story of the city from its geological roots to the people, music and politics that shaped the modern-day city.

This is definitely not a 'do not touch' place, and the kids will love it.

GO ROUND THE GARDENS
Sheffield Winter Garden
sheffield.gov.uk
Surrey Street, S1 2HH
0114 2053547 | Open Mon–Sat 8–8, Sun 8–6

Sheffield's Winter Garden is one of the largest glasshouses to be built in the UK during the last hundred years. Next to the Peace Gardens and the Millennium Galleries, it is home to more than 2,500 plants from 150 species, including big palms from Central America, Madagascar and China.

GET INDUSTRIAL
Abbeydale Industrial Hamlet
simt.co.uk
Abbeydale Road South, S7 2QW
0114 2722106 | Open Mon–Thu 10–4, Sun 11–4.45

Step back in time and catch a glimpse of life at home and at work in a rural scythe-making plant and steelworks dating back to the 18th century. Workers' houses, water wheels, steel furnaces, tilt hammers and workshops make up one of the largest water-powered industrial complexes on the River Sheaf. The family events programme offers traditional crafts and demonstrations, living history tours and activities. Join in the annual Steam Gathering in early October, when goliath steam engines congregate to show off their paces.

PLAY A ROUND
Sheffield's golf courses have a wide diversity. Beauchief Golf Club is a pay-and-play course with natural water hazards. The rolling land of the course looks west to the Pennines, and a 12th-century abbey adorns the course. The Birley Wood Golf Club is an undulating meadowland course with varied features, easy walking and good views.

The challenging Blue Monster parkland course of the Rother Valley Golf Centre features a variety of water hazards. Notable holes include the seventh, with its island green fronted by water and dominated by bunkers to the rear. And look out for the water on the par 5, 18th. At some 500 feet above sea level, the beautiful Hillsborough Golf Club is a moorland and woodland course. It has a challenging first four holes, which are into a prevailing wind, and a tight, testing 14th hole.

Tinsley Park Municipal Golf Club is another of Sheffield's undulating parkland courses, with plenty of trees and rough and a signature hole of the par 3, 17th. Abbeydale Golf Club is a well presented undulating parkland course set in the Beauchief Estate, with fine views over Sheffield and the Derbyshire countryside.

Beauchief Golf Club
beauchiefgolfclub.co.uk
Abbey Lane, S8 0DB
0114 2367274 | Open daily

Birley Wood Golf Club
sheffieldgolf.co.uk
Birley Lane, Birley, S12 3BP
0114 2647262 | Open daily

Rother Valley Golf Centre
rothervalleygolfcentre.co.uk
Mansfield Road, Wales Bar,
S26 5PQ | 0114 2473 000

Hillsborough Golf Club
hillsboroughgolfclub.co.uk
Worrall Road, S6 4BE | 0114 2349
151 (Sec) | Open Mon–Fri, Sun pm

**Tinsley Park Municipal
Golf Club**
sheffieldgolf.co.uk
High Hazels Park, Darnall, S9 4PE
0114 2448 974 | Open daily

Abbeydale Golf Club
abbeydalegolfclub.co.uk
Twentywell Lane, Dore, S17 4QA
0114 2360 763 | Open Mon–Tue,
Fri, Sun

EAT AND DRINK
Broadfield Ale House
thebroadfield.co.uk
452 Abbeydale Road, S7 1FR
0114 255 0200
Silent movie-goers and steam
railway passengers were
among the first customers at
the Broadfield, built just before
Queen Victoria died. Millhouses
and Ecclesall station no longer
exists, but this pub is still very
much in business. No fewer
than nine handles proffer the
discerning ale enthusiast a
wonderful choice, from the
likes of Stancill, Acorn, Black
Iris and Blackjack breweries.
Pride is taken in the food too.

The Fat Cat
thefatcat.co.uk
23 Alma Street, S3 8SA
0114 2494 801
Built in 1832, it was known as
The Alma Hotel for many years,
then in 1981 it was the first
Sheffield pub to introduce guest
beers. The policy continues,
with constantly changing,
mainly microbrewery, guests
from across the country, two
handpumped ciders, unusual
bottled beers, Belgian pure fruit
juices and British country
wines. The pub's own Kelham
Island Brewery accounts for
at least four of the eleven
traditional draught real ales.
The smart interior is very much
that of a traditional, welcoming
back-street pub, with real fires,
while outside is an attractive
walled garden with Victorian-
style lanterns.

Kelham Island Tavern
62 Russell Street, S3 8RW
0114 2722 482
This 1830s backstreet pub was
built to quench the thirst of
steelmakers who lived and
worked nearby. The semi-
derelict pub was rescued in
2001 by Lewis Gonda and
Trevor Wraith, who transformed
it into a small treasure. The
pub is located in a conservation
and popular walking area,
with old buildings converted
into stylish apartments, and
The Kelham Island Museum
round the corner. The real
ale list is formidable: four
residents including Barnsley
Bitter and Bradfield Farmers

Blonde are joined by ten ever-changing guests, as well as Westons Old Rosie cider, and a beer festival is held every year at the end of June. Good-quality pub grub is available six days a week and includes a great veggie choice. Great in the summer, the pub has won awards for its beer garden and floral displays.

Nonnas ●

nonnas.co.uk

535–541 Ecclesall Road, S11 8PR

0114 268 6166

Nonnas is a bustling, good-natured Italian restaurant with friendly staff, cafe-style marble-topped tables and green walls. Many of the staples are made in-house, from pasta to ice cream, using Yorkshire produce and ingredients flown in from the homeland, and the menu is a celebration of modern Italian cooking. This is an imaginative kitchen turning out properly cooked, highly original dishes.

Rafters Restaurant ●●

raftersrestaurant.co.uk

220 Oakbrook Road, Nethergreen, S11 7ED | 0114 230 4819

After over 20 years as a dining hotspot in the city, Rafters continues to go from strength to strength. Located on the first floor of a shop in a green part of Sheffield, there are leafy views to be had and some seriously good cooking to be enjoyed. The room has capacious windows and a smart finish, with richly upholstered,

high-backed chairs and tables laid with white linen cloths. The cooking is modern and the menu is packed with interesting combinations.

The Sheffield Tap

sheffieldtap.com

Platform 1B, Sheffield Station, Sheaf Street, S1 2BP | 0114 273 7558

For more than 30 years disused, derelict and vandalised, the former Edwardian refreshment room and dining rooms of Sheffield Midland Railway Station have become a much praised Grade II listed free house. Painstakingly restored to its former glory by the current custodians, with help from the Railway Heritage Trust, The Sheffield Tap is now a beer hotspot with its own on-site microbrewery, offering ten real ales, one real cider, a dozen keg products and more than 200 bottled beers from around the world. Food is limited to bagged bar snacks, and children are welcome until 8pm every day.

▶ **PLACES NEARBY**

One of the beauties of Sheffield is its close proximity to the fabulous Peak District National Park. Britain's first National Park is only minutes away from the city centre by car – and can be reached by train too. Here you'll find a whole range of walking and cycling on offer, providing an interesting contrast to the more northerly National Parks of Yorkshire.

Visit www.peakdistrict.gov.uk for more information.

Whitley Hall Hotel ◉◉

whitleyhall.com
Elliott Lane, Grenoside, S35 8NR
0114 245 4444

Surrounded by rolling countryside, Whitley Hall is a solid stone, ivy-clad mansion dating from the 16th century (it has a priest's hole) with 20 acres of grounds including lakes and immaculate gardens. In surroundings like these, it's no wonder the place is a popular wedding venue. The restaurant may have a whiff of formality, but the kitchen keeps ahead of the game with a thoroughly modern British menu, superbly cooked and exquisitely presented.

The Wortley Arms ◉

wortley-arms.co.uk
Halifax Road, Wortley, S35 7DB
0114 288 8749

This is a traditional Georgian coaching inn, with a reassuring interior of panelled walls, oak beams, open fires, hunting-themed pictures and a jumble of furniture – in short, an appealing spot to enjoy a pint of locally brewed ale or an ice-cold lager and some straightforward modern gastro pub cooking. The kitchen keeps a clear focus on local ingredients and seasonality in its menus, which take in timeless pub staples and up-to-date ideas.

▶ Skipton MAP REF 327 D4

Skipton fairly buzzes with life, a busy market filling its main street with stalls four days out of seven. It has modern shops, ancient inns, churches, a museum, restaurants and hotels, as well as a Norman castle that's over 900 years old but still in a superb state of preservation.

Skipton Castle is one of the most complete and well-preserved medieval castles in England. It was the birthplace of the indomitable Lady Anne Clifford and bears the Clifford family motto of Desormais (Henceforth) in large lettering above the splendid main entrance gate. Lady Anne (1590–1676) is Skipton's hero – born in the castle, she grew up to be a feisty, independent-minded lady who travelled frequently between several homes around the country and fought legal battles to reclaim her inheritance. Her colourful diary is still widely available in print, and makes a very readable record of her interesting life and her era.

Beside the castle is Holy Trinity Church, which dates mainly from the 14th and 15th centuries. It contains the tombs of many members of the Clifford family (though not Lady Anne), and a fine Tudor roof and screen.

The castle and church stand at the top of the High Street; halfway down is the Craven Museum and Gallery, housed in the town hall. There is a small exhibition relating to one of

Skipton's most famous sons, Thomas Spencer, of Marks and Spencer, who co-founded the company.

The oldest building in Skipton's High Street is the Red Lion Inn. It was built in either the late 14th or early 15th century and was once partly a farm. It is said to have been owned at one time by Richard III. In the forecourt of the inn you can see a grisly relic of what once passed for entertainment – a bear-baiting stone.

Skipton, like Settle, is a place whose back streets need to be explored. There are also some pleasant walks to be enjoyed along the canal towpaths. The Leeds and Liverpool Canal passes through the town, joining on its way the Ellerbeck and Springs Canal, adding to the sense that Skipton, for centuries, really has been the 'Gateway to the Dales'.

TAKE IN SOME HISTORY

Skipton Castle

skiptoncastle.co.uk
BD23 1AW | 01756 792442
Open Mar–Sep Mon–Sat 10–5
Sun 11–5, Oct–Mar Mon–Sat 11–4,
Sun 12–4

Although the castle dates from much earlier, it is strongly associated with the Civil War, when it withstood a siege for three years. By the time the troops had left in 1645, the structure was almost totally destroyed by cannon fire – the gatehouse that stands robustly at the head of the main street today is the result of painstaking restoration work. Some of the original Norman building remains, but most dates from the 13th century,

▼ Skipton Castle

renovated by Lady Anne Clifford in the mid-17th century. There are plenty of events to look out for, including re-enactments of battles and life in the castle in medieval times, performances of Shakespeare plays and a clog-dancing festival.

VISIT THE MUSEUM
Craven Museum and Gallery
cravenmuseum.org
Town Hall, High Street, BD23 1AH
01756 706407 | Open Mon, Wed–Sat 10–4
The local museum depicts life – ancient and modern – in Skipton and the surrounding Craven area, with displays on social history, archaeology, costume and art. One of the most remarkable exhibits is a piece of cloth found in one of the Bronze Age graves nearby – it's believed to be the oldest piece of cloth to be discovered in Britain.

TAKE A TRAIN RIDE
Embsay & Bolton Abbey Steam Railway
embsayboltonabbeyrailway.org.uk
Embsay Station | 01756 710614 (general), 01756 795189 (talking timetable)
Embsay lies to the east of Skipton. Its station dates from 1888, and steam trains run from here to the station at Bolton Abbey. It's still a 1.5-mile walk to the abbey ruins (see page 68), but is a pleasant way to travel through the Dales. Trains run daily in high summer, and most Sundays through the year.

EXPLORE BY BIKE
The Yorkshire Dales Cycleway is an almost circular route of 130 miles around the Yorkshire Dales National Park (see page 318), which begins and ends in Skipton. It mostly follows the back road, and is waymarked with blue signs that carry a white cycle and a large direction arrow. It is suggested that the average cyclist could tackle the route in six days, each day's stage being between 18 and 25 miles. A folder, containing full details and laminated maps for each section, is available from National Park Centres and other outlets.

Dave Ferguson Cycles
davefergusoncycles.com
3 Albion Yard, BD23 1FD
01756 795367
A wide range of cycles, suitable for all ages, from toddlers to adults, can be hired and they can arrange delivery and collection of them too.

TAKE A BOAT TRIP
Leeds and Liverpool Canal
Several companies run boat trips along the canal, including Skipton-based Pennine Boat Trips.

Pennine Boat Trips
penninecruisers.com
19 Coach Street, BD23 1LH
01756 795478

▶ **PLACES NEARBY**
If you're looking for somewhere to dine out, you're spoiled for choice around Skipton.

The Angel Inn ◉◉
angelhetton.co.uk

Hetton, BD23 6LT | 01756 730263

The Angel was a drovers' inn about 500 years back, and must have presented as welcoming a sight to fatigued farmworkers then as it does to modern gastronomes today. Clad in red and green clambering foliage, it's a warren of little corners and crannies, with winter fires and cask ales to warm the cockles. This country pub offers inspired, imaginative cooking and decent wines.

The Bull at Broughton
thebullatbroughton.com

Broughton, BD23 3AE

01756 792065

The Bull is part of the historic Broughton Estate, 3,000 acres of prime Yorkshire parkland and countryside, owned by the Tempests for nine centuries. Their family seat, Broughton Hall, is close by. While essentially a dining pub, The Bull still loves to see beer drinkers, as its good selection of real ales proves – Dark Horse Hetton Pale Ale and Thwaites Original – and a real cider, Westons Stowford Press. The chefs rely on carefully chosen local producers for modern English dishes such as seafood, game or ham sharing platters. Theres also a comprehensive gluten-free menu.

Devonshire Arms at Cracoe
devonshirecracoe.co.uk

Grassington Road, Cracoe, BD23 6LA | 01756 730237

Midway between Skipton and Grassington, this convivial and lovingly renovated 17th-century inn is conveniently located for the Three Peaks and has excellent views of Rhylstone Fell. Its claim to fame is as the original setting for the Rhylstone Ladies WI calendar – a story memorably portrayed in the film *Calendar Girls* (2003). Enjoy a rotating selection of award-winning real ales; the drinks list also offers a generous choice of wines sold by the glass, and an eclectic collection of rare bottled refreshments. The inn's menus feature rare breed meats alongside classics pub meals. The provenance of all ingredients is reassuringly identified on the menu; and if you would like to pre-order something special, it can be sourced for you with just a few days' notice.

The Tempest Arms
tempestarms.co.uk

Elslack, BD23 3AY | 01282 842450

A local landmark, the Tempest dates to the coaching days of the 17th century. The rolling Yorkshire Dales and surrounding countryside draw walkers and cyclists, who come to enjoy the pub's warm welcome and convivial atmosphere. Wood fires, comfy cushions, quiet corners and alcoves and dining spaces set the interior's comfortable mood, completed by an array of Yorkshire ales at the bar and a vast menu of pub food.

▸ Sleights   MAP REF 338 C3

Sleights (pronounced Slites) straddles the River Esk in a sheltered dip in the landscape, on the road between Whitby and Pickering. There are few buildings here to attract the eye, but it's a convenient spot from which to explore the surrounding countryside – whether you head for open moors or the environs of the Esk – Yorkshire's only salmon river. Ruswarp, between Sleights and the sea, marks the tidal limit of the River Esk.

A minor road from Sleights leads to a hamlet with the name of Ugglebarnby, which means 'the farm of old owl beard'. Continue past Ugglebarnby to Littlebeck, on a road that snakes through this delightful village. Here you can enjoy a couple of fine walks, one along May Beck and the other to the south to see Falling Foss, an exquisite waterfall in the woods.

▸ Spurn Head National Nature Reserve

MAP REF 333 F5

ywt.org.uk

Kilnsea, HU12 0UH | 01964 650533

Spurn Head – also called Spurn Point – is the narrow sand-spit sticking out of the East Riding of Yorkshire. It reaches into the North Sea to form the north bank of the Humber estuary, curling round for more than three miles. Anchored by little more than marram grass, it's a National Nature Reserve. A vast number of migrating birds, blown down from Scandinavia or on their way north from Africa, know it as a great stop-off place for a breather. To get to the nature reserve at the tip you'll need to walk or cycle – but be careful, the sea washes over the beach here and access is not always possible. There's a visitor centre, and hides are set along the spit for birders to watch from. Dogs aren't allowed here – not even in your car.

▼ Spurn Head

▶ Staithes MAP REF 338 B1

You could easily miss the Staithes turning off the main A174 coast road, but drive half a mile, park in the pay-and-display car park and proceed on foot, and you'll soon see why Staithes is so special.

This perfectly preserved Yorkshire fishing village is divided into two by Cowbar Beck and the steep-sided gorge through which it runs. For centuries the people of Staithes have had to cope with the twin problems of an inhospitable site and the ravages of the North Sea – and they've made their living from the sea, while always taking care to respect its awesome power.

The Staithes you see today is a village that would have been immediately familiar to the young James Cook, who spent an impatient 18 months working at the counter of a draper's shop in the village before realising his ambition to go to sea. The whitewashed houses, pantiled roofs, fishing cobles and lobster pots would make him feel at home.

It may seem that time has stood still here, but the battering from the sea has been relentless. Despite the shelter given by its steep cliffs, Staithes has lost many buildings to its stormy seas. The little draper's shop was washed away; a house near the Cod and Lobster pub bears a commemorative plaque but has been rebuilt since James Cook lived and worked here. The pub itself backs on to the harbour wall and has suffered more than its fair share of storm damage – it's been rebuilt three times, most recently in 1953.

On a sunny summer's day, it is hard to imagine such destruction. You would have to make your visit in winter, when a strong northeasterly gale is blowing, and the waves are hammering against the harbour wall, to understand why the people of Staithes have earned a reputation for self-reliance. To have maintained a viable community here, despite the drawbacks, is remarkable.

It's small wonder that painters and photographers are attracted here in droves. The village used to have a railway station; both station and line are gone, leaving just the trackbed and the stanchions of the old viaduct over the gorge as reminders of the scenic line from Saltburn to Scarborough.

To the north of Staithes are Boulby Cliffs. At more than 656 feet they are the highest, if not the most dramatic, on England's east coast and offer excellent views. Close by is the Boulby Potash Mine, the deepest mine in Europe. The extent of the mining operation here can be gauged by the fact that tunnels extend almost three miles out under the North Sea.

VISIT THE MUSEUM
Captain Cook and Staithes Heritage Centre
captaincookatstaithes.co.uk
High Street, Staithes, TS13 5BQ
01947 841454 | Open Feb–Dec daily 10–5, Jan Sat–Sun 10–5
The best museums are often those run by enthusiasts – and this is no exception. Reg and Ann Firth have a wealth of knowledge about the world-famous seaman to share, alongside the Cook memorabilia and nautical items in this fascinating museum, located in the imposing former Methodist chapel.

▶ PLACES NEARBY
Just a few miles up the coast is the Cleveland Ironstone Mining Museum, and a spot of sailing.

Cleveland Ironstone Mining Museum
ironstonemuseum.co.uk
Deepdale, Skinningrove, Cleveland TS13 4AP | 01287 642877
Open late Mar–early Nov Mon–Fri 10–3.30, Sat 1–3.30; organised groups at other times
Discover the history of ironstone mining and its influence on the people's lives at this museum. Ironstone mining in the area had a major

impact on the growth of Teesside as a whole, and this is the place to find out more on a fully guided tour and even head briefly underground.

Scaling Dam Sailing Club
scalingdam.org
Scaling Dam Reservoir, Whitby

Moor Road, Easington, Saltburn-by-the-Sea, TS13 4TP
01287 643026
Indulge in a range of watersports on this reservoir, owned by Northumbrian Water. There are also some lovely walks taking in the wildlife around the area.

▶ Stokesley MAP REF 337 E3

Now bypassed by the modern A172, Stokesley maintains the unhurried character of a market town. The broad verges of West Green create a little space between the Georgian facades of the houses and the main street that winds through the town. Stokesley still has regular markets, held every Friday on the cobbled edges of the main street. There are also monthly farmers' markets, and each September it's the site of one of the largest agricultural shows in the area.

The big open spaces include College Square and the market square. Behind them is Levenside, where the River Leven – little more than a stream at this point – follows its tranquil winding course between grassy banks and underneath a succession of little bridges. The oldest of these is the handsome arch of a fine old packhorse bridge; close by is a ford.

The National Park boundary makes a detour to exclude the town and neighbouring Great Ayton. While many of Stokesley's inhabitants commute to industrial Teesdale immediately to the north, Stokesley has, nevertheless, kept its own identity.

The Cleveland Hills form a backdrop to the south as you drive northeast along the A172 between Osmotherley and Stokesley. Once tramped by drovers, packhorse men, pedlars and monks visiting their outlying granges, the paths of the Cleveland Hills are now used by weekend walkers.

▶ Studley Royal
see **Fountains Abbey & Studley Royal**, page 102

▶ Sutton Bank MAP REF 337 E6

The view from the top of Sutton Bank is one of the finest in Yorkshire. Below you, spread out like a vast picnic blanket, is the flat plain of the Vale of York. It would be hard to imagine a sharper division between the rich, arable farmland that lies to the south and the heather moors of the Hambleton Hills immediately to the north. On a clear day, you can see York Minster and the Three Peaks of the Yorkshire Dales – if you have a pair of binoculars. Gormire Lake, directly below and almost hidden by trees, was once imagined to be bottomless.

The A170 marks the midway point between the market towns of Thirsk and Helmsley by making a long 1-in-4 climb to the top of Sutton Bank. You can watch cars and lorries labouring up what is one of the steepest stretches of road in the country. For those who want to stretch their legs and enjoy the view, or for those whose engines overheat, there is a car park and information centre conveniently sited at the top. From here there is a splendid – and undemanding – walk along the edge of Sutton Bank.

The Yorkshire Gliding Club operates from the top of the bank, and on summer weekends the sky will be filled with slim, silent planes exploiting the thermals rising up the scar. Powered planes tow the gliders over the edge – a moment that would moisten the palms of all but the most nonchalant of flyers. With the addition of microlight aircraft, hang-gliders and, of course, soaring birds, the skies beyond Sutton Bank can get very busy indeed.

The walk continues along the top of Roulston Scar, offering beautiful views all the way, to Kilburn's White Horse (see page 160) – a landmark which looks best from a distance.

SADDLE UP
Boltby Trekking Centre
boltbytrekking.co.uk
Johnstone Arms, Boltby, YO7 2DY
01845 537392

Boltby is perched on the edge of Sutton Bank, and you'll find this trekking centre based on a working farm in the village itself. It has access to a wide variety of bridleways through forestry, over hills and moorland trails. You can choose from a number of different horses and ponies, and absolute beginners are welcome.

EAT AND DRINK
The Hare Inn ●●●
thehare-inn.com
Scawton, YO7 2HG
01845 597769

The Hare has the look of a proper moorland inn; a sturdy white-painted construction built to withstand the worst the climate can throw at it. It's very much a pub, with real ales at the pumps and a fire in the grate, but stick around to sample the food and you'll discover The Hare is a little dynamo of culinary endeavour. Scawton lies east of Sutton Bank, off the A170.

▶ Sutton-on-the-Forest MAP REF 329 E2

This small village between York and Easingwold has a notably long name – the forest in question was the royal hunting demesne of Galtres, which was largely chopped down in the 17th century. You'll see an attractive main street of mellow old houses overlooking a green, with a handsome church – where Laurence Sterne served as vicar from 1738 to 1768 – a couple of excellent pubs, and there's a stately Georgian manor house, Sutton Park, to explore.

The village changed ownership many times, with the Nevill and Fauconberg families prominent. During World War II there was an airfield here, operating bombers flown by the Royal Canadian Air Force – you can see a sundial memorial to those who never returned in the garden that was the old village pound.

TAKE IN SOME HISTORY
Sutton Park
statelyhome.co.uk
YO61 1DP | 01347 810249
See website for opening times, house guided tours only
This early Georgian house contains fine furniture, paintings and porcelain. Large parts of the collection originally came from Buckingham House, now known worldwide as Buckingham Palace. The grounds have superb terraced gardens, including a lily pond and a Georgian ice house. There are also delightful woodland walks.

EAT AND DRINK
Miss Daisy's Tea Rooms
missdaisystearooms.co.uk
Sutton Park, YO61 1DP
01347 810852
Opened in 2003, these tea rooms are situated in the beautiful grounds of Sutton Park stately home, and feature, as much as possible, locally sourced food. In fact the eggs, meat, chutneys, preserves and the fruit and vegetables are all from local North Yorkshire producers. From light bites and soups to afternoon tea, there's something here for everyone.

The Rose & Crown
theroseandcrownyork.com
Main Street, YO61 1DP
01347 811333
There's no shortage of period charm at The Rose & Crown, with the 200-year-old inn still packing a punch when it comes to period features (wooden floors, low-beamed ceilings and the like), but it is looking pretty spruce these days, fit-for-purpose as a 21st-century dining pub. The culinary output is focused on seasonal and local ingredients. Outside is an African-style gazebo and a large south-facing rose-filled garden with sofas and recliners. There are regular quiz nights on Tuesdays and an Open Mic Night on Thursdays.

▶ Swaledale MAP REF 335 D3

At the northern tip of the Yorkshire Dales National Park, the unspoiled valley of Swaledale winds its way from the high moors on the Cumbria–Yorkshire boundary to the market town of Richmond, where the valley meets the lowlands.

It's easy to leave modern life behind in Swaledale. With miles of hills, moorland and mountains to explore, and few modern distractions, you can walk, cycle or ride, and tour to your heart's content.

Walk in any direction and you'll find fields of native wild flowers, waterfalls, grouse and hares, curlews and lapwings, along with the little stone hay barns unique to this area. For the best in colour, June and early July are when those spectacular wildflower meadows are a blaze of colour. When night draws in, head for the scenic stone villages and spend a relaxing hour in a traditional tea room or a quiet country pub.

Swaledale is famous for its hardy breed of sheep. Swaledales are noted for their off-white wool and curled horns, and found widely throughout the more mountainous parts of Britain.

Swaledale village names are mostly short and sharp, from their Norse origins: Muker, Keld, Thwaite, Reeth, Angram. Even the longer ones are spat out with those same short Norse vowels: Gunnerside, Arkengarthdale. Most of the villages in this area are short and sharp too, strung out along the B6270 like knots in a rope, but they will certainly welcome you and offer lots of places to shop and eat, as well as a range of local craft studios. Beyond Keld, the 'knots' end, and the lonely road crosses the fells to Nateby and Kirkby Stephen at the northern end of the valley of Mallerstang, as it opens out into the lovely Vale of Eden.

Travelling from Reeth, Gunnerside is the first sizeable community you reach. It is an appealing place with grey stone cottages – once the homes of lead miners – looking down on the River Swale with high-rising moors. Lead mining brought prosperity to the area, and the remains of several mines can be found just a short distance from the centre of the village. Another walk is to the unusual Ivelet Bridge.

▼ View over Muker, Swaledale

Beyond Ivelet is Muker, a collection of stone cottages clustered in jigsaw streets that zigzag steeply up from the main road. Plaques on the church wall commemorate Richard and Cherry Kearton, brothers who were born in Thwaite and went to school in Muker. They devoted their lives to watching wildlife and became early pioneers of wildlife photography.

Less than a mile west of Muker is Thwaite, where the cottage in which the Kearton brothers were born stands. This idyllic place hides the tragedy of the fearsome flood of 1899, when the waters of Thwaite Beck swept down from Stock Dale in the west and almost wiped out the entire community. It is said that flowers washed from Thwaite's cottage gardens were later found growing in Muker.

The last Swaledale village is Keld, quietly going about its business, set back from the main road in a dead end that leads down to the River Swale and some of the valley's most impressive falls. The Pennine Way passes the edge of Keld before heading northwards up Stonesdale to the lonely outpost that is Tan Hill (see page 277).

SEE A LOCAL CHURCH
Keld Chapel
nationaltrust.org.uk
Keld Lane, Shap, CA10 3NW
01768 361893
Thought originally to be the chantry for Shap Abbey, this remote 16th-century building seems to have been used as a cottage and a meeting house at various points during its long history. And if you want to look inside, the key to the door can be found hanging by the front door of the house opposite – just return it afterwards.

EAT AND DRINK
Ghyllfoot Tearoom
ghyllfoot.co.uk
Lodge House, Gunnerside,
DL11 6LA | 01748 886239
Home-baking and local specialities mark out this delightful tea-shop in the centre of Gunnerside. There's a terrace and garden at the back facing out on to fields towards Gunnerside Gill, or you can eat inside.

Muker Village Store and Tea Shop
mukervillage.co.uk
Muker, DL11 6QG
01748 886409
This cosy tea-shop is a part of the Dales landscape. The store looks after the needs of the local community as well as stocking a good range of local produce, while the tea room has a tempting menu of home made snacks and cakes. Muker has a special place in the lives of walkers in the area, as it is on both the Pennine Way and the Coast to Coast walks. Indeed Swaledale was said to be Alfred Wainwright's favourite dale – and walkers can enjoy the offer of bed-and-breakfast too.

▶ Tadcaster   MAP REF 329 D5

There's often a certain – not unpleasant – odour hanging over Tadcaster, emanating from the three famous breweries based in the town: John Smiths (with its distinctive Victorian brick chimney); the Tower Brewery (ultra-modern looking; Molson Coors, previously Bass); and Samuel Smith's (Yorkshire's oldest, established in 1758, and still delivering locally via horse-drawn dray cart). Tadcaster is second only to Burton-upon-Trent as a centre for English brewing, which started up here in the 14th century.

Tadcaster was originally founded by the Romans, who named it Calcaria – from the Latin word for lime. This reflected the large deposits of limestone in the area, and from which many significant buildings have been constructed, including York Minster (see page 305). The town grew up at a crossing point over the River Wharfe.

The oldest building in Tadcaster is probably the half-timbered Ark on Kirkgate, which takes its name from the carved heads on its front, believed to show Noah and his wife. The Pilgrim Fathers apparently met here in the early 17th century to talk over their move to North America.

▶ PLACES NEARBY

West of Tadcaster is a fine Queen Anne mansion.

Bramham Park
bramhampark.co.uk
LS23 6ND | 01937 846000
Open Mon–Fri by appointment only – see website for booking
Bramham Park was built by Robert Benson and is the home of his descendants. The landscape remains virtually unchanged from that time, and there's a garden with ornamental ponds, cascades, temples and avenues. You're most likely to visit for a festival – The Leeds Rock Festival fills the park in August, and Bramham International Horse Trials take place here in June.

▶ Tan Hill Inn   MAP REF 334 C2

tanhillinn.com
Tan Hill, DL11 6ED | 01833 628246

It's not often that a pub gets a main entry in a guide like this, but the Tan Hill is an exception – mainly as there is no village. In fact, there's nothing else around for miles, with the pub standing on bleak, wild moorland at the head of Arkengarthdale, truly miles from anywhere. There's no public transport, so car, bike or Shanks' pony is the order of the day to get there – but check the opening hours before you set off

The pub is reached via a hairpin road from Keld, four miles to the south, and is the highest pub in Britain at some 1,732 feet above sea level. So proud are its clientele of its status as a great Yorkshire pub that there was outrage when boundary changes in 1974 moved it into County Durham – it was soon moved back.

You don't want to get lost up here in snow, ice or fog – but no matter the weather outside, there's always a welcome as warm as the open fires inside. Bar food is designed to satisfy the hunger of passing Pennine Way-farers. Good ale and a series of weekend music and motoring events means you'll seldom be short of good company.

▶ Thirsk   MAP REF 337 D6

Thirsk might be a typical North Yorkshire market town, with a square overlooked by the Victorian town clock, but most people today don't just visit for the market on Mondays and Saturdays – good as it is – or indeed for the characterful Edwardian Ritz Cinema, beautifully preserved and run by volunteers. They come to see Skeldale House in Kirkgate – on the right as you return from the church to the Market Square. This was the surgery of local vet Alf Wight (1916–95). Not heard of him? He's better known by his pen name, James Herriot, and for the entertaining series of memoirs he published from 1970 onward, later filmed and televised with huge success as *All Creatures Great and Small*. His surgery is now an award-winning museum, The World of James Herriot – and this was where Wight worked for all his professional life. Thirsk itself is a major character in the books, appearing lightly disguised as Darrowby.

James Herriot is not Thirsk's only famous son – cricketer Thomas Lord (1755–1832), the founder of Lord's Cricket Ground in London, hailed from the town too. His birthplace is now the town's museum. The local cricket team have rather different resources, of course – they play their matches on the nice flat green area in the middle of the racecourse.

VISIT THE MUSEUM
The World of James Herriot
worldofjamesherriot.com
23 Kirkgate, YO7 1PL
01845 524234 | Open Mar–Oct
10–5, Nov–Feb 10–4
The museum has reconstructions of what the surgery and the family rooms were like in the 1940s, and tells the history of veterinary science. Whether or not you're a fan of the Herriot tales, which began with *If Only They Could Talk* in 1970, you'll find it a fascinating and nostalgic tour.

MEET THE ANIMALS
Monk Park Farm
Visitor Centre
monkparkfarm.co.uk
Bagby, YO7 2AG | 01845 597730
Open Feb–Oct daily 10–5, Nov
Fri–Sun 11–3
The monks are long gone, and
this farm is now a favourite for
children. There is something for
all ages on the farm, with a
variety of animals from guinea
pigs and alpacas to goats and
donkeys. There are indoor and
outdoor viewing and feeding
areas – and the all-important
adventure playground too.

MEET THE BIRDS
Falconry UK –
Birds of Prey Centre
falconrycentre.co.uk
Sion Hill Hall, Kirby Wiske, YO7 4EU
01845 587522 | Open Mar–Oct
daily 10.30–5; displays (weather
permitting) at 11.30, 1.30, 3.30
Enjoy the excitement of falconry
with over 70 birds and 30
species, with three flying
displays daily – weather
permitting. After each display,
birds are brought out for
visitors to handle.

GO TO THE RACES
Thirsk Racecourse
thirskracecourse.net
Station Road, YO7 1QL
01845 522276
Hosting some 16 flat fixtures
per year between April and
September, including five
Saturday afternoon and three
evening meetings, Thirsk
Racecourse attracts high-class
runners and jockeys from
across the country.

▶ PLACES NEARBY
Get out and about at Yorkshire
Outdoors in Felixkirk.

Yorkshire Outdoors
yorkshire-outdoors.co.uk
Felixkirk, near Thirsk, YO7 2DP
01845 537766
Take some 4x4s, expert
instruction and a 45-acre
course, and you're ready for a
great day of off-road action –
wallowing through deep mud
and water, climbing impossibly
steep hills, creeping over
breathtaking crests in a 4x4.
Or perhaps bouncing over
extreme terrain on a quad bike
is more your thing?

▶ Thorton-le-Dale   MAP REF 338 C5
Thorton-le-Dale is certainly one of the prettiest villages in
the county – despite being chopped in half by the busy A170 –
and the quaint thatched cottage beside Dalby Beck must be
the most photographed dwelling in Yorkshire, making
countless appearances on calendars and biscuit tins. And
when the boundary of a National Park makes a special detour
to include a village, you know it's worth a visit. You are advised
to come outside the busier holiday periods if you can, as
Thornton-le-Dale is best explored in tranquillity, when the
crowds have gone home.

The pace of life here is characterised by the beck, which meanders a steady course through the village, punctuated by a succession of tiny bridges. You'll find a slender market cross and a set of wooden stocks on the village green near the crossroads. On the opposite side are Lady Lumley's Almshouses, a block of 12 dwellings built in 1670 and still retaining their original use. There's a small but appealing motor museum to discover, too.

Thornton-le-Dale's churchyard is the last resting place of Sir Richard Cholmeley of Roxby, a swarthy, larger-than-life figure known as the Black Knight of the North. When not fighting Scottish invaders off the coast or causing upset at home, he served as constable of Scarborough, and died in 1583.

To explore further afield, take the Forest Drive (toll payable) through Dalby Forest, which is easily accessible by driving north from the village. You can enjoy the numerous walking trails, mountain-bike routes, fishing areas and picnic places.

GET OUTDOORS
Dalby Forest
forestry.gov.uk
YO18 7LT | 01751 472771
Dalby Forest has walking trails for every ability, dedicated cycling trails with bike hire available on site and several different adventure play areas. You'll soon see why Dalby Forest is a great day out. Bring a barbeque to one of the special picnic areas, play ball games, discover about the area in the refurbished visitor centre and eat in the cafe.

WALK THE HIGH ROPES
Go Ape! Dalby
goape.co.uk
Low Dalby, YO18 7LT | 0845 643 9215 | Open Apr–Oct Wed–Mon, (daily during school holidays), Nov Sat–Sun (pre-booking advised)
Swinging from the tree-tops on hilltop-to-hilltop zip wires and a plunging valley below is all part of the Go Ape! Dalby Forest experience. Unleash your inner monkey and enjoy an ape-tastic day.

EXPLORE BY BIKE
Dalby Bike Barn
dalbybikebarn.co.uk
1 Pickering Road, Thornton-le-Dale, YO18 7LG | 01751 460049
All sorts of bikes are available for hire here, including a great range of cycles and buggies for children.

EAT AND DRINK
The New Inn
the-new-inn.com
Maltongate, YO18 7LF
01751 474226
Right on the crossroads in the middle of Thornton-le-Dale, this family-run Georgian coaching house dates back to 1720. The old-world charm of the location is echoed inside the bar and restaurant, with real log fires and exposed beams. Enjoy well-kept

Theakston Best Bitter and guest ales, bitters, lagers and wines, and tuck into hearty home-cooked pub food.

Warrington House
warringtonhouse.co.uk
Whitbygate, YO18 7RY
01751 475028
A traditional tea room in a former coaching inn – it's a perfect place to enjoy afternoon tea, with home made cakes and scones, or ploughman's lunch.

▶ **PLACES NEARBY**
The Fox and Rabbit Inn at Lockton, north of Thornton-le-Dale, is an archetypal North Yorkshire Moors pub.

The Fox & Rabbit Inn
foxandrabbit.co.uk
Whitby Road, Lockton, YO18 7NQ
01751 460213
This traditional pub – all heavy orange pantiles and honey limestone dressed with creepers – is set on a secluded junction at the fringe of Dalby Forest, north of Thornton. The owning Wood brothers are keen supporters of local microbreweries, with beers from brewers such as Cropton and Wold Top slaking the thirst of the cyclists and ramblers with whom the pub is a very popular stop. The seasonally adjusted menus have a distinctly Yorkshire pedigree.

▶ Wakefield MAP REF 323 F1

Wakefield owed its earliest prosperity to its role as an inland port and trading centre, linked to the canal network and thus the East Coast ports. Three canals came through here – the Aire and Calder, the Calder and Hebble Navigation, and the Barnsley Canal. Trade in cattle and grain was overtaken by manufacturing – based around textiles, glass and engineering. In the 19th century, coal mining around the city brought huge changes – and considerable prosperity which is reflected in some of Wakefield's grander Victorian civic buildings.

The mines are now consigned to history, and the city has undertaken some major regeneration projects in the 21st century, including new shopping malls and redevelopment around the old canalsides. As a measure of its success, in 2013 Wakefield was named by *The Telegraph* as one of the 'Top 20 arty places to live' – mainly because of its position at the heart of the so-called Yorkshire Sculpture Triangle, an area shared with Leeds, showcasing the work of over 200 artists across four iconic venues. Wakefield's major artist daughter is the internationally acclaimed sculptor Barbara Hepworth (1903–75), whose name was given to a gallery opened in 2011 to celebrate her legacy. The gallery recently expanded with the unveiling of The Calder, an exhibition space located in a 19th-century former textile mill, next door to the original building.

Wakefield is also the capital of the 'Rhubarb Triangle' – an area of West Yorkshire famous for producing early forced rhubarb. At one time 90 per cent of the world's early rhubarb came from this area – and in 2005 a sculpture was erected in Holmfield Park to celebrate the city's connection.

VISIT THE MUSEUMS AND GALLERIES

The Hepworth Wakefield
hepworthwakefield.org
Gallery Walk, WF1 5AW
01924 247360 | Open 10–5
The Hepworth Wakefield is an exciting and inspiring art gallery. It celebrates the area's artistic legacy as the birthplace of Barbara Hepworth, and explores the work of major contemporary artists – as well as rarely seen works by Hepworth herself. Special events and exhibitions are on offer throughout the year, and don't forget about the building itself – composed of 10 trapezoidal blocks, it's the largest purpose-built gallery outside London.

Yorkshire Sculpture Park
see highlight panel opposite

Wakefield Museum
wakefield.gov.uk
Wakefield One, Burton Street, WF1 2EB | 01924 305356
Open Mon–Tue 9–6, Wed 9–8, Thu–Fri 9–7, Sat 9–5
Housed in the new Wakefield One building at the heart of the city, this museum tells the story of Wakefield thematically, as seen through the eyes of the people involved. A popular display is devoted to the world's first eco-warrior, the 19th-century naturalist Charles Waterton, who was born locally.

SEE A LOCAL CHURCH

Wakefield Cathedral
wakefield-cathedral.org.uk
Northgate, WF1 1HG
01924 373923
Wakefield's Cathedral is a prominent landmark – and not just because the 247-foot spire is the tallest in Yorkshire. People began to worship on this site in Saxon times, and the Normans started to build the first stone structure in around 1150. Today, the cathedral offers regular services as well as an oasis of calm in the modern world.

GET ON THE WATER

Pugneys Country Park
wakefield.gov.uk
Asdale Road, WF2 7EQ
01924 302360
When you're left with an open cast mine and a quarry next to each other, what can you do with them? Simple – turn them into a country park, offer watersports on the big lake, and create a 24-acre nature reserve. Watersports available include canoeing, sailing and windsurfing – and a new

▶ Yorkshire Sculpture Park

MAP REF 323 E2

ysp.co.uk
West Bretton, WF4 4LG | 01924 832631 | Open summer daily 10–6,
winter daily 10–5

Opened in 1977 and set in the beautiful grounds and gardens of a
500-acre, 18th-century country estate, the Yorkshire Sculpture
Park is one of the world's leading open-air galleries of modern
sculpture – and Yorkshire's artistic jewel. There's always
something new to see, as the YSP organises a number of
temporary exhibitions throughout the year in five magnificent
galleries. The visitor centre provides useful all-weather facilities,
including a good restaurant, an audio-visual auditorium, a coffee
bar and the inevitable shop. Even for those who don't 'get' the art
on offer, the park is fantastic to walk around, with excellent vistas
of the valley, lakes, estate buildings and bridges – and it's all free
(though you'll pay for the car park). You can even take your dog on
the outdoor cultural tour.

5 top free attractions in Yorkshire

▶ **National Coal Mining Museum**, Overton. Travel deep underground down one of Britain's oldest working mines, in a rural setting near Wakefield. A genuine insight into the hard life of miners through the ages.
page 284

▶ **Royal Armouries Museum**, Leeds. The UK's national collection of arms and armour. Live demos, re-enactments, handling collections, jousting tournaments and thousands of exhibits.
page 174

▶ **Sheffield Winter Garden and Millennium Gallery** The Winter Garden is a stunning verdant world in the heart of the city, linking the Millennium Gallery, Tudor Square and the Peace Gardens. It is the largest temperate glasshouse in any European city centre.
page 261 and page 260

▶ **Museums Quarter**, Hull. Four museums in the historic old town. Hull and East Riding Museum of Archaeology; The Streetlife Museum of Transport; Wilberforce House; and the *Arctic Corsair*.
page 142

▶ **National Science and Media Museum**, Bradford. Museum devoted to film, photography, TV, science and the web, with IMAX screen and Animation Gallery.
page 74

Watersports Centre provides excellent facilities during your visit.

PLAY A ROUND

Wakefield has two notable courses; Normanton Golf Club is a championship course occupying 145 acres of the Hatfield Hall Estate. A blend of parkland and elevations, the course incorporates impressive lakes. Wakefield Golf Club is a well-sheltered meadowland and parkland course with easy walking and good views.

Normanton Golf Club

normantongolf.co.uk
Hatfield Hall, Aberford Road, WF3 4JP | 01924 377943
Open daily (weekend restrictions)

Wakefield Golf Club

wakefieldgolfclub.co.uk
28 Woodthorpe Lane, Sandal, WF2 6JH | 01924 258778
(secretary) Open daily

▶ **PLACES NEARBY**

Attractions near Wakefield include an industrial museum, a medieval priory and Waterton Park Hotel.

National Coal Mining Museum for England

ncm.org.uk
Caphouse Colliery, New Road, Overton, WF4 4RH | 01924 848806
Open daily 10–5
This industrial museum lies southwest of the city. You can't really have a coal mining museum just above ground – which is why at the NCM you'll

be taken 150 yards underground by one of the experienced local miners. Deep in the tunnels of the former Caphouse Colliery, you'll discover the underground workings, where models and machinery depict methods and conditions of mining from the early 1800s to the present day. There's plenty above ground, too, including the Hope Pit, pithead baths, Victorian steam winder, nature trail, adventure playground and ponies. But you'll need to wear sensible footwear and warm clothing.

Nostell Priory and Parkland

nationaltrust.org.uk
Doncaster Road, WF4 1QE
01924 863892 | Gardens open
Mar–Oct daily 11–5.30; house
1–5.30; park 9–7

Built on the site of a medieval priory, Nostell has been the home of the Winn family for 300 years. The house was built by James Paine in the middle of the 18th century, with an additional wing by Robert Adam dating to 1766. Furniture maker Thomas Chippendale was born nearby, and some of his best work can be seen in the house, along with a cute 18th-century dolls' house. Even if the house is closed, don't miss the fantastic walks through the 300 acres of grounds, with rhododendrons and azaleas in bloom in late spring.

Waterton Park Hotel ◉

watertonparkhotel.co.uk
Walton Hall, Walton, WF2 6PW
01924 257911

The location of this Georgian hotel must be unique. It stands on an island in a 26-acre lake, with a modern extension on the shore accessed via a bridge, which explains where the Bridgeman restaurant gets its name from. Dishes are admirably understated and flavours are to the fore.

▶ Wensley MAP REF 335 F4

Wensley is one of the small villages that many people pass through on their way to other attractions in the dale that took its name. It's a big ask to imagine that this little place – scarcely more than a cluster of stone houses around a squat-towered church – was once the main settlement in Wensleydale, being the first place to receive a market charter way back in 1202 – and it stayed the only market in the whole of the valley for the next 100 years. In fact, Wensley flourished until plague struck the village in 1563, when the focus of valley life shifted a mile to the east, to Leyburn, and later westward to Askrigg and then Hawes. When Bolton Hall was built nearby in 1678, Wensley began its regrowth as an estate village – the present hall (private) is set in fine parkland west of the village.

The Church of the Holy Trinity is a reminder of that era of importance, with parts of the building dating back to 1240. Its sturdy stone tower was built in 1719, and inside you will find an 18th-century pulpit and an even earlier font. There's also an elaborate canopied pew used by the Scrope family from nearby Castle Bolton – a nifty piece of recycling, it incorporates bits rescued from Easby Abbey (see page 229).

There's a small waterfall on the river, and Wensley Mill. Today, this houses the White Rose Candle Workshop, where you can watch the process of candle-making.

VISIT THE WORKSHOP
White Rose Candles
whiterosecandles.co.uk
Wensley Mill, DL8 4HR
01969 623544
This family-run business was established in 1971, and manufactures candles from beeswax and paraffin wax for all sorts of events, from dinner parties to weddings. You can buy them, of course, along with hand-crafted and floral candle holders – they come in every colour of the rainbow, and a range of popular fragrances. Call ahead or visit the website for opening times.

▶ Wensleydale MAP REF 335 D4

Most of the Yorkshire Dales are named after their main rivers, but you'll search the maps in vain for a River Wensley – this dale takes its name from the former market town, Wensley, now simply a big village (see page 285). Thanks in modern times to the publicity generated by the hugely popular Aardman animated characters Wallace and Gromit, the valley is synonymous with the famous crumbly white cheese produced here since the 12th century.

Highlights of this broad sweeping valley – threaded by the River Ure, which becomes the Ouse some time before reaching York – include the towns of Middleham, Hawes and Leyburn, and villages such as Aysgarth, Castle Bolton and Wensley itself. There are spectacular waterfalls at Aysgarth, Hawes and Askrigg, and great walking over the hills.

The majority of the dale is located within the Yorkshire Dales National Park, and as such can get quite busy at peak times as well as in lovely weather. The lower part of Wensleydale below East Witton, however, is in the Nidderdale Area of Outstanding Natural Beauty (AONB) and therefore is often much quieter – despite being as stunning.

If you want further unspoiled and tranquil scenery, then discover Bishopdale and Coverdale – both are Wensleydale tributaries and are secret gems waiting to be explored.

▶ Cauldron Falls, Wensleydale

▶ West Burton MAP REF 335 E4

This attractive village is found just off Wensleydale, its houses scattered around an extensive green. West Burton lies at the point where Walden Beck flows out of Waldendale and into Bishopdale – there's a pretty waterfall, Burton Force, just a short stroll from the village centre, which was painted by J M W Turner after a visit here in 1816. Below the fall is a packhorse bridge, which adds to the charm of the scene.

At West Burton's centre is one of the largest village greens in the country – a great expanse like a grassy lake, its sloping sides lined by old stone cottages, with tree-clad hills rising up behind them. Many of the houses were built for workers in the nearby quarrying and lead-mining industries. The village centre is a quiet, almost timeless place – mostly thanks to the main road bypassing the area. This means children can play and horses can graze, and visitors can feel they have stepped back at least 50 years in time. Set on the green is a tall and imposing cross, which was originally erected in 1820 and rebuilt in 1889. This is believed to replace a more ancient affair, probably marking the location of a weekly market. On one side of the green is a pub, on the other the Cat Pottery: Moorside Cats, which specialises in life-like ceramic felines.

EAT AND DRINK
Fox and Hounds
foxandhoundswestburton.co.uk
DL8 4JY | 01969 663111

This is a traditional pub which overlooks that large village green – parents can happily sit at the front and enjoy a drink while keeping an eye on their children playing out on the swings. It's a proper local, with men's and women's darts teams and a dominoes team; in summer customers can play quoits out on the green. Real ales – some from the Black Sheep Brewery down the road – are served, and you can enjoy home made food prepared from fresh ingredients.

▶ Wetherby MAP REF 328 C4

Wetherby is a curious place – at first glance, it looks like it can't decide which part of Yorkshire it should belong to. For example, most of the houses are built of pale stone, topped with red-tiled roofs – North Yorkshire, you would say. But the riverside developments and its overall air of prosperity firmly place it in West Yorkshire – which is where this old market town officially stands. Its two features most pleasing to the eye are the arched stone bridge over the River Wharfe and the handsome Georgian-fronted town hall on the marketplace. Today,

Wetherby is a prosperous backwater, helped perhaps by the reputation of its famous racecourse.

Wetherby lies equidistant between Leeds and York, and also midway between London and Edinburgh – the Great North Road passed through the town, and so it became an essential coaching stop, with dozens of inns flourishing. Most of these have now disappeared, or changed their function. Even the Great North Road has been rerouted – it's the A1(M), snaking round to the east.

GO TO THE RACES
Wetherby Racecourse
wetherbyracing.co.uk
York Road, LS22 5EJ | 01937 582035
The Romans started Wetherby's racing tradition, with the first meeting at the present course held somewhat later, in 1891. This is one of the country's leading jumping tracks, and it hosts a range of events through the season.

▸ PLACES NEARBY
Wetherby's nearest neighbour to the southeast is Boston Spa which, like Ilkley (see page 146), became a prosperous spa town on the River Wharfe, based on the supposed health-giving properties of its sulphurous mineral waters. With some splendid Georgian buildings, the town has an air of elegance and is well worth a look.

Stockeld Park
stockeldpark.co.uk
Stockeld, LS22 4AW | 01937 586333
Opening times vary – check website in advance
Selling trees from Yorkshire's biggest Christmas tree plantation is one of the ways that the owners make this vast agricultural estate pay its way. Other ways are even more inventive – there are regular themed 'adventures' set up in the grounds and gardens, aimed squarely at families. The Palladian-style stately home at its centre is not open to the public, but doubled as Thrushcross Grange in a 2009 TV version of *Wuthering Heights*. Stockeld lies northwest of Wetherby.

Wood Hall Hotel & Spa ◉◉
handpickedhotels.co.uk/ woodhall
Trip Lane, Linton, LS22 4JA
01937 587271
Southwest of Wetherby, and built as a country retreat for the Vavasour family, Wood Hall retains some grand Georgian features blended with more modern comforts. High on a hill, with fine views, this is the sort of country-house hotel where you'll want to linger. Dating from 1750, the property retains a number of original details, while furnishings and decor have been chosen with guests' comfort and well-being in mind. The Georgian Restaurant is as elegant as the other rooms, with its relaxing colour

scheme, upholstered chairs and drapes at the windows. The rigorous pursuit of Yorkshire produce – beef from local farms, lamb from the moors, produce from the garden – eschews over-elaboration and unnecessary garnishes in favour of a simple approach, so the cooking is marked out by clear, distinct flavours.

▶ Wheeldale MAP REF 338 B4

The Romans have left little sign that they spent much time on the heights of the North York Moors, but there are indications that they built a road across the middle to link up a settlement at Malton with their signal stations on the coast near Goldsborough and Whitby.

The section of road on Wheeldale Moor, just over a mile in length and known as Wade's Causeway, is said to be the best-preserved Roman road in the country – though doubts have been expressed in recent years, suggesting that it's even older. The route gradually fell into disuse, eventually

disappearing beneath the encroaching heather and bracken, until it was rediscovered in 1914.

Find it by driving north from Pickering on an unclassified road. Once past the village of Stape, follow the Wheeldale Road, with Cropton Forest on the right and the expanse of Wheeldale Moor on your left. Park near to the watersplash at Wheeldale Bridge, and the old Roman road is immediately ahead. The Roman road over Wheeldale is also signposted from Goathland, west of the A169.

We all learned about the Romans' innovative road-making skills at school, yet this particular road looks to be a rather rocky thoroughfare. That's because what you can see today is merely the road's foundations, made up of large stones set into gravel. The original road surface would have been much smoother, and overlaid with finer aggregate. The road is cambered so that water drains off to the edges and is carried away in culverts or ditches. You can follow the route and decide for yourself whether or not you are walking in the footsteps of those Roman legions.

▶ Whernside MAP REF 334 B5

This long ridge on the Cumbrian border is the highest point in the Dales, reaching to 2,415 feet/736 metres. Like its fellows in the Pennine range, Ingleborough and Pen-y-Ghent, it owes its existence to the time when, some 300 million years ago, this part of the world was a tropical sea. The seabed became thick with the shells of dead creatures, and now forms the Great Scar limestone that lies up to a depth of 600 feet underneath much of this region – you'll get the best idea of the scale at Malham Cove. The Great Scar was mostly buried under sandstones, shales and other limestones deposited by the rivers that drained into the ancient sea. These extra deposits, known as the Yoredale series of rocks, form the tops of the Three Peaks and cover much else in the Dales.

There are a number of approaches to Whernside, but the two most popular are from the Ribblehead Viaduct (see page 226) and Chapel-le-Dale (see page 152). If you're climbing Whernside as part of the Yorkshire Three Peaks Challenge, then the Ribblehead route is the one to choose. From the top, on a clear day, you can see across to the Lancashire coast and Morecambe Bay – perhaps one of the attractions for the people who built a huge hill fort up here in prehistoric times.

◀ Wade's Causeway

▶ **Whitby** MAP REF 338 C2

Whitby is a seaside town that offers much more than most. To start with, it has a long and illustrious history as one of the country's most important seaports, and can claim associations with a remarkable variety of historical figures. Even Whitby's setting is dramatic, with houses clinging to the steep slopes on either side of the River Esk. Whitby traditionally offered the only safe harbour between the rivers Tyne and Humber. The town's large harbour is still at the heart of the town, though today there are more pleasure craft passing the breakwaters than fishing cobles.

You get a good overview of the town from the elevated bridge that now carries through-traffic on the A171. From this vantage point you can see the Esk broaden into a large marina full of yachts. Beyond the swing bridge is the harbour, overlooked spectacularly on the southern flank by St Mary's Church and the ruined abbey – a landmark for miles around. The scene is always one of bustle and activity. Whitby has thrived when other fishing towns and villages have declined, and new building projects emphasise that the town is looking to the future as well as the past.

Whitby has always looked out to sea – for centuries it was isolated from the rest of the county by poor roads and the wild expanse of moorland that surrounds it on three sides. By the 18th century it had become a major port, with shipbuilding, fishing and whaling all contributing to a maritime prosperity that lasted into the early years of the 20th century. This is where the fine Georgian houses at the west end of the town came from, built by wealthy shipbuilders and fleet owners.

▼ Whitby Harbour

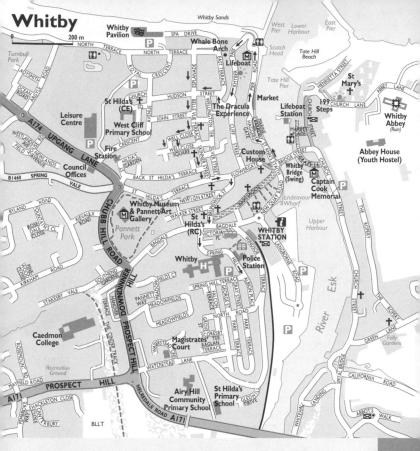

Whitby

The more traditional whitewashed cottages, with their typical red-tiled roofs, housed fishermen and their families. Space was at a premium, so their houses were crammed up the steep slopes on the eastern side of the Esk. They are linked by ginnels and steps, which are a delight to explore on foot.

Whitby also prospered during the 17th and 18th centuries with the mining and refining of alum – a vital ingredient in the dyeing of wool. Coal was shipped in to fire the cauldrons that separated alum from rock, and stone was needed for building; this increase in trade required the building of a better harbour.

In 1753, a company was set up in the town to undertake whaling expeditions, using the sturdy ships already being built here. The whalers spent many weeks at sea in the distant, inhospitable waters of the Arctic. The trade was lucrative for those who survived the hardships. Almost 3,000 whales were brought back to Whitby up to 1833, and seals, walruses and polar bears also featured in these hauls. The whale blubber was rendered down on the quayside to make oil. Even the streetlamps of the town were lit with gas refined from whale oil. An arch formed from the jawbone of a whale looks down on the harbour today in commemoration.

Smaller boats sailed out of Whitby to net herring, and its fish market was one of the busiest. Fishing is still a part of the modern Whitby, but on a much reduced scale – and many of the boats that leave the harbour today are carrying sea anglers and other visitors.

The town has a special place in ecclesiastical history. In AD 655 King Oswy of Northumbria celebrated a heady victory in battle by promising his daughter as a bride of Christ. He founded a monastery on Whitby's eastern cliff, overlooking the town, and the first abbess was Hilda, who presided over a community of nuns and monks. Her goodness and piety passed into legend, and she was recognised as a saint. In AD 664 the Synod of Whitby convened in the town to decide whether Northumbria should follow Catholic or Celtic Christianity. In the event the Catholic Church triumphed. The most notable member of this community was a monk, Caedmon, 'the Father of English poetry'. A shy man, he preferred to keep his own company as a cowherd instead of singing with the choir. His poem, 'The Song of Creation', is the earliest known poem written in English. A sandstone cross standing by St Mary's Church commemorates Caedmon's life.

▼ Whitby

Sharing the abbey's windswept site is St Mary's Church, built to cater for the spiritual needs of the village that grew up around the abbey. St Mary's still serves, although its congregation has to tackle the famous 199 steps that lead up to the church. Parts of the building date back to the 12th century; fortunately, the fabric of the church suffered none of the indignities meted out to the abbey. Make sure you have a look inside St Mary's – the interior was fitted out during the 18th century with wooden galleries, high-sided box pews and a splendid three-decker pulpit. The effect is quite startling, with a distinctly nautical feel as the craftsmen were more accustomed to fitting out ships.

At the bottom of Church Stairs is the oldest part of town. Little fishermen's cottages huddle together as if to keep out the bitter weather. Narrow alleyways lead off from the tiny market square, and if those 199 steps have taken their toll you can enjoy a drink in one of the harbour-side pubs.

In summer, steam trains puff into Whitby Station from the North Yorkshire Moors Railway.

Whitby jet, used for jewellery since the Bronze Age, was popularised by Queen Victoria who wore it during her decades of mourning for Prince Albert. Jet is actually fossilised wood, which turns from its natural brown colour to the deepest black ('jet-black', as we say) once it is polished, and Whitby proved a particularly fruitful site. This craft trade expanded as jet ornaments became the fashion statement of their day, but popular taste proved fickle, and by the time of Victoria's death in 1901 the demand for Whitby jet was much reduced. Today, you can see original pieces of jewellery displayed in Whitby Museum in Pannett Park, and for sale in the town's antiques shops. Some modern jet jewellery is being made now, too.

Few graveyards enjoy a more panoramic view than the one surrounding St Mary's Church. But if the wind is whipping around the gravestones and the full moon is shrouded by clouds, it can have a more menacing atmosphere. Bram Stoker realised its potential and avid readers of his horror novel, *Dracula* (1897), will recognise some of the settings from Whitby. Look out for the skull and crossbones gravestones near the topmost gate – these are said to have directly inspired the novel.

Whitby holds several major festivals each year which bring in visitors from far and wide – they include the summer rowing regatta, the twice-yearly Gothic Weekend (if you want to blend in, then dress to impress), and the famous Folk Week of song and dance in August.

TAKE IN SOME HISTORY
Whitby Abbey
see highlight panel opposite

VISIT THE MUSEUMS
AND GALLERIES
Captain Cook
Memorial Museum
cookmuseumwhitby.co.uk
Grape Lane, YO22 4BA
01947 601900 | Contact museum
for details of opening times
On Grape Lane, by the
harbour, you'll find the home
of ship owner and Quaker,
Captain John Walker, to
whom the young James
Cook was apprenticed in
1746, before joining the Royal
Navy. Today, the building
houses the Captain Cook
Memorial Museum.

Lifeboat Museum
rnli.org.uk
Pier Road, YO21 3PU
01947 602001 | Open Easter–Oct
10–5, Nov–Dec 11–4, Jan–Mar
Sat–Sun 11–4
A stark reminder that Whitby's
success was built on the perils
of the sea, the Lifeboat Museum
is small but full of interest. It's
star is the self-righting lifeboat
of 1919, the *Robert and Ellen
Robson* – you can usually see
its vivid orange, high-tech
and all-weather modern
successor, *George and Mary
Webb*, in the harbour.

Whitby Museum and
Pannett Art Gallery
whitbymuseum.org.uk
Pannett Park, YO21 1RE | 01947
602908 | Open Tue–Sun 9.30–4.30

A great little museum,
stuffed with curiosities and
telling the history of the town
and the geology of the East
Yorkshire coastline. Find out
about Whitby's whaling
background, as well as fabulous
marine fossils, items relating to
Captain James Cook, exquisite
flint tools left by our Stone Age
forebears on the moors, and
lively paintings of sailing ships
through the ages.

ENTERTAIN THE FAMILY
The Dracula Experience
draculaexperience.co.uk
9 Marine Parade, YO21 3PR | 01947
601923 | Open Easter–Oct daily
9.45–5, Nov–Easter Sat–Sun 9.45–5
Enjoy the spine-chilling thrills
as the myth is brought to life,
with animations, live actors
(at peak times, anyway) and
lots of special effects. Then
hit the souvenir shop and get
the T-shirt.

TAKE A BOAT TRIP
Various different operators
offer trips round the bay,
fishing trips and even
whale-watching tours,
leaving from the West Pier
in season.

Whitby Coastal Cruises
whitbycoastalcruises.co.uk
The Brewery Steps, Lower Harbour,
YO21 3PR | 07981 712419

Whitby Fishing Trips
whitbyfishingtrips.co.uk
New Quay Road, YO21 3BQ
07866 249927
(Address for satnav purposes only)

▶ **Whitby Abbey** MAP REF 338 C2

english-heritage.org.uk

Abbey Lane, YO22 4JT | 01947 603568 | Open Apr–Sep daily 10–6,
Oct–Mar Thu–Mon 10–4, 18–24 Feb daily 10–4, 25 Feb–Mar & Nov to
mid-Feb Sat–Sun 10–4

Uncover the full story of these atmospheric ruins in their
impressive clifftop location above the town. St Hilda's original
abbey was destroyed by Viking raiders. The abbey that replaced it
was begun in the 11th century and was rebuilt on several occasions
before being dismantled at the Dissolution; this is what you can see
today, starkly silhouetted against the sky. The ruin suffered further
damage in 1914, when two German battleships shelled the town
and inadvertently hit the west front.

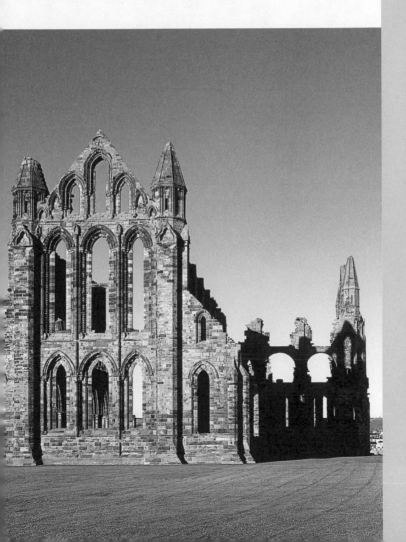

GO WHALE WATCHING
Whitby Whale Watching
whitbywhalewatching.net
Departs from Brewery Steps, St Ann's
Staithe, Whitby | 07941 450381
Head out into the North
Sea from the port of Whitby
in search of minke, sei, fin
and even humpback whales.
Seals, porpoises and dolphins
provide the icing on the cake.

GET SCARED
Whitby Walks
whitbywalks.com
Walks start from the whalebone
arch, West Cliff, YO21 3HA
07880 801957
A thousand years of
ecclesiastical and maritime
heritage are waiting to be
discovered in the historic
port of Whitby. Follow as Dr
Crank leads you through
secret courtyards and winding
alleyways, telling gruesome
tales of murder, mystery
and suspense.

PLAY A ROUND
Whitby Golf Club
whitbygolfclub.co.uk
Low Straggleton, Sandsend Road,
YO21 3SR | 01947 600660
Open daily
This seaside course has
four holes along the clifftops
and over ravines. It offers
good views and a fresh
sea breeze.

EAT AND DRINK
Elizabeth Botham and Sons
botham.co.uk
35–39 Skinner Street, YO21 3AH
01947 602823

The invitation to take tea at
Botham's is irresistible,
involving wonderful cakes and
pastries made from authentic
Victorian recipes, and a huge
range of rare and fine teas.
Established in 1865 by Elizabeth
Botham, it's still run by her
great-grandchildren. Afternoon
tea comes with the house
Resolution Tea, or you can try
China Yunnan, Java Gunpowder,
Darjeeling First Flush
Badamtam and many others on
the superb tea menu.

The Magpie Cafe
magpiecafe.co.uk
14 Pier Road, YO21 3PU
01947 602058
It must be difficult to keep hold
of an acclaimed reputation for
North Yorkshire's 'best-ever
fish and chips' – but the Magpie
Cafe first gained its reputation
during the late 1930s and now
serves an exhaustive list of fish
and seafood dishes. Perhaps
enjoy Whitby crab pâté with
French bread and home made
chutney together with a pint of
Cropton – but there's no shame
in partaking in your choice of
fish, simply battered and served
with chips. There's a takeaway
hatch too – but it's popular, so
be prepared to queue.

Teare Woods Luxury Ice Cream Parlour & Cafe
tearewoods.co.uk
9 St Ann's Staithe, YO21 3PW
A day out in Whitby isn't
complete without fish and chips
topped off with an ice cream
from this artisan parlour. Real

hand-crafted luxury Jersey ice cream with all the usual flavours and some rather interesting ones too. How about Country Apple Crumble, Malteser or Chilli Chocolate?

▶ PLACES NEARBY

Whitby's many closed railway lines offer some great cycling – for example the Whitby–Scarborough rail trail – and if you need a bike, Trailways Cycle Hire will have one for you.

Trailways Cycle Hire
trailways.info
The Old Railway Station, Hawsker YO22 4LB | 01947 820207
Easter–Nov daily 9.30–6, phone ahead at other times
Hire a bike to ride along the Whitby–Scarborough rail trail. The company is based in an old railway carriage, and has lots of leaflets to help you plan your route. Hawsker is southeast of Whitby, on the route to Robin Hood's Bay (see page 239).

▼ Whitby harbour

▶ York MAP REF 329 E4

This strikingly beautiful walled medieval city straddling the River Ouse is one of Britain's top sights, with a multitude of museums and buildings spanning a range of historic periods. Much of York's compact heart is pedestrianised, so it's great to explore on foot, allowing you to absorb its wealth of interesting shops and enjoy the vibrant street performers. Among the most evocative streets are The Shambles, originally a street of butchers' shops and retaining overhanging, jettied, timber-framed buildings; and Stonegate, where shop signs and frontages span several centuries. A circuit of the medieval walls gives great views over the city and beyond – it's a walk of about two-and-a-half miles.

You can't miss the wonderful Minster, of course – started in around 1080, it's the largest Gothic cathedral in Northern Europe, and many would say the most beautiful – but look out, too, for York's distinguished clutch of medieval churches. One of the best is Holy Trinity in Goodramgate, with its inward-facing box pews and 15th-century stained glass. Of course, York is the seat of the Archbishop of York, a leadership role second only to that of the Archbishop of Canterbury in the Anglican Church. The current incumbent is the charismatic Ugandan-born Dr John Sentamu, who has declared that part of his job is to reconnect the Church of England with England – hear him lead a service in the Minster if you can.

York was founded on the marshy banks of the River Ouse by the Roman army in AD 71 as the town of Eboracum. The Roman fortress and the roads that led to it form the basis of the city's outline today, and a few remains are still visible – such as the walls of the fortress in the foundations of York Minster. It became the Roman capital of northern Britain, and Constantine the Great was proclaimed Emperor in the city in AD 306. After the Romans left, the city declined in status but was occupied by the Angles. King Edwin of Northumbria proclaimed it as his capital, but the Vikings had other ideas and seized the town in AD 866, changing the name to Jorvik. Under Danish rule it became a major inland port, part of the extensive Viking trading network across Europe – find out the full story in the entertaining, family-friendly Jorvik Centre. The Vikings established the city's gateways and named the streets, many of them following the Roman lines. Erik Bloodaxe was the last of the Viking kings to rule here, and after his defeat in AD 954 at the hands of King Edred, York became part of a united Anglo-Saxon kingdom.

▲ The water tower by the abbey

Over the next centuries, the city prospered on trade with the Low Countries and the Baltic. Things went badly for York in the Civil War, when Parliamentarian troops laid siege, destroying many houses outside the city and even threatening to blow up the walls – a rescue attempt by the flamboyant Prince Rupert was crushed at Marston Moor, and in 1644 the city handed itself over to Sir Thomas Fairfax. Yet York recovered, and prospered once more as a cultural centre – many of the city's most elegant buildings, including the Mansion House, the Assembly Rooms and the Theatre Royal date from the Restoration period – and so does the famous racecourse.

With the introduction of the railway in the 19th century came engineering – learn more at the outstanding National Railway Museum – and the development of a chocolate-making industry. Scholarship came later – unlike other medieval centres, York had to wait until 1963 for its university – which is world class, and brings a vibrancy to the whole place. Its campus is just outside the centre at Heslington, and the students, like everybody else, bike in and out of the city – be on the lookout for and extra careful of cyclists if you're driving here.

You could easily build a whole week around the attractions in and around York – covering everything from the ancient history to railway history, religion to chocolate. Catch it in Festival time if you can, to see the extraordinary cycle of medieval mystery plays performed by a local cast in different locations around the city – an unforgettable experience.

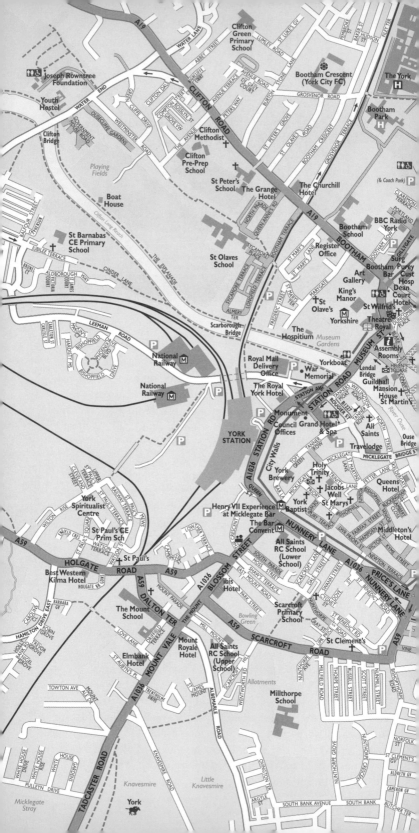

TAKE IN SOME HISTORY
City Walls

You get an immense sense of historic continuity in York, which is enclosed by its virtually complete wall, pierced by bars (gateways). The section between Bootham Bar (on the site of the Roman gateway) and Monk Bar gives some of the choicest views of the old city. Monk Bar, the best-preserved gateway, houses the Richard III Museum (Mar–Oct daily 9–5; Nov–Feb 9.30–4), giving you a chance to reach your own verdict about a monarch who was much admired in Yorkshire. The heads of criminals and enemies were placed on spikes on Micklegate Bar during the Wars of the Roses (1455–85), and there's a small social history display inside.

York Minster

yorkminster.org
Deangate, YO1 7HH | 01904 557200
Open from 7am for services
for visitors, Mon–Sat 9–5 (9.30–5 in
winter), Sun 12.45–5

Dating from 1220–1472, York Minster is dedicated to St Peter, and its twin western towers and dominant central square tower can be seen for miles around. It's built out of magnesian limestone which gleams white in sunlight. Come here for evensong when the choir is in residence if you can, or perhaps to an organ recital, to sit and enjoy the building's interior at its glorious best. The stone choir screen is carved with images of English monarchs from William I to Henry VI, while around the nave and choir are painted stone shields dating from the time when Edward II held a parliament in York. Look up to admire the vaulted roof, with its huge carved wooden bosses picked out in gilt and rich colour.

The Minster's medieval stained glass represents a quarter of all the stained glass of this period to be found in England. Look out for the Five Sisters within a quintet of lancet windows, and for the depictions of Genesis and Revelation in the superb east window of c.1250 – the world's largest area of medieval stained glass within a single window. The stone tracery of the west window incorporates a distinctive heart shape. A modern display point called The Orb helps you to get up close to some of the images in the glass.

There are separate admission charges for certain parts of the Minster, including the undercroft with its interactive displays. The foundations reveal an absorbing cross-section of history, from the remains of a Roman fort to drastic building works carried out in the 1960s to support the collapsing central tower, whose foundations turned out to be completely inadequate. The long climb up the central tower today is rewarded by a panoramic view over the city. If you're visiting with young children, borrow one of the Explorer Backpacks, which are equipped with all sorts of fun things to help youngsters engage with this fabulous building.

Fairfax House

fairfaxhouse.co.uk
Castlegate, YO1 9RN | 01904 655543
Open mid-Feb–Dec, Tue–Sat 10–5, Sun 12.30–4; Mon guided tours only at 11 and 2

In 1759, Charles, Viscount Fairfax of Emley, purchased a house and land at Castlegate, overlooking the River Ouse, for his daughter, Anne, the sole survivor of his nine children. The gift was made to compensate Anne for her disappointment in marriage: at the eleventh hour, when the bridal parties were already assembling in London, he stopped her marriage to William Constable of Burton Constable, on the grounds that the groom was not assiduous enough in his attendance at weekday Mass (Fairfax himself was a devout Catholic). He poured a fortune into designing a fine new town house where the family could entertain at the hub of York society – Fairfax House. The architect of his day, John Carr, was involved in the elegant interiors.

The house changed hands many times, and was purchased by the York Civic Trust in 1981 and restored to its full Georgian glory, the perfect home for the Noel Terry collection of 18th-century furnishings and fine art.

▼ Merchant Adventurers' Hall

Merchant Adventurers' Hall

merchantshallyork.org

Fossgate, YO1 9XD | 01904 654818

Open Sun–Fri 10–4.30, Sat 10–1.30

Discover one of the best preserved medieval guildhalls in the world, dating back to 1357. You can see the Great Hall, undercroft and chapel, along with unique collections of art, silver and furniture.

Mansion House

mansionhouseyork.com

Coney Street, YO1 9QN

01904 552 036 | Open Feb–Dec Wed–Sun 10.30–5; Guided tour 11am

The present Mansion House – the red-painted civic building on St Helen's Square – dates from 1960. It's a complete restoration of the original 1446 building, which was virtually destroyed during a bombing raid in 1942. You can see various civic treasures, and it's used as a venue for concerts and other special events.

Treasurer's House

nationaltrust.org.uk

Minster Yard, YO1 7JL

01904 624247 | Open mid-Feb–late Dec Sat–Thu 11–4.30

Named after the Treasurer of York Minster and built over a Roman Road, this mellow medieval house is not all it seems – the size, splendour and contents of the house are a constant surprise to visitors, as are the ghost stories. Wealthy industrialist Frank Green did much to restore the house, furnishing each room in a different period style – eclectic treasures include the Wedgwood cauliflower-shaped tea service and a 17th-century chandelier of Venetian glass.

York Cold War Bunker

english-heritage.org.uk

Monument Close, YO24 4HT

01904 797935

See website for opening times

English Heritage's most modern, most unusual and probably most spine-chilling site dates back to the Cold War. 'No.20 Group Royal Observer Corps HQ' is the semi-subterranean secret bunker which was built to monitor nuclear explosions and fallout in the Yorkshire region. It's not only the control rooms you can explore beyond the bomb-proof doors of this 20th-century time capsule, but also the dormitories and the decontamination chamber.

VISIT THE MUSEUMS AND GALLERIES

Jorvik Viking Centre

jorvikvikingcentre.co.uk

Coppergate, YO1 9WT | 01904 615505 | Open Apr–Oct daily 10–5, Nov–Mar 10–4

Explore York's Viking history on the very site where archaeologists discovered remains of the city of Jorvik. See over 800 of the items discovered on site and meet the famous Jorvik Vikings in the three exciting exhibitions – journeying through a reconstruction of Viking streets.

A new exhibition displays the only two skeletons found at the Coppergate excavation. Look out for special events throughout the year, including Europe's biggest Viking Festival, held in February.

National Railway Museum
see highlight panel opposite

York Castle Museum
yorkcastlemuseum.org.uk
The Eye of York, YO1 9RY
01904 687687 | Open daily 9.30–5
Fascinating exhibits are imaginatively displayed through reconstructions of period rooms and Victorian indoor streets – complete with cobbles and a Hansom cab. There's masses to see here – and your ticket covers you for 12 months, so come and enjoy it a bit at a time. The museum is housed in the city's former prison and is based on an extensive collection of 'bygones' acquired at the beginning of the 20th century. It was one of the first folk museums to display a huge range of everyday objects in an authentic scene. The Victorian street includes a pawnbroker, a tallow candle factory and a haberdasher's. There's even a reconstruction of the original sweet shop of York chocolate manufacturer, Joseph Terry, for you to explore. An extensive collection of many other items ranges from musical instruments to penny-in-the-slot machines. The museum has a fine collection of militaria, and a special exhibition called 'Seeing it Through' explores the life of York citizens during World War II.

Barley Hall
barleyhall.org.uk
2 Coffee Yard, YO1 8AR
01904 615505 | Open daily Apr–Oct 10–5, Nov–Mar 10–4
This stunning reconstructed medieval town house was once home to the Priors of Nostell and the Mayor of York. The building shows its original splendour, with exposed timber frames. It's a hands-on kind of place and you can make yourself at home – sit on the chairs, handle the objects and experience what life was like in medieval England. Check the website for themed events that you can join in.

Clifford's Tower
english-heritage.org.uk
Tower Street, YO1 1SA
01904 646940 | Open daily Apr–Sep 10–6, Oct 10–5, Nov–Mar 10–4
In its dominating position atop a grass-covered mound, Clifford's

▼ Clifford's Tower

▶ National Railway Museum

MAP REF 329 E4

nrm.org.uk

Leeman Road, YO26 4XJ | 08448 153139 | Open daily 10–6

The National Railway Museum is the world's largest railway museum. From record breakers to history makers, it's home to a vast collection of gleaming locomotives, restored carriages and wagons, including the Royal Trains, a replica of Stephenson's *Rocket*, the only Bullet Train to be seen outside Japan, and *Mallard* – the fastest steam locomotive in the world. With three enormous galleries, interactive exhibits and daily events in summer, the museum mixes education with fun, and is a 'must see' – even for non-train-buffs. The viewing gallery above the workshop known as The Works provides a fascinating vantage point to watch engineers at work maintaining and restoring locomotives.

Tower is a memorable landmark, all that's left of York Castle. In 1190 it was the scene of one of the most bloody incidents in the city's history: the Jewish population was rounded up and put into the castle, which was then burned to the ground. A second castle was quickly built on the site, which involved raising the mound – originally built in about 1070 from layers of clay and marl, gravel and stones, and timber – to its present height of about 60 feet. The new tower did not last long – it was blown down in a gale in 1228. Henry III ordered that a third tower should be built, and the stone quatrefoil-shaped keep seen today was erected on top of the mound. The castle was obsolete by the end of the 17th century – the rest of the site was rebuilt as a prison, and is now the Castle Museum.

Henry VII Experience at Micklegate Bar

richardIIIexperience.com

Micklegate, YO1 6JX | 01904 634436

Open daily Feb–Sep 10–4, Oct–Nov 11–3

Micklegate Bar has stood sentinel for over 800 years, and was originally the main entrance into the city, so many a monarch have passed through these gates. Visit the museum in this ancient gateway to explore the pageantry and history that has unfolded inside these walls.

ENTERTAIN THE FAMILY
DIG

digyork.com

St Saviour's Church, St Saviourgate, YO1 8NN | 01904 615505

Open daily 10–5

Grab a trowel and dig to see what you can find in the excavation pits at this homage to archaeology. Rediscover for yourself some of the amazing finds that have been discovered under the streets of York, and understand how people lived in Roman, Viking, medieval and Victorian times. Touch real artefacts and work out what they would be used for, and look out for the special events.

The York Dungeon

thedungeons.com/york

12 Clifford Street, YO1 9RD

0871 423 2260 | See website for opening times

Those with young people interested in the more horrible of histories will love this – delve into the city's most despicable past, and laugh your socks off at the same time. It's a mixture of fear and fun as actors join with special effects to give you a sense of being transported back to those black, bleak times. Tours last 70 minutes, and it's popular – book ahead to save money and queuing.

York's Chocolate Story

yorkschocolatestory.com

King's Square, YO1 7LD

01904 527765 | Open daily 10–6.30; tours every 30 mins

Whatever became of Terry's Chocolate Apple? Find the answer to this and other pressing questions on this innovative guided tour through York's sweet-making history. Learn how chocolate was made here, how to taste it like an expert and the story behind some of the world's favourite chocolate brands – in the home of Rowntrees and Terry's. Chocaholics can watch chocolate being made at a demonstration, and of course, buy it in the giftshop...

TOUR THE BREWERY
The York Brewery Co Ltd
york-brewery.co.uk
12 Toft Green, YO1 6JT
01904 621162 | Open Mon–Sat, tours at 12.30, 2, 3.30 and 5
One of the north's finest independent breweries now offers a tour of its premises inside the city walls. Observe all the processes that go into producing beers like Centurion's Ghost, Yorkshire Terrier and Guzzler, and if you're made intolerably thirsty by the sight of all this brewing expertise, you'll be glad to know that the adult ticket price includes a pint of beer.

SEE A LOCAL CHURCH
All Saints Church
North Street, YO1 6JD
Tucked away from York's city centre, near the River Ouse and next to a row of 15th-century timber-framed houses, lies this fine medieval Anglo-Catholic church – you'll recognise it from the lacy octagonal lantern tower. It has a small hermitage at the west end, where a female hermit lived in the early 15th century. Once inside, look up to see the beautifully decorated ceiling, with brightly painted angels bearing emblems and musical instruments. There's a 15th-century oak stall with a fine carving of a pelican, and the stained glass gives a vivid insight into the clothing and customs of medieval times.

▼ Inside All Saints Church

Holy Trinity Church

holytrinityyork.org

Micklegate at Priory Street, YO1 6EN

Open daily 10–4

The walls of the nave and the central tower is all that remain of a substantial Benedictine priory church founded in 1089. Most of the surviving older stonework is 13th-century, but the church decayed after the Dissolution and had to be rebuilt in the 19th century. As if to make up for its lost heritage, the church now has a fascinating display on the Monks of Micklegate, focusing on the beautiful 13th-century illuminated *Book of Beasts* they created (currently in St John's College, Oxford). In the Middle Ages, Holy Trinity was the starting point for the celebrated York Mystery Plays.

St Martin Coney Street

stmartinsyork.org.uk

Coney Street, near junction with New Street, YO1 9QL

St Martin's was burnt out in World War II, in bombings, known as the 'Baedeker raids' which targeted historic cities – only the tower and the south aisle survived. After extensive rebuilding, the church was re-hallowed as a chapel of peace and reconciliation, and a walled garden was created from the remaining shell. Some strikingly modern elements have taken their place alongside the old. A suitably fiery east window depicting the burning of the church soars above a gold-painted aluminium sculpture of the Last Supper, the figures angular and twisted. However, the old west window remains. Dating from about 1440, and the largest of any parish church in York, it had fortunately been removed into storage in 1940 for safety.

St Wilfrid's Catholic Church

Duncombe Place, YO1 7ED

St Wilfrid's Catholic Church is known as the Mother Church of the city of York. It's also the first Catholic church to have been constructed here, built in the Gothic Revival style (1862–4). The arch over the main door has the most detailed Victorian carving in the city. The tower, visible around much of York, is designed to appear taller than the Minster in the background, even though it is not.

CATCH A PERFORMANCE

Grand Opera House York

atgtickets.com/york

Clifford and Cumberland Street, YO1 9SW | 0844 871 3024

This is York's major entertainment hub, and in the spectacular surroundings of the restored music hall-cum-theatre you'll find West End musicals, live bands, stand-up comedians and family shows.

York Theatre Royal

yorktheatreroyal.co.uk

St Leonard's Place, YO1 7HD

01904 623568

Watch a range of plays both innovative and traditional at

this long-established theatre. The Christmas pantomime is a local institution.

TAKE A BOAT TRIP
City Cruises York
citycruisesyork.com
Lendal Bridge, YO1 7DP
01904 628324
The River Ouse is central to York's history, and a relaxing river cruise is a great way to get a different perspective, and escape the hustle and bustle of the city. Choose from a range of trips – the evening cruise is recommended.

GO TO THE RACES
York Racecourse
yorkracecourse.co.uk
The Racecourse, YO23 1EX
01904 620911
This is the Ascot of the north – there has been horseracing at York since 1709, and since 1730 on the current Knavemire course. The most prestigious meeting is the Yorkshire Ebor Festival held in August – with a very popular Ladies Day.

PLAY A ROUND
York has a range of great courses. Fulford Golf Club is a flat parkland and heathland course well-known for the top quality of its turf, particularly the greens, and famous as the venue for some of the best professional golf tournaments in the British Isles in recent years. Forest of Galtres Golf Club is a level parkland course in the heart of the Forest of Galtres, with mature oak trees and interesting water features coming into play on the 6th, 14th and 17th holes. There's also some great views of York Minster. The York Golf Club is a pleasant, well-designed,

▼ The River Ouse, York

heathland course with easy walking between holes. The course is well bunkered with excellent greens, and there are two testing pond holes.

Fulford Golf Club
fulfordgolfclub.co.uk
Heslington Lane, YO10 5DY
01904 413579 | Open Mon–Fri, Sun

Forest of Galtres Golf Club
forestofgaltres.co.uk
Skelton Lane, Skelton, YO32 2RF
01904 766198 | Open daily

York Golf Club
yorkgolfclub.co.uk
Lords Moor Lane, Strensall,
YO32 5XF | 01904 499840 (sec)
Open Mon–Fri, Sun

EAT AND DRINK

Dean Court Hotel ◉
deancourt-york.co.uk
Duncombe Place, YO1 7EF
01904 625082

Sitting on the corner of Petergate, Dean Court is an amalgam of Victorian buildings originally put up to house clergy at the celebrated Minster, adjacency to which is a powerful selling-point for today's privately run boutique hotel. Neither Gothic medievalism nor Victorian interior design have been carried through to the dining room, which is a clean-lined, light-coloured contemporary haven. The modern styling gives a clue to the orientation of the cooking, where Yorkshire produce is put to effective use.

Bettys Cafe Tea Rooms
bettys.co.uk
6–8 St Helen's Square, YO1 8QP
01904 659142

In 1936 Frederick Belmont, founder of Bettys, travelled on the maiden voyage of the *Queen Mary*, during which time he was planning a new cafe in York. The luxury liner provided the required inspiration, and the ship's interior designers were commissioned to re-create the magnificent panelling, pillars and mirrors in the elegant new premises. Favourite dishes to accompany a fine selection of well-chosen teas include Swiss rösti, Yorkshire sausages, Alpine macaroni, and Yorkshire rarebit, plus a fine selection of cakes, patisserie and desserts. The curd tart is exemplary. Children have always been welcome, and there's a 'Little Rascals' menu, books, toys, organic baby food and baby-changing facilities for mums and dads. A range of musical events is hosted throughout the year.

Bettys Stonegate
bettys.co.uk
46 Stonegate, YO1 8AS
01904 622865

This is the smallest of the Bettys tea rooms, and perhaps the cosiest. The cafe is reached via a flight of winding stairs, and has a delightful interior with wooden beams and roaring fires. Hot dishes, speciality sandwiches and an extensive range of cakes and patisserie are served, with the Yorkshire

Fat Rascal – a large fruity scone with citrus peel, almonds and cherries – a house speciality.

The Blue Bell
53 Fossgate, YO1 9TF
01904 654904

It's easy to miss this charming pub because of its slimline frontage, but don't – it's the smallest in York and has been serving customers in the ancient heart of the city for 200 years. In 1903 it was given a typical Edwardian makeover, and since then almost nothing has changed – so the Grade II listed interior still includes varnished wall and ceiling panelling, cast-iron tiled fireplaces, and old settles. The only slight drawback is that the pub's size leaves no room for a kitchen, so don't expect anything more complicated than lunchtime sandwiches. However, there's a good selection of real ales: no fewer than seven are usually on tap, including rotating guests – so that more than makes up for it.

The Churchill Hotel ⊛⊛
churchillhotel.com
65 Bootham, YO30 7DQ
01904 644456

The set-up is all rather civilised in this Georgian mansion, set in its own grounds just a short walk from the Minster. The Churchill blends the airy elegance of its period pedigree with the sharp looks of a contemporary boutique city hotel in a dining room that looks through those vast, arching Georgian windows into the garden, where the trees are spangled in fairy-lights. Laid-back live music floats from a softly tinkling baby grand piano as the soundtrack to cooking that hits the target with its imaginative modern pairings of top-grade regional produce.

Le Cochon Aveugle ⊛⊛
lecochonaveugleyork.com
37 Walmgate, YO1 9TX
01904 640222

With no bar and just 16 covers, this converted shop in the centre of York deserves its 'small but perfectly formed' tag. With its black-and-white chequered floor, simple wooden furniture and linen napkins, there is an old-school French bistro feel to the place, although the contemporary cooking has considerably more flair and ambition than that. The limitations of the tiny open kitchen means that only a fixed-price six-course tasting menu is served. While the flavours may be classical, the execution and presentation is thoroughly modern.

The Grange Hotel ⊛⊛
grangehotel.co.uk
1 Clifton, YO30 6AA | 01904 644744

Behind the pillared frontage of this classic 1829 townhouse is a designer-led interior of some panache, with inviting sofas, paintings on the walls, open fires and heavy curtains. The restaurant itself is divided into three distinct sections, all flamboyantly decorated, with walls and ceiling painted to create a tented effect, a horseracing mural, theatrical drapes at the windows in the red area and corners, and alcoves with silver birch branches covered in lights.

Guy Fawkes Inn ◉

gfyork.com
25 High Petergate, YO1 7HP
01904 466674

The Gunpowder Plotter, Guy Fawkes, was born on this spot in 1570, in the shadow of the Minster – a fact which adds a frisson to the pub that has been here for centuries. It's a dark, atmospheric, history-steeped den with an inside rather like stepping into an Old Master painting; there are roaring log fires, a timber staircase, wooden floors, gas lighting, tables nestling in candlelit nooks and crannies, and cheerful service that suits the buzzy vibe. Menus change regularly to reflect the seasons and daily chalkboard specials follow a hearty modern pub grub course, treating great local produce with honest, down-to-earth simplicity.

Hotel du Vin & Bistro York ◉

hotelduvin.com
89 The Mount, YO24 1AX
01904 557350

The York billet of the HdV group is a late Georgian town house in the vicinity of the Minster's Gothic splendour and the city racecourse, a location referenced in the equestrian

pictures that adorn the bistro dining room. Bare tables and floor fit in with the unbuttoned ethos, and the menu offers sturdy French domestic fare with minimal flounce.

The Judge's Lodging ◉

judgeslodgingyork.co.uk
9 Lendal, YO1 8AQ
01904 638733

This Georgian town house, just a stone's throw from the great York Minster, has been creatively retooled as a modern hotel with a plethora of eating and drinking options. Dining can be elegantly panelled or domestic-cosy, as you fancy, and the all-day menus trade in a wide range of international favourite dishes.

Lamb & Lion Inn ◉

lambandlioninnyork.com
2–4 High Petergate, YO1 7EH
01904 654112

Built quite literally into the ancient city walls, and sitting in the shadow of the Minster, this offers everything you could reasonably ask of a historic pub: a labyrinth of cosy little rooms takes in a bar bristling with hand-pulled real ales and kitted out with church pews, bare wooden tables and a real fire; while skinny corridors lead to the back snugs and Parlour dining room. The undisputed classic of the kitchen is a steak pie to be proud of, and Sunday roasts are a reliable draw too, offering topside or pork loin with Yorkshires and proper stock-pan gravy.

Middlethorpe Hall & Spa ◉◉

middlethorpe.com

Bishopthorpe Road, Middlethorpe, YO23 2GB | 01904 641241

Middlethorpe Hall is part of the National Trust's portfolio of historic buildings, but this William and Mary-era property is a country-house hotel, not a museum. The majestic building stands in 20 acres of gardens and parkland that have been extensively restored and replanted, while the interior designers have achieved a classy 18th-century look within – but there's a modern spa, too. The oak-panelled restaurant matches the smart and traditional mood of the house with a refined formality that extends to the service.

Oxo's on The Mount ◉◉

oxosrestaurantyork.com

The Mount Royale Hotel, 119 The Mount, YO24 1GU | 01904 619444

Set in a pair of Regency-era houses, The Mount Royale creates the atmosphere of a country-house venue within the confines of the city. Its softly lit main dining room extends into an outdoor terrace called the Gazeover. The kitchen celebrates fine Yorkshire produce in contemporary dishes that pay a clear homage to French classics.

▶ PLACES NEARBY

Seven miles southeast from the city centre is the Yorkshire Air Museum; 10 minutes from there is the small Derwent Light Railway at Murton; carry on the air theme at the Lysander Arms in Rawcliffe.

Yorkshire Air Museum and Allied Air Forces Memorial

yorkshireairmuseum.org

Halifax Way, Elvington, YO41 4AU

01904 608595 | Open summer daily 10–5, winter daily 10–4

This big independent museum is based around a former World War II Bomber Command Station at nearby Elvington, which was shared by the RAF and French squadrons. There's so much to see here, with a restored tower, an Air Gunners display, Squadron Memorial Rooms and much more. Among the exhibits are replicas of the pioneering Cayley Glider and Wright Flyer, along with a fully restored Halifax bomber and modern jets like the Harrier GR3, Tornado GR1 and GR4 – some 60 aircraft in all. 'Against the Odds' tells the story of the RAF Bomber Command, while the history of aviation and its notable Yorkshire connections can be explored in the 'Pioneers of Aviation' display.

Lysander Arms

lysanderarms.co.uk

Manor Lane, Shipton Road, YO30 5TZ | 01904 640845

This pub and restaurant stands on a former RAF airfield north of York, where No. 4 Squadron's Westland Lysander aircraft were based in World War II. The bar has a pool table and the restaurant serves fresh, locally sourced British food.

▶ Yorkshire Dales National Park MAP REF 327 D3, 334 C5

The Yorkshire Dales became Britain's seventh National Park in 1954 – and there are some potentially confusing points to clear up about its name. For starters, not all of the National Park is actually in Yorkshire – part of the western side actually falls in Cumbria. And then not all of the area traditionally known as the Yorkshire Dales is included in the boundaries of the National Park – Nidderdale (see page 202) is a notable example.

What definitely isn't confusing is why this magnificent upland region dominated by gritstone and limestone is so popular. A recent survey suggested that 75 per cent of visitors wanted to drive around the area and 65 per cent to walk – and eight million visitors a year can't be wrong.

There's such a lot to explore, either by car, on foot or by bike. The National Park covers a vast area, with Leeds and Bradford lying to the south, Kendal to the west, Darlington to the

northeast and Harrogate to the southeast. A small sliver of
land originally separated the Dales from the Lake District
National Park, but since Yorkshire Day 2016 (1st August), the
newly extended park is only separated from its Lakes cousin by
the M6. The extension, of course, means the Yorkshire Dales
National Park has entered the land of the old foe... Lancashire.
The National Park is crossed by several long-distance routes
including the Pennine Way, the Dales Way, the Coast to Coast
Path and the Pennine Bridleway. Cycling is also popular, with
several biking initiatives in the park to provide a number of
cycleways, which have proved very successful.

The park has its own museum – the Dales Countryside
Museum (see page 126) – housed in a conversion of the
Hawes railway station, as well as five visitor centres located
in major destinations in the park.

One of the best ways to see the Yorkshire Dales National
Park is by rail. The Settle to Carlisle Railway starts at Leeds

▼ The Ribblehead Viaduct crossing the Ribble Valley

and makes its way up to Settle, skirting the boundary of the park, before entering just after Langcliffe. Horton-in-Ribblesdale station (see page 135) is the stop for an attempt at Pen-y-Ghent, the lowest of the Yorkshire Three Peaks. The other two Peaks are best tackled from Ribblehead (see page 226). Garsdale is the last station stop in the National Park just before the line heads to Kirkby Stephen and on to Carlisle.

If you're staying in the area for a while, Northern Rail's North West Rover is great idea, allowing you any four in eight days' travel across the region, including starting from Leeds, at a discounted price. There's a seven-day Rover as well. Full details are available at northernrailway.co.uk

▼ Green How Hill

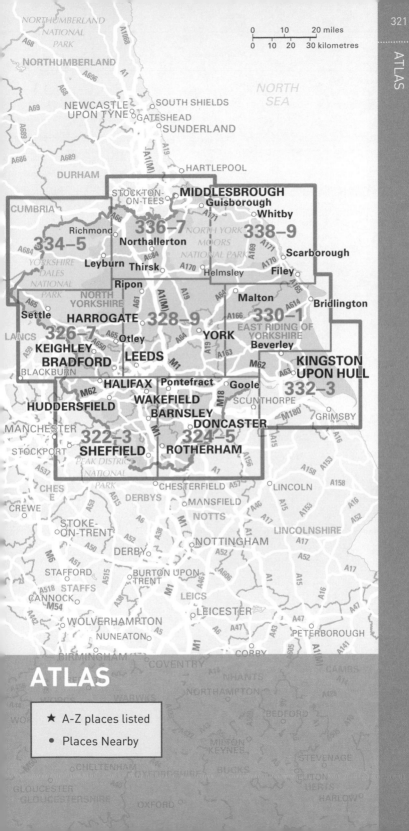

ATLAS

- ★ A-Z places listed
- • Places Nearby

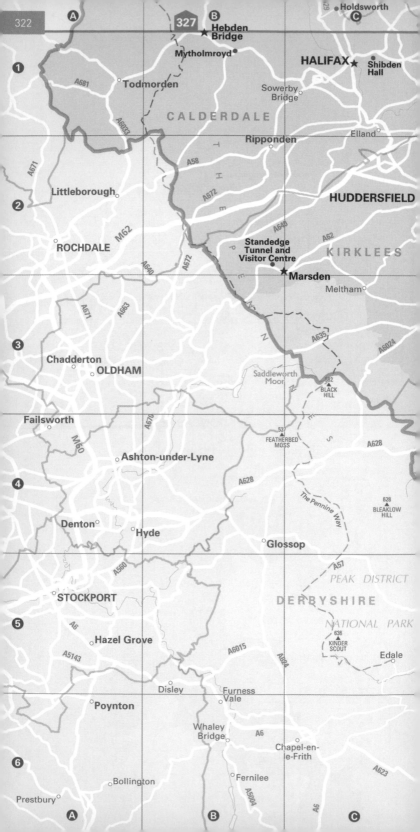

RSP **A** Nature Reserve
Fairburn Ings

B

C

329

A1041

A19

River Aire

1

Diggerland

Castleford

Brotherton

A162

Carlton

**Xscape
Yorkshire**

Knottingley

A645

Pontefract ★

A645

Darrington

M62

**Nostell Priory
and Parkland**

A639

A638

Wentbridge

A19

Ackworth
Moor Top

2

A1

Askern

Hemsworth

A628

South
Elmsall

River Don

ston

Adwick
Le Street

A18

Cudworth

**Brodsworth
Hall and Gardens**

A638

Doncaster
Racecourse

A630

**Monk
Bretton
Priory**

3

**Little
Houghton**

Thurnscoe

A635

**Cusworth
Hall**

A1(M)

DONCASTER ★

mbwell

323

**Yorkshire
Wildlife Park** ★

Elsecar
Heritage
Centre

**Wath upon
Dearne**

Mexborough

**Potteric Carr
Nature
Reserve**

and
er

**Conisbrough
Castle**

Swinton

Conisbrough

A638

4

A630

M18

A60

Tickhill

Bawtry

**Wentworth
Woodhouse**

Rawmarsh

A629

M1

★ **ROTHERHAM**

Maltby

A614

A631

A634

A631

M1

Thurcroft

**Roche
Abbey**

5

A618

A60

A1

Dinnington

**Tropical
Butterfly
House**

A634

A57

A57

6

Eckington

A57

A618

M1

A619

Worksop

A60

A57

eld

A **Staveley**

Clowne

A616

B

Whitwell

C

A Ribblehead★
Viaduct

B

C

★ Hubberholme

1

White Scar
Cave

e Falls

723

Ingleborough

Ingleton

A65

334

Pen-y-Ghent ★

Ingleborough
Cave

Horton-in-
Ribblesdale

Arncliffe

★ Clapham

Austwick

Malham
Tarn

2

m

Settle
Falconry

Stainforth

River Ribble

Giggleswick

★ **Settle**

Malham
Cove

Malham
National Park
Centre

★ **Malham**

Airton

The Pennine Way

T
H

Long Preston

3

Stocks
Reservoir

Hellifield

A65

Gargrave

Slaidburn

Broughton

A682

4

Gisburn

Elsack

Barnoldswick

A59

A56

Earby

Waddington

Chatburn

A682

5

Clitheroe

A6068

Hurst
Green

LANCASHIRE

Barrowford

Colne

Trawden

Nelson

Whalley

A6068

Brierfield

518
BOULSWORTH
HILL

A59

Padiham

BURNLEY

A666

Great
Harwood

A678

M65

6

A682

A646

Accrington

BLACKBURN

A56

A

B

C

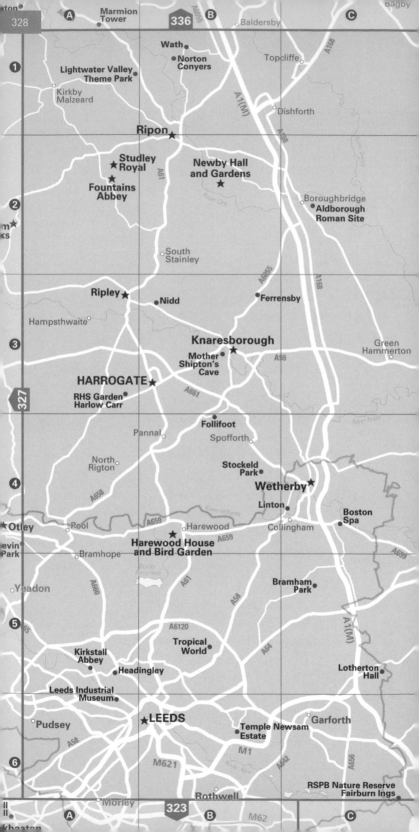

D **E** **F**

Flixton

Hunmanby

339

Filey Bay

Reighton

1

Burton
Fleming

Bempton
Cliffs ★

Flamborough Head
Heritage Coast

Bempton

Flamborough

**Flamborough
Head** ★

Rudston

Sewerby Hall
and Gardens ●

★ **Bridlington**

2

Carnaby

Kilham

Bridlington Bay

★ **Burton Agnes
Hall**

Barmston

Driffield

3

L S

O

Skipsea

Beeford

N

North
Frodingham

A164

Atwick

Brandesburton

★ **Hornsea**

4

Hornsea
Mere ●

Leven

River Hull

Tickton ●

A1035

332

★ **Beverley**

H

Aldbrough

5

A1174

O

Burton
Constable
Hall ●

L

Sproatley

D

A164

Cottingham

E

**KINGSTON
UPON HULL** ★

A1033

R

N

6

E

Hedon

S

S

Hessle **D**

E

F

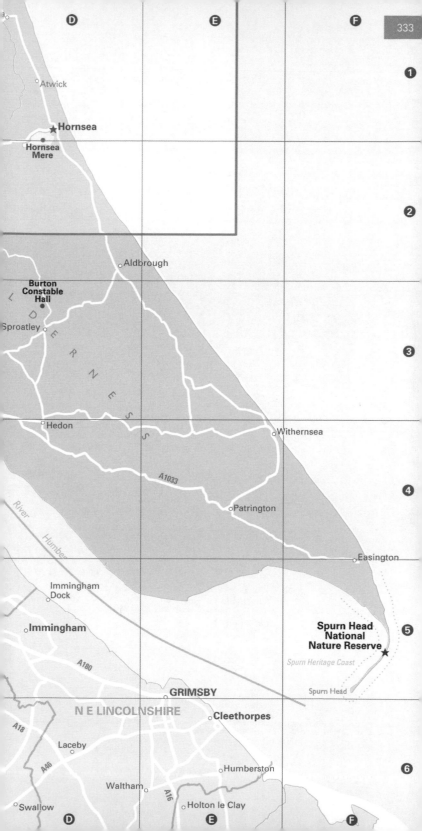

D · E · F
1
2

Atwick

★ **Hornsea**
Hornsea Mere

○Aldbrough

Burton Constable Hall

3

H O L D E R N E S S

Sproatley ○

○ Hedon

○Withernsea

A1033

4

○Patrington

River Humber

○ Easington

Immingham Dock ○

○ **Immingham**

A180

5

Spurn Head National Nature Reserve ★

Spurn Heritage Coast

Spurn Head

○ **GRIMSBY**

N E LINCOLNSHIRE

○ **Cleethorpes**

A18

Laceby ○

A46

○Humberston

Waltham ○

A16

○ Swallow

○ Holton le Clay

6

A B C

1

Warcop ○
Brough ○

A66

Soulby ○

A685

Kirkby Stephen ○

2

CUMBRIA

617
▲ BASTIFELL

Tan Hill Inn ★

A685

547
▲ TAILBRIDGE
HILL

Ravenstonedale ○

Birk Dale

710
▲ HIGH
SEAT

Keld ●

3

A683

Thwaite ○

713
▲ GREAT
SHUNNER FELL ★
The Buttertubs

675
▲ LOVELY
SEAT

Sedbergh ○

**Garsdale
Head** ●

**Hardraw
Force** ★

Garsdale A684

Hardraw ★

Hawes ★

4

Dent ○

The Pennine Way

614
▲ WETHER
FELL

Barbon ○

686
▲ CRAGHILL

YORKSHIRE

★

★

NATIONAL ★

736
▲

528
▲ BLEA
MOOR

5

Whernside ★

Ribblehead ★
Viaduct

**White Scar
Cave** ●

723
★

The Falls ★

Ingleborough

693
▲
Pen-y-Ghent ★

Ingleton ★

Ingleborough
Cave ●

326

**Horton-in-
Ribblesdale**

A687

A65

6

**Low
Bentham** ●

★ **Clapham**

High
Bentham ○

Austwick ○

Stainforth ○

**Settle
Falconry** ●

A B C

D **E** **F**

1

Wolviston ○

Billingham ●

Redcar

Marske-by-the-Sea

STOCKTON-ON-TEES

A66

Saltburn-by-the-Sea

A174

Skelton

2

★ **MIDDLESBROUGH**

Eston ○

Tocketts Watermill ●

Guisborough Priory ●

CLE

Ormesby Hall ●

Captain Cook Birthplace Museum ●

A171

Guisborough ★

Yarm ○

A1044

322

★ Roseberry Topping

★ **Great Ayton**

A174

A19

A67

A173

★ Kildale

Crathorne ○

Stokesley ★

★ Castleton ★

3

D

THE CLEVELAND HILLS

★ Cleveland Way

A172

454
URRA MOOR

338

Seave Green ○

4 ★

Mount Grace Priory ●

Bilsdale ★

N O R T H

★ Bransdale

★ Osmotherley

399
BLACK HAMBLETON

Farndale

The Hambleton Hills

Hawnby ●

5 tt le-H

Carlton ○

Kirkby

Boltby ●

Kirkdale ●

A19

Yorkshire Outdoors ●

Rievaulx Abbey ★

Helmsley ★

Sutton Bank ●

Scawton ●

Helmsley Walled Garden

Helmsley Castle ★

A170

Thirsk ★

Monk Park Farm Visitor Centre ●

Harome ●

Sowerby ○

Baghy ○

Oldstead ●

6

Num Hall ★

Kilburn ★

Byland Abbey ●

Ampleforth ○

Oswaldkirk ○

A168

329

Coxwold ★

E Newburgh

D **F**

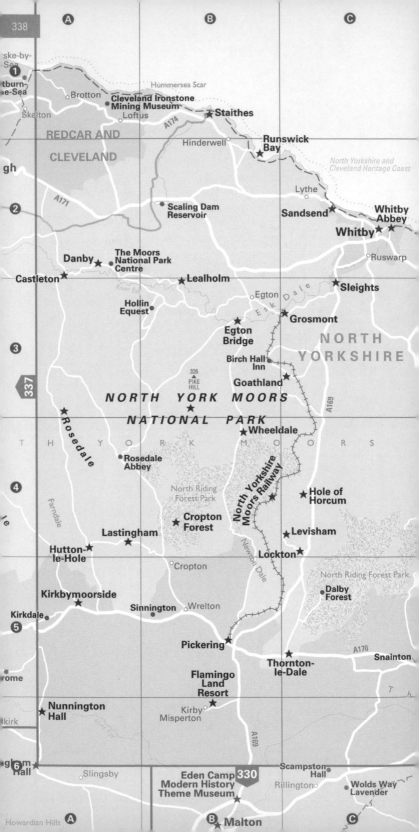

D

E

F

1

2

NORTH

SEA

Hawsker

★ Robin Hood's
Bay

Robin Hood's
Bay

3

★ Ravenscar

A171

Cleveland Way

★

Pesky
Husky ●

○ Cloughton

Cromer Point

4

Langdale
End ●

Hackness ★

Scalby ○

A165

● Sea Life and Marine Sanctuary
● North Bay

★ Scarborough
● South Bay

East Ayton ○

A165

● Cayton Bay

5

Seamer ○

Cayton ○

Filey Brigg

★ Brompton

C a r r s

★ Filey

Flixton

Filey Bay

Staxton ○

A1039

River Derwent

A64

Sherburn ○

Hunmanby ○

331

Reighton ○

6

D

E
Burton
Fleming ○

F

Be

★

Index, themed

Page numbers in **bold** refer to main entries

Index, places

Page numbers in **bold** refer to main entries, page numbers in *italics* refer to maps

The Automobile Association wishes to thank the following photographers and organisations for their assistance in the preparation of this book.

Abbreviations for the picture credits are as follows – (t) top; (m) middle; (b) bottom; (l) left; (r) right; (c) centre; (AA) AA World Travel Library.

4tl AA/D Clapp; 4tr AA/J Tims; 4b AA/T Mackie; 5l AA/T Mackie; 5r AA/J Hunt; 8–9 AA/J Tims; 11 AA/M Kipling; 12t AA/D Clapp; 12b Courtesy of Yorkshire Sculpture Park/Jonty Wilde; 13t Courtesy of Yorkshire Wildlife Park; 13m AA/P Bennett; 13b Courtesy of Royal Armouries; 14t AA/T Mackie; 14b Courtesy of The Deep, Hull; 15t Courtesy of North Yorkshire Moors Railway/Mike Nicholas; 15b AA/M Kipling; 16t Courtesy of National Railway Museum, York; 16m Courtesy of Flamingo Land/ Jonathan Pow; 16b Courtesy of Eden Camp; 17 AA/D Clapp; 18 AA/M Kipling; 19 AA/D Clapp; 20 AA/C Molyneux; 22 AA/T Mackie; 23 AA/D Clapp; 24 AA/J Morrison; 26-7 Mike Kipling Photography/Alamy; 29 AA/J Tims; 30 AA/J Morrison; 33 AA/J Tims; 34 Ian M Butterfield (Yorkshire)/Alamy; 36 AA/L Whitwam; 37 AA/D Clapp; 38 AA/J Tims; 39 AA/J Tims; 41 AA/T Mackie; 42 AA/J Tims; 45 AA/J Tims; 46 AA/M Kipling; 48 Courtesy of Leeds Festival/Giles Smith; 50 AA/A Burton; 52–3 AA/T Mackie; 55 AA/T Mackie; 56 AA/T Mackie; 62 AA/D Clapp; 67 AA/J Gillham; 68 AA/J Morrison; 69 AA/L Whitwam; 71 AA/T Mackie; 72 AA/J Morrison; 79 AA/T Mackie; 82 AA/M Kipling; 87 AA/J Morrison; 89 AA/M Kipling; 90–91 AA/M Kipling; 97 AA/S Day; 98 Courtesy of Yorkshire Wildlife Park; 101 AA/D Clapp; 103 AA/L Whitwam; 104 AA/D Tarn; 109 AA/M Kipling; 113 AA/M Kipling; 115 West Yorkshire Images/ Alamy; 118 AA/L Whitwam; 123 travellinglight/Alamy; 125 AA/J Morrison; 126 AA; 127 AA/J Tims; 129 AA/T Mackie; 132 AA/M Kipling; 137 AA/S & O Mathews; 140 incamerastock/Alamy; 143 Courtesy of The Deep, Hull; 145 Robert Christopher/ Alamy; 148 Aisle / Alamy; 151 AA/T Mackie; 152 AA/T Mackie; 155 Ian Lamond/ Alamy; 156 West Yorkshire Images/Alamy; 159 Andrew Kearton/Alamy; 165 AA/T Mackie; 169 AA/M Kipling; 174 Courtesy of Royal Armouries; 180 AA/J Hunt; 184–5 AA/T Mackie; 187 AA/P Bennett; 188 Courtesy of Eden Camp; 190 Courtesy of Flamingo Land/Jonathan Pow; 197 AA/D Tarn; 202 AA/D Tarn; 203 AA/M Kipling; 204–5 AA/M Kipling; 206–7 AA/J Mottershaw; 209 AA/M Kipling; 212 AA/J Tims; 215 AA/T Mackie; 216 AA/J Tims; 218 Robert Christopher/Alamy; 221 AA/P Wilson; 225 AA/J Hunt; 226-7 AA/T Mackie; 231 AA/M Kipling; 235 AA/T Mackie; 238 AA/M Kipling; 243 AA/M Kipling; 244 Darren Galpin/Alamy 248–9 AA/M Kipling, 265 AA/T Mackie; 268 Stephen Fleming/Alamy; 269 AA/M Kipling; 274–5 AA/T Mackie; 283 Courtesy of Yorkshire Sculpture Park/Jonty Wilde; 287 Gavin Dronfield/Alamy; 290 AA/S Gregory; 292 John Bentley/Alamy; 294 AA/L Whitwam; 297 AA/L Whitwam; 299 BJ Bromley/Alamy; 300 AA/D Clapp; 304 AA/D Clapp; 306 AA/D Clapp; 308 AA/D Clapp; 309 Courtesy of National Railway Museum, York; 311l AA/R Newton; 311r AA/R Newton; 313 AA/D Clapp; 318–9 Ribblehead Viaduct/Alamy; 320 AA/ TMackie; 352 AA

Every effort has been made to trace the copyright holders, and we apologise in advance for any unintentional omissions or errors. We would be pleased to apply any corrections in any following edition of this publication.

Series editor: Rebecca Needes
Author and updater: Andrew White
Project editor: Jackie Bates
Proofreader: Dawn Bates

Designer: Tom Whitlock
Digital imaging & repro: Ian Little
Art director: James Tims

Additional writing by other AA contributors. Lore of the Land feature by Ruth Binney. Some content may appear in other AA books and publications.

Has something changed? Email us at travelguides@theaa.com.

YOUR TRUSTED GUIDE

The AA was founded in 1905 as a body initially intended to help motorists avoid police speed traps. As motoring became more popular, so did we, and our activities have continued to expand into a great variety of areas.

The first edition of the AA Members' Handbook appeared in 1908. Due to the difficulty many motorists were having finding reasonable meals and accommodation while on the road, the AA introduced a new scheme to include listings for 'about one thousand of the leading hotels' in the second edition in 1909. As a result the AA has been recommending and assessing establishments for over a century, and each year our professional inspectors anonymously visit and rate thousands of hotels, restaurants, guest accommodations and campsites. We are relied upon for our trustworthy and objective Star, Rosette and Pennant ratings systems, which you will see used in this guide to denote AA-inspected restaurants and campsites.

In 1912 we published our first handwritten routes and our atlas of town plans, and in 1925 our classic touring guide, *The AA Road Book of England and Wales*, appeared. Together, our accurate mapping and in-depth knowledge of places to visit were to set the benchmark for British travel publishing.

Since the 1990s we have dramatically expanded our publishing activities, producing high-quality atlases, maps, walking and travel guides for the UK and the rest of the world. In this new series of regional travel guides, we are drawing on more than a hundred years of experience to bring you the very best of Britain.